A CENTURY OF SERVITUDE:
Pribilof Aleuts Under U.S. Rule

Dorothy Knee Jones

UNIVERSITY
PRESS OF
AMERICA

University Press of America, Inc.

P.O. Box 19101, Washington, D.C. 20036

Printed in the United States of America

ISBN: 0-8191-1349-2 (Perfect)

ISBN: 0-8191-1348-4 (Cloth)

Library of Congress Catalog Card Number: 80-1407

TABLE OF CONTENTS

PREFACE v

CHAPTER 1. INTRODUCTION—FROM RUSSIAN TO AMERICAN ADMINISTRATION 1

CHAPTER 2. THE REIGN OF THE TREASURY AGENT, 1870-1889. 15

CHAPTER 3. FROM WAGE EARNERS TO WARDS, 1890-1909 35

CHAPTER 4. SOLE FEDERAL JURISDICTION, 1910-1918 51

CHAPTER 5. A COLONIAL REGIME, 1918-1942. 65

Photographs 88

CHAPTER 6. REFUGEES 107

CHAPTER 7. TURNING POINT, 1945-1960 119

CHAPTER 8. THE ABANDONMENT POLICY, 1961-1970 139

CHAPTER 9. CENTENNIAL, 1971-PRESENT. 159

CHAPTER 10. IN SUM, WHAT HAPPENED ON THE PRIBILOFS? 173

BIBLIOGRAPHY 179

INDEX 185

PREFACE

By accident really, I discovered a scandalous federal government abuse that began in the nineteenth century and continued until very recently. We purchased Alaska shortly after the Civil War, fought partly on the issue of slavery. Yet, within three years of the purchase, the federal government established a slave-like relationship with the Aleuts on Alaska's remote Pribilof Islands in the Bering Sea. The government promoted and sponsored a system of hidden, internal colonialism that flourished decade after decade despite dramatic and progressive reforms in the rest of the country. How did such a condition arise? What forces sustained it, and what signalled its end? These questions prompted this book.

The Pribilof Islands have been inhabited by a small group of Aleuts—200 at the beginning of this story in 1867 and about 650 at the time of telling it in 1978. The human tragedy these Aleuts experienced was stark and pervasive. But why, the reader may ask, is it important to read about a tragedy that affected so few people when contemporary problems affect millions? The story is significant not because of the number of people involved but because it shows the extremes to which even an enlightened democratic government can and did go, the totalitarian condition it established and continued until recently. Moreover, as an extreme case, the Pribilof story highlights some of the processes of deprivation and oppression that operate less visibly in other parts of the United States—in urban ghettos and rural backwashes where people are held in fixed economic and social traps.

The reader may also wonder why we need yet another story of government mistreatment of American Indians; after all, that is an old, familiar, and oft-told tale. In broad strokes, the government's historical relations with Pribilof Aleuts did resemble those it had with other American Indians. But there was a critical difference. The government did not want the Aleuts' land as it did with other Indian groups; it wanted and coerced their labor. And to this end, the government came to control virtually every aspect of the Aleuts' lives—social, political, economic—even to the choice of marriage mates and freedom of movement.

The Pribilof story is significant, then, because it is an extreme case in United States' Indian history, it focuses general processes of oppression, and it shows the mechanisms of a democratic government at its worst.

The government needed the Aleuts' labor to harvest fur seals. About four-fifths of Pacific fur seals make an annual migration to the Pribilofs to breed. The Russians had developed a profitable seal industry on the islands. Eager to protect this profitable industry and to prevent the unregulated slaughter of the seals, the United States in 1869 declared the Pribilof Islands a federal reservation. In essence, the Pribilofs were the country's first national wildlife refuge. The United States sent Treasury Department agents to the islands to manage both the seals and the Aleut people on whose labor the seal industry depended. What happened to the Aleuts was integrally intertwined with the conditions of the seals as well as with the characteristics of the institutions that administered the islands. The interplay between these three main actors—seals, people, and institutions—provided the structure for this story.

Heretofore, the Pribilof story constituted an unwritten chapter in Alaskan and American history. Until World War II, the government surrounded its Pribilof operation with a wall of secrecy. However, during the war and the evacuation of the Pribilof Aleuts to southeastern Alaska, parts of the story leaked out, and a demand for change emerged. Since then, only bits and pieces of this history have been related, never the full story.

Then in 1975 I was presented with an opportunity to investigate and write the entire history of the United States government's relations with the Pribilof Aleut people. This is how the opportunity arose. In 1963 when I married the manager of the Aleutian Islands National Wildlife Refuge (not connected with the Pribilof Islands refuge), my seven-year-old son and I moved to the Aleutian area, to Cold Bay, which is on the western end of the Alaska Peninsula and encompasses in its glorious view several Aleutian Islands. I was forty years old and thoroughly urban, having lived until then in Chicago and Los Angeles. Politically, I was an activist, primarily involved in minority group causes. Professionally, I was a psychiatric social worker, especially interested in the research aspects of my job. I loved the Aleutians from a sensory, aesthetic, and life-style perspective, but I suffered keenly from the loss of my professional and political identities and activities. What to do in a town of 150 people, nearly all transients (Cold Bay's *raison d'etre* is to maintain an international airport). After my first visit to an Aleutian fishing village, I knew what I wanted to do. Intrigued by the Aleuts I met—their gentleness and humor—and fascinated by their adjustment to rapid culture change, I wanted to understand and write about these people. Believing I needed more credibility and training than a master's degree afforded to conduct research on Aleut culture, I returned to school for a doctor's degree. For six years after receiving it, I studied Aleut villages, becoming familiar with eight of the twelve remaining. The Pribilof villages—St. Paul and St. George—were not included in my research itinerary, but I maintained an intense curiosity about them, having heard about their history of oppression and about the persisting traces of this oppression. For example, until 1962 the government still paid part of Aleuts' wages in kind. As late as 1964 the government still required permission to visit the islands: an Aleut legislative candidate was refused permission that year. And alcoh prohibition prevailed in the Pribilofs until 1963.

The chance to slake my curiosity about the Pribilofs came in 1975. The Pribilof Aleuts were involved in a suit against the United States for damages, charging seventy-six years of servitude. Technically, the suit was called violation of the Fair and Honorable Dealings clause of the Indian Claims Commission Act. The Justice Department, defending the government, asked me through one of its attorneys to write a social and economic history of the Pribilofs. I was selected because I was one of the few sociological-anthropological investigators publishing about contemporary Aleuts. I faced a dilemma. I felt a deep compassion for the Aleut people and wrote about the wrongs that had been perpetrated against them. I was committed to their cause and felt uncomfortable at the prospect of working for the "other side." I confided my bias and discomfort to the Justice Department attorney responsible for the case. After his assurances (by which he stood) that I was free to write the truth as I saw it, that there would be no censorship of my work, and that I would have propriety rights to it, I decided to take the assignment.

Precisely because they have been a government reserve for over one hundred years, a voluminous amount of data exists on the Pribilof Islands--Congressional hearings, specialized reports, censuses, an enormous correspondence file, records of the Aleuts' grievances, agents' annual reports—a gold mine for a research investigator.

From these records, I and my colleague, economist George Rogers, ably assisted in library research by Mariana Foliart, prepared the report for the Justice Department. The report was largely descriptive and covered the years 1870 to 1946. George and I were vitally interested in updating the report and converting it into an analytical work. We applied to the National Endowment for the Humanities for a grant to write this book and received a favorable response.

Because of pressing time commitments, George did not co-author this book, but the material he contributed to the Justice Department report as well as his consultation on the subsequent work form a vital part of this book. George is considered by many to be the father of Alaska economics and has done considerable work in fisheries economics. In addition to George, Thomas Morehouse, political scientist at the Institute for which George and I work—University of Alaska's Institute of Social and Economic Research—consulted on the project. Thomas is widely published in the areas of Alaska and federal political institutions, including fishery organizations. He made an invaluable contribution not only in advice and ideas but in a lengthy analytical memorandum which has since been woven into the book. Mariana Foliart, who continued working on the book, also made an important contribution. An incredibly capable library researcher, she delighted us with the discovery of significant obscure sources. She also did some of the fieldwork and reviewed the manuscript.

In addition to the above project staff, I was assisted by many others. First are the Pribilof Aleuts who during fieldwork shared their experiences and confidences as well as their historical records. Fredericka Martin, former resident of the islands and publisher of two books about them, made a unique contribution. She generously shared her abundant files including correspondence with Aleuts and government officials. Her material afforded an intimate view of life on the Pribilofs that otherwise would not have been available. My husband, Bob Jones, gave consistent moral support throughout the preparation of the book and uncomplainingly reviewed each draft. Other reviewers who made valuable contributions were Richard Pierce, Professor of History at Queen's University in Kingston, Ontario, and publisher of the Limestone Press; Howard Baltzo, Program Director, Pribilof Islands, during the 1960s; Lillian Rubin, a dear friend and author of three major sociological books in recent years; Julie Cruikshank, also a close friend and a Canadian anthropologist; Scott Goldsmith, economist at the Institute of Social and Economic Research; and Agafon Krukoff and Larry Merculieff, Pribilof Aleut leaders.

Ron Crowe, editor; Kandy Crowe, editorial assistant; and Teresa Dignan, research assistant, all of the Institute of Social and Economic Research, greatly facilitated the preparation of the manuscript.

Finally, I want to express special thanks to William and Regina Browne for use of their photographic collection of the Pribilof Islands. The Brownes lived and taught at St. Paul for nine years.

CHAPTER 1

INTRODUCTION

FROM RUSSIAN TO AMERICAN ADMINISTRATION

The Pribilof story takes place out in the Bering Sea, far from centers of human abundance. The Pribilof Islands lie between the mainlands of Siberia and Alaska, about 200 miles north of the islands of the Aleutian chain [1] (See Figure 1). Until the twentieth century, the only outside contact occurred when sailing vessels and steamers called once or twice a year. The islands are unique from several aspects. Their severe weather and unusual setting cast a strange and exciting spell; typically fog lies close to the ground, and high winds and storms lash the rocky, treeless terrain. Until the Russians discovered them in the eighteenth century, the Pribilof Islands were uninhabited, probably because of the absence of natural harbors and fish-bearing streams and insufficient natural resources.[2] Commercially valuable resources were also sparse, limited primarily to the Pacific fur seal (*Callorhinus ursinus*). The migratory fur seal utilizes the beaches of the Pribilofs for a birthing and breeding area. The animals arrive during the early summer and accomplish both processes in a relatively short time, then depart to warmer marine areas. Other commercially utilized marine resources such as halibut are available but are not commercially attractive because of their greater abundance in other parts of the Bering Sea-Aleutian area.

These stormy, windswept, isolated islands with a narrow resource base captured the United States' interest; in fact, the Pribilof fur seal industry was one of the government's main motivations for purchasing Alaska from Russia in 1867. Though many visitors raved about Alaska's rich resources--fossil ivory, whales, walrus, many species of cold water fish, vast amounts of timber, and numerous fur-bearing land and sea mammals—only the Pribilof fur seals, estimated at two million animals, produced commercial profits of any significance. During Congressional hearings in 1868, experts gave glowing accounts of the profits from the industry. In the last years of Russian administration of the territory, the Russians insured their animal skins for one million dollars a year. [3] These were primarily seal skins, as the rest of the Russian fur trade had collapsed by then.[4] In the first two sealing seasons after the purchase, San Francisco traders who bought skins from Aleut sealers for 35 to 40 cents each sold them raw for $6.50 in London and $4.50 in San Francisco. A customs officer said that one West Coast company alone reported profits of over one-half million dollars from the fur seal trade in a single year, 1868. Another customs officer estimated an annual revenue to the government of $100,000 from the industry. [5]

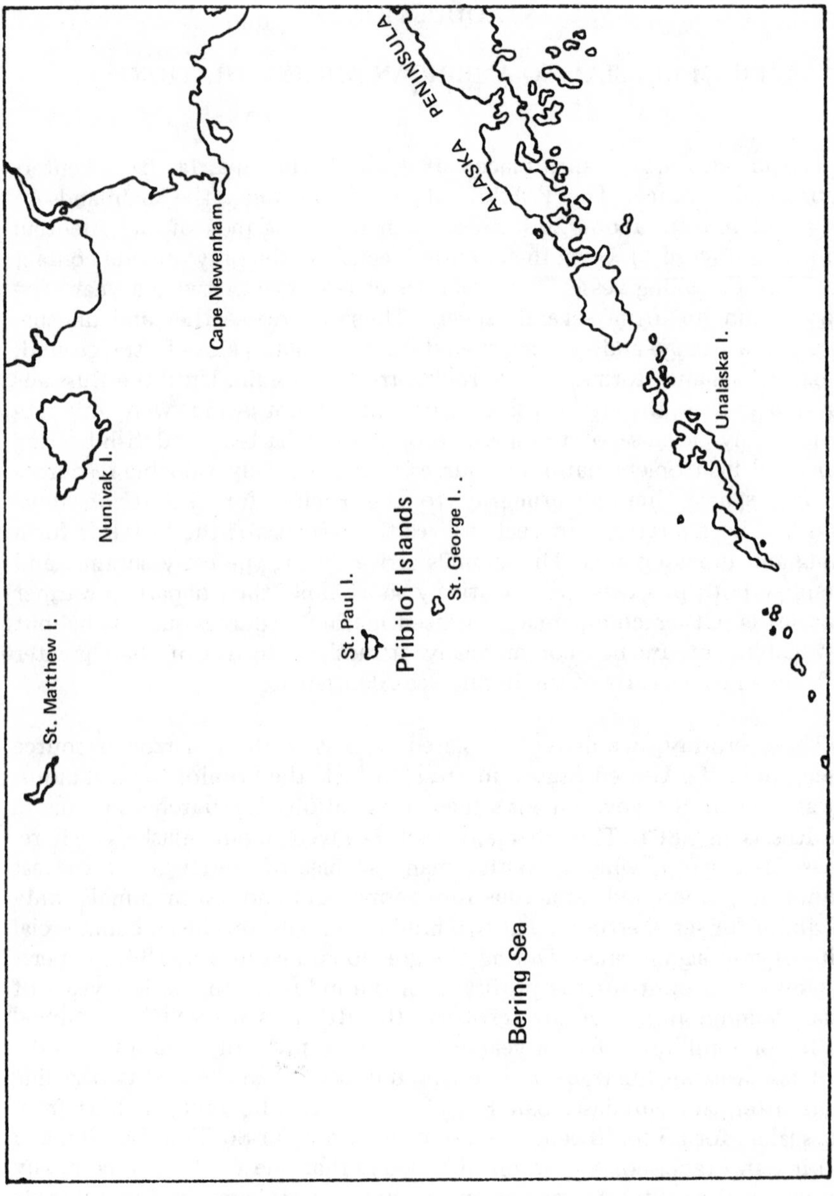

Figure 1 — The Pribilof Islands in Relation to the Mainland

The promise of wealth in Alaska sparked keen interest among government officials sensitive to recent charges that the purchase of Alaska was "Seward's folly." Opponents of the purchase contended that the resources of Alaska were of dubious value and the costs of administering the territory would drain the treasury. The minority report of the Congressional committee debating the purchase echoed these views: "The possession of the country (Alaska) is of no value to the government . . . it will be a source of weakness instead of power, and a constant annual expense for which there will be no adequate return."[6] Undoubtedly, officials realized that government revenues from the fur seal industry would silence the voices of opposition once and for all and exonerate the proponents of the purchase, especially with the high level of profits expected; some predicted that revenues from the seal industry would, in a few years, equal or exceed the original $7,200,000 purchase price of Alaska. The pressure to prove and realize the economic value of Alaska had a powerful influence on the evolution of Pribilof management policies and generated interest in natural resource conservation long before it attracted national attention, for revenues from sealing were inextricably bound to protection of the seal resource.

After the purchase the Pribilof fur trade operated similarly to that in other parts of Alaska. In line with the prevailing *laissez-faire* economic principle, the fur trade was in the hands of individual traders who set up posts and stores and traded with the native populations, exchanging store goods and later credit at the store for pelts. The traders had no responsibility for the welfare of the natives. No one raised objections to this system in the rest of Alaska where the fur trade was relatively inconsequential, but officials questioned its application to the Pribilofs where the potential for substantial revenues to the government existed and where free trade threatened the survival of the resource producing the revenue.

In 1867 and 1868 Pacific Coast companies plundered the seal rookeries. Rival traders took an estimated 240,000 seals in 1868 alone.[7] At that rate the seals would be extinct in a relatively short time. Public officials expressed alarm. The seal herds, they warned, were seriously endangered by indiscriminate slaughter. Congress responded quickly with legislation prohibiting the killing of fur seals except those needed for the Aleuts' food, estimated at 30,000 seals a year.[8]

Nonetheless, the seal slaughter continued. The following year, to assure permanent regulation of the seals, Congress declared the Pribilof Islands a special government reservation and barred persons from landing there without permission from the Secretary of the Treasury[9] (in whose department lay administrative responsibility for the Pribilofs). The Secretary granted landing permission to only two companies, ostensibly to take care of their properties which they had purchased from the Russians. Once there, however, these two companies reaped an excessive harvest, estimated at 100,000 seals, in complete disregard of the 30,000 limit.[10] Clearly more stringent federal regulations were needed.

Officials' thoughts turned to the Russians' successful experience in seal management. What was its history? What had it entailed in terms of conservation practices, government relations with private industry, and private industry's relations with the Aleut sealers? The Treasury Secretary assigned a Russian-reading employee to translation of Russian works and secured the cooperation of the Smithsonian Institution in furnishing other translations. Congressmen sought information not only about Russian management of the Pribilofs but about its entire fur trade on this continent, because the Pribilofs were not an isolated case; they were an integral part of the total North American administration by the Russians. Here is the background.

After Vitus Bering first sighted the Aleutian Islands in 1741, a steady stream of fur hunters from Siberia came to the Aleutians. Later, they extended their operations to other coastal parts of Alaska and even established a settlement as far away as Fort Ross in California. In the first fifty years of Russian occupation, the free trade period, Russian fur hunters brutally mistreated the Aleuts and at the same time commanded their labor.[11] The Russians stole the Aleuts' wives, slaves, and possessions, and slaughtered any who resisted their domination.[12] They sent Aleut men on long sea hunting expeditions from which many never returned and during which many women and children, left alone in the villages, suffered severe deprivation.[13] This mistreatment, combined with the diseases the Russians introduced, nearly decimated the Aleut population. In the first thirty years of Russian contact, the Aleut population declined from an estimated 12,000 to about 1,900.[14]

The fur traders plundered not only the Aleuts but also marine resources, especially the sea otter which produced the most valuable skins. After several decades of fierce competition between Russian companies, the sea otter population showed serious decline. In addition to competition with their own countrymen, the Russians also became concerned about the threat of competition from fur traders from other countries, especially the United States and Great Britain.

Eager to prevent ruinous competition between its companies, to regulate traders' treatment of the natives, and most importantly, to protect and expand its sovereignty in Russian America (its first overseas colony), the Russian government in 1799 granted a monopoly to a private firm, the Russian-American Company. The government gave the company not only a monopoly on trade but authority to govern and garrison the new territory. Apparently the Russians applied the experience of the British East India

Company in using a private business as an instrument of government. The establishment of an outright Russian government administration in North America might have provoked conflict with the United States and Great Britain, which was averted by establishing a company administration.[15]

The first charter granted to the Russian-American Company contained no definite regulations about the status and treatment of natives other than an injunction to treat them amicably and convert them to Christianity. [16] The second and third charters, in 1821 and 1844, however, specified natives' political status. Aleuts and other natives under company administration were declared Russian subjects: "Tribes inhabiting the places administered by the company are . . . Islanders, Kurils, Aleuts, and others. . . . As Russian subjects they shall conform to the general laws of the empire and shall enjoy the protection thereof."[17] The protection was hardly forthcoming. The Russian government was thousands of miles away, and it stationed no officials in the territory to oversee company activities.

Russian citizenship probably meant little to the Aleuts. They were faced with a more serious political problem—the threat company managers posed to their traditional political institutions. Aleut political authority consisted of a chief and council of elders in each village. Experts hold disparate views about the hereditary or elective basis of chieftainship,[18] but this became a moot question under company administration. The company set up a system of joint village administration by its village manager and the chief, but it was a very unequal partnership. Managers changed the one-chief system to a hierarchy of three chiefs, apparently in an effort to diffuse the chiefs' prestige and power. Further, managers appropriated authority to appoint and remove chiefs, thereby undermining the Aleuts' political integrity. They reduced the chiefs' powers in other ways, for example, by eliminating their role in the administration of justice if one of the parties to a suit were a Russian or Creole (persons with native and Russian ancestry).[19] Semen Okun, a Soviet historian, claimed that the company "bought off" chiefs by paying them an attractive salary in exchange for which they performed policing functions and organized work parties for the company.[20] Nevertheless, chiefs retained considerable authority, especially because Aleuts continued to rely on the first chief and to turn to him for arbitrating disputes, making important community decisions, and organizing community activities. The Aleuts' political system was less damaged by company policies than other elements of their social structure and autonomy, such as their cycle of work and lack of freedom to choose their places of residence.

Before the Russian occupation the Aleuts lived in hundreds of villages in the Aleutian chain and western end of the Alaska Peninsula. The company resettled many Aleuts into *artels* at or near the sources of furs, and consolidated some villages for ease of administration. By 1834 only twenty-seven villages remained.[21] The company apparently considered the *artels* temporary settlements, judging by its censuses which listed Aleuts from their villages of origin. Nonetheless, the *artels* and consolidated villages became permanent settlements.

The organization of *artels* reflected the Russians' dependence on Aleut labor, a dependence that grew from two sources. The paucity of Russian settlers in the territory was one. The existence of serfdom in the mother country limited emigration. To compound the problem, the Russian government restricted the residence of emigrants to seven years, although later in its administration, it liberalized this constraint.[22] In 1818 only 400 Russians resided in Russian America; by 1867 their numbers had grown to only 812.[23] The second source of this dependence was the Russian fur hunters' failure to master the Aleuts' seamanship and sea hunting skills—their ability to sail small skin boats, *baidarkas*, in rough seas, and use spears, darts, and throwing boards to capture sea mammals, including whales.

The company recruited an Aleut labor force by appropriating the Aleuts' slaves as permanent employees and commanding the labor of Creoles (whom it educated) for ten to fifteen years of compulsory service. But the bulk of its workers were full-blooded Aleuts compelled to labor not only by the company but by government edict as reflected in the charters to the company. The charters issued in 1821 and 1844 required half the Aleut men in every village between the ages of eighteen and fifty to labor for the company for three years at whatever pay the company fixed, usually merchandise or scrip for the company store.[24] Actually, the work obligation was worse than that. Four-fifths of the men in the villages were usually recruited and the three-year work limitation was often overlooked.[25] In addition to the work obligation, the company compelled old men, women, and children to perform other services for it, such as producing a specified number of bird-feather parkas every year. Furthermore, the company forbade Aleuts to sell furs or meats to any other firms, restricted their subsistence fishing along the shores of their villages, and prohibited them from leaving their villages without official permission.[26]

The Aleuts' economic status under the Russians was influenced in part by the institution of serfdom. The condition of Russian serfs varied at different times in history, in different regions, and in the practices of different lords. Generally the landlords required *barshchina*, a work obligation, usually three days a week of compulsory labor at no pay, and *obrok*, a cash payment, as well as lesser services such as providing produce from the land the serfs farmed. Serfs had virtually no rights; they were not even allowed to petition the state regarding abuses by the landowners; they could own no real property; they had no freedom of movement (they could not leave the estate without the landowner's permission); and they could be sold like chattels. Furthermore, the owner exercised wide judicial and police powers extending even to the serfs' private lives and choice of marriage partners.[27]

The Russian-American Company had failed to secure serfs of its own, probably because of opposition from the nobility. But in practice, Aleuts belonged to the company as much as Russian serfs belonged to the landowning nobility. The power to compel the Aleuts to labor, force their resettlement, and confine them to their villages certainly bespeaks possession.

In many respects, then, the Aleuts' economic status resembled that of Russian serfs. But it also differed in a fundamental way. Unlike the lord's relationships to his serfs, the company paid Aleuts for labor performed—75 kopeks for a seal skin in the 1860s, equivalent to about 40 to 50 cents in American money.[28] This rate was as high as that which American traders paid the Aleut sealers for several decades after the transfer of the territory. In this aspect, in paying a wage for labor performed, the Russian company treated Aleuts like other American wage workers were treated at that time.

In yet another way, in the manner the company distributed wages, it treated the Aleuts uniquely. The Aleuts' traditional distributive system was essentially egalitarian. Aleuts shared the products of the hunt with the entire village and looked after the welfare of all individuals. In line with this tradition, company managers paid the Aleuts' wages into a community fund which the chiefs divided among the sealers according to their work classification and apparently also according to their need.[29]

Considering the extreme domination the company exercised over the Aleuts' lives, it is puzzling why the company respected this Aleut institution. Of course, such methods cost the company nothing, and it seems reasonable to assume that because the company depended on the Aleuts' labor, it wanted to avoid alienating them; on this issue the Aleuts probably harbored intense feelings, for communal sharing was an integral and highly valued feature of their way of life.

In sum, then, the Aleuts' economic status under company administration was part serf, part proletariat, and part traditional Aleut.

The company's administration of the Pribilof Islands was not unique, although the fate of the Pribilof Aleuts differed from that of the others. This becomes apparent as we trace the evolution of the two Pribilof communities, St. Paul and St. George. Of the many fur-bearing animals in Russian America, Russian fur hunters' primary interest lay in two—sea otters and seals. Sea otters were easily captured in the water along the shores, but the best approach to fur seals was on their breeding grounds, where they concentrate on beaches. At first the location of the breeding grounds was not known, but in 1786 Gerasim Pribilof, a navigator on a Russian ship, discovered one, an island with tens of thousands of seals. He named it George Island after his ship. The following year fur hunters on George Island discovered another island about thirty miles to the north which they named Peter and Paul Island.[30] These two islands, now known as St. George and St. Paul, are the two main sealing islands in the Pribilof group and the only two on which humans reside.

Grigor Shelikhov, president of a large trading firm that preceded the Russian-American Company, at first harvested seals with imported labor from the Siberian port of Okhotsk. However, this system apparently failed, and he substituted imported Aleutian workers, primarily from the villages of Atka and Unalaska. Importing laborers made economic sense because of the highly seasonal nature of sealing, which was the main commercial activity on the Pribilofs. True, other species were harvested—blue and white foxes and sea lions for their fur, walruses for their tusks, and whales for their bones—but these were not sufficiently valuable to warrant year-round activity. At first the Russian-American Company followed Shelikhov's practice of importing Aleut laborers, but by the 1820s it had established permanent villages, evidently to ease administration and avoid the expense and trouble of carrying Aleuts to and from their villages.

Permanent villages meant a juncture for the Aleuts, turning those on the Pribilofs to a different path from the rest. With the coming of the Russians, all Aleuts were forced into specialized activities in the fur trade. Most became pelagic (open sea) hunters roaming along the coasts of northwest North America for part of the year and subsistence hunters in their villages for the rest of the year. Thus, they were able to maintain their aboriginal skills as boatmen, hunters, and fishermen. Those consigned to the Pribilofs suffered a different fate. Although they did some hunting and fishing, they basically became gatherers and processors on an industrial assembly line with a specialized division of labor that involved driving, slaughtering, and skinning seals on land, activities far removed from their traditional marine hunting. Furthermore, sealing occurred during the summer months, the prime time for many subsistence activities. As a result of confinement to the islands and assembly line work during the summers, the Pribilof Aleuts lost many of their aboriginal skills.

When it came to seal management, the Russian-American Company did an exemplary job. The Russian fur traders' senseless and unsystematic destruction of sea otters had threatened their survival. To protect the fur seal trade, the company, from the outset, established conservation measures. It suspended seal hunting in various periods and limited the harvests to males of two and three years of age.[31] The purpose of the age limitation was to restrict harvests to the age groups whose skins were prime, but the prohibition against taking females reflected social characteristics of the seal population. Successful reproduction of seals requires only a small proportion of males who live in harems. Most males do not breed, and their slaughter does not affect the viability of the herd. Harvests can be limited to males of a certain age because seals sort themselves on beaches in ways that make age, sex, and breeding status apparent. Observing these conservation practices, the Russian Company was able to harvest seals consistently, averaging about 20,000 animals a year during the last forty years of its administration.[32] At the time of the transfer of the territory, the seal herd was thriving with a population estimated at over two million.

In sum, the Russian system in its North American colony involved private monopoly of the fur trade with: (1) a private company having political and administrative authority over the territory; (2) labor practices characterized by a combination of serf-like, proletariat, and uniquely Aleut features; and (3) relatively advanced conservation practices.

How did this system strike American government officials? Undoubtedly they were impressed by the Russians' success at both seal conservation and operating a profitable business. But what did they think about the human abuses that occurred under the same system? They expressed humanitarian concern for the Aleuts. In fact, Secretary of the Treasury George Boutwell, in urging a public monopoly in the Pribilofs, stressed the importance of establishing humanitarian institutions for the care and welfare of the natives.[33] Despite the lack of precedence for government control of a profit-making industry, other officials, in the name of humanitarianism, called for a public monopoly. But it is doubtful that humanitarian interests were the primary motivation; more likely it was rhetorical justification to mask economic interests. Special Indian Commissioner Vincent Colyer argued that "as it will require the same amount of governmental . . . expense to protect the (private) lessors as it would for the government to manage the concern itself; it would seem practical economy for our government to take charge of the operations."[34] In more blatant terms, Frank Wicker, special Treasury agent sent to investigate the fur seal operation, underscored the economic rationale for a government monopoly.

> The habits and peculiarities of the fur seals are such that any deviation from the old established custom adopted by the "Russians" would have a tendency to drive them away from their rookeries; consequently, *the necessity of surrounding this mine of wealth with the strong arm of government should be made apparent to all.* This method not only insures a handsome revenue to the government, but at the same time does away with private monopolies, which are always obnoxious to the people.[35]

Clearly, the government had a vested economic interest in the Pribilofs, which it sought to protect by public monopoly and which it justified in terms of humanitarianism.

Counteracting these few officials was the louder and more persuasive voice of the fur trade lobby. Its spokesmen argued that a private lease was congruent with American sentiment and furthermore that it would still assure Treasury revenues in the form of rent and taxes.[36] John Miller, one of the most persistent spokesmen for a private monopoly, was president of the recently organized Alaska Commercial Company (formed by a merger of several trading firms including the two that had purchased property from the Russians and been given permission to land on the islands in 1869). A former military officer and friend of General Grant, Miller had access to many legislators as well as to the President.[37]

Given the tenor of those times, Miller's agitations fell on receptive ears. It was a period of rapid industrial development, great land steals made possible by prodigious corruption in government circles, and the growth of giant corporations accompanied by intense exploitation of laborers who had no power to bargain individually; it was the era of the post Civil War robber barons; it was the gilded age of capitalism.

In this national mood, Congress in 1870 enacted legislation instructing the Secretary of the Treasury to grant an exclusive private lease.[38] The Secretary awarded the lease to the Alaska Commercial Company which, although the lowest bidder (in terms of rent and royalties to the government), had the advantages of already possessing property on the Pribilofs, experience in the fur trade, and influence in the White House.[39]

The American version of private monopoly control of the Pribilofs did not duplicate that of the Russians'. The legislation gave the company a monopoly on trade only; the government retained authority to regulate the seals and the Aleut sealers. In essence, the legislation and the lease that followed it established a dual system of government-company administration of the Pribilofs. How did this system affect the Aleut people? Did it protect them from forced labor, from serf-like features of the Russian system, from political domination? Which part of this dual system proved more fateful for the Aleut people—the reality of economic monopoly or the reality of protection by a democratic government? What sort of organzational forms did the government develop to monitor the private lease and manage the seals and the Aleut people? And what priorities did it set among its three main goals—seals, profits, and people?

Endnotes

1. The Pribilof group of islands occupies an isolated portion of the Bering Sea between 56°35’ and 57°11’ north latitude and 169°35’ and 170°24’ west longitude. The Pribilofs lie between Unalaska Island in the Aleutian archipelago, about 214 miles southeast; St. Mathew Island, about 220 miles northwest; and Cape Newenham on the mainland, 309 miles northeast. St. Paul and St. George, the two islands of concern, are approximately the same size. St. Paul Island, 13-1/2 by 7-2/3 miles, has 45 miles of coastline and 43 square miles of area; St. George Island, 12 by 4—1/2 miles, has 30 miles of coastline and almost 36 square miles of area. Tom F.W. Barth, "Geology and Petrology of the Pribilof Islands, Alaska," Biological Survey Bulletin 1028-F (Washington, D.C.: Government Printing Office, 1956), p. 101-102; David Starr Jordon, et al., The Fur Seals and Fur-Seal Islands of the North Pacific Ocean (Washington, D.C.: Government Printing Office, 1898), p. 31. (Also issued as Treasury Department Doc. No. 2017)., Wilfred Osgood et al., The Fur Seals and Other Life of the Pribilof Islands in 1914. Bulletin of the Bureau of Fisheries, Vol. xxxiv, 1914, p. 17. (Also issued as Bureau of Fisheries Doc. No. 820, 1915 and Senate Doc. No. 980, 63rd Cong., 3rd sess.).

2. The archeological record reveals no signs of human habitation prior to the Russians' discovery of the islands. There were a few signs of recent visitation—a clay pipe, a copper sword hilt, and evidence of recent fires, suggesting that the Aleuts did visit or camp on the islands. Alan L. Bryan, "An Archeological Reconnaisance of the Pribilof Islands" (Anchorage: Alaska Department of Natural Resources, Division of Parks, n.d.), Osgood, et. al., The Fur Seals and Other Life of the Pribilof Islands, p. 132. Ivan Veniaminov, Russian Orthodox priest in the Aleutians from 1825 to 1834, recorded a story indicating that Aleuts knew of the existence of the Pribilofs long before the advent of the Russians. The tale recounts the experience of a man from the Aleutian Island of Unimak, carried northward in his boat by a tempest, who landed his *baidarka* (skin boat) on St. Paul and spent the winter there. In the spring he sighted the peaks of Unimak Island several hundred miles distant, set out in his *baidarka*, and returned home. Ivan Veniaminov, Notes on the Islands of the Unalaska District, 3 vol. (St. Petersburg, 1840), trans. Richard Geogehan, vol. 2, p. 223.

3. Vincent Colyer, Report of the Honorable Vincent Colyer, United States Special Indian Commissioner, on Indian Tribes and Their Surroundings in Alaska Territory from Personal Observation and Inspection, 1869. H. Exec. Doc. No. 1414, 41st Cong., 2nd sess., 1869, pp. 1052-1054.

4. Petr Tikhmenov, Historical Review of the Formation of the Russian-American Company and Its Activity to the Present Time, 2 parts (St. Petersburg: St. Petersburg Printing Office of Edward Weimar, 1861). Part I trans. Michael Dobrynin, Berkeley: Bancroft Library, University of California, pp. 308, 407, Part II. trans. Dmitri Krenov, Seattle: Works Public Administration, 1939-1940, p. 254. (Recently issued as A History of the Russ-

ian-American Company, trans. and ed. Richard A. Pierce and Alton S. Donnelly (Seattle and London: University of Washington Press, 1978).

5. U.S. Treasury Department, Special Agents Division, Seal and Salmon Fisheries and General Resources of Alaska, 4 vol. (Washington, D.C.: Government Printing Office, 1898), Vol. I: Reports on the Conditions of Seal Life on the Pribilof Islands by Special Treasury Agents and Others from 1868 to 1895 Inclusive, pp. 7-13.

6. U.S. Congress, House, Committee on Foreign Relations, Minority Report No. 37 (Washington, D.C.: Government Printing Office, 1869), 50th Cong., 2nd sess., 1869, p. 65.

7. U.S. Congress, House, The Alaska Commercial Company, H. Rpt. No. 623, 44th Cong., 1st sess., 1876, p. 99.

8. 15 Stat. 241 (July 27, 1868).

9. 15 Stat. 348 (March 3, 1869).

10. Colyer, Report on Indian Tribes, p. 988; U.S. Congress, House, Fur Seal Fisheries of Alaska, H. Exec. Doc. No. 136, 41st Cong., 2nd sess., 1869, p. 3; Frank N. Wicker to the Honorable Herbert C. Schenck, H. Misc. Doc. No. 11, 41st. Cong., 2nd sess., 1869, p. 2.

11. Aleuts of the Aleutian Islands and the western end of the Alaska Peninsula and Koniags of Kodiak Island whom the Russians classified as Kodiak Aleuts comprised the bulk of the company's American Indian employees. William Sarafian, Russian-American Company Employee Policies and Practices, 1799-1867 (Ann Arbor: University Microfilms, 1970), p. 150.

12. The Aleuts' slaves were prisoners of war, taken in raids on other villages (Aleut and Eskimo). Slaves were accorded diverse treatment. Some became wives or adopted children and were integrated into the community. Others remained in slave status and were used or abused according to the inclination of the owner. He might liberate them, add them to a dowry, torture them, or burn them alive. An entire family of slaves might be murdered at funerals or during mourning rites. Dorothy Jones, Aleuts in Transition: A Comparison of Two Villages (Seattle: University of Washington Press, 1976), p. 14.

13. Semen B. Okun, The Russian-American Company (Boston: Harvard University Press, 1951), trans. Carl Ginsburg, pp. 175, 200.

14. Aleš Hrdlička, The Aleutian and Commander Islands and Their Inhabitants (Philadelphia: Wistar Institute of Anatomy and Botany, 1945), pp. 32-33.

15. Vladimir Gsovski, Russian Administration of Alaska and the Status of Alaska Natives (Washington, D.C.: Government Printing Office, 1950), p. 9. (Also issued as S. Doc. No. 152, 81st Cong., 2nd sess., 1950).

16. Ibid., p. 5.

17. 1821 Charter, Sections 42, 44; 1844 Charter, Sections 247, 250. In Gsovski, Russian Administration, pp. 44, 49.

18. Margaret Lantis, "The Aleut Social System from 1750 to 1810," in Margaret Lantis (ed.) Ethnohistory of Southwestern Alaska and the Southern Yukon (Lexington: University of Kentucky Press, 1970), pp. 250-251.

19. 1844 Charter, Section 277, in Gsovski, Russian Administration, p. 51.
20. Okun, Russian-American Company, pp. 198-200.
21. Hrdlicka, The Aleutian and Commander Islands, p. 41.
22. Okun, The Russian-American Company, pp. 172-174.
23. Svetlana G. Fedorova, The Russian Population in Alaska and California, Late Eighteenth Century—1867 (Kingston, Ontario: Limestone Press, 1973), p. 151.
24. 1821 Charter, Sections 51, 53; 1844 Charter, Sections 265, 266. In Gsovski, Russian Administration, pp. 44, 51; Tikhmenev, Historical Review, Part I, p. 292.
25. Sarafian, Russian-American Company, pp. 150-178; Veniaminov, Notes, trans. Geogehan, p. 228.
26. Okun, The Russian-American Company, pp. 196-201.
27. Jerome Blum, Lord and Peasant in Russia from the Ninth to the Nineteenth Century (Princeton: Princeton University Press, 1961).
28. Source for Aleuts' rate of pay is Tikhmenev, Historical Review, Part I, pp. 319, 320, 399. In the 1860s there were 100 kopeks to the paper ruble; only paper rubles were used in Russian America and the nominal value of the paper ruble then was 75 cents. S.R. Tompkins, Alaska, Promyshlennik and Sourdough (Norman: University of Oklahoma Press, 1945), p. 185; The Alaska Commercial Company, H. Report No. 623, p. 7.
29. Veniaminov, Notes, trans. Geogehan, p. 234.
30. Ibid., pp. 223-225.
31. Tikhmenev, Historical Review, Part I., pp. 307, 403.
32. Ibid., Part I, pp. 308, 407; Part II, p. 254.
33. The Alaska Commercial Company, H. Rpt. No. 623, p. 12.
34. Colyer, Report, p. 991.
35. Frank N. Wicker, Special Agent, Treasury Department, to George S. Boutwell, Secretary of the Treasury, November 4, 1869, in Fur Seal Fisheries of Alaska, H. Exec. Doc. No. 136, p. 4.
36. See, for example, Seal and Salmon Fisheries of Alaska, Vol. I, p. 12.
37. The Alaska Commercial Company, H. Rpt. No. 623, pp. 23-24.
38. 16 Stat. 180. (July 1, 1870).
39. U.S. Congress, House, Fur Seal Fisheries of Alaska, H. Rpt. No. 3883, 50th Cong., 2nd sess., pp. vi, vii, 91.

CHAPTER 2

THE REIGN OF THE TREASURY AGENT, 1870-1889

At Congressional hearings in 1888 to investigate the Alaska Commercial Company, Treasury Department agents repeatedly asserted their sovereignty over the Pribilof Aleuts. Here are some examples.

> I am the representative of the Government. . . . The agents have absolute control of the natives. . . . *The Government Agents are required to see that the natives are kept in subjection** and that they perform their duties toward the lessee.[1]

> *The Government agent is a sovereign* there and his word is law.[2]

> I issued an order—there *the agent is supreme ruler* and when an agent issues orders, they are generally obeyed promptly.[3]

Supreme rulers, sovereigns—how did such domination come to pass? Not a single word appeared in either the 1870 Act to Prevent the Extermination of Fur Seals or in the lease to the Alaska Commercial Company that even hinted at dictatorial powers for the agents or for any representatives of the government or the company. On the contrary, the legislation required the Secretary of the Treasury "to make all needful rules and regulations . . . for the comfort, maintenance, education, and protection of the natives of said islands."[4] Yet, autocratic rule by Treasury agents emerged as the dominant mode of interaction with Aleuts. This pattern was given impetus and shape by a confluence of forces—the characteristics of the administering institution, the priorities it set, and prevailing national attitudes about Indians and Indian welfare—which will become clear as we trace developments on the islands.

The 1870 Act contained three primary objectives as well as the means to achieve them: (1) to protect the seals, it established the Pribilofs as a permanent government reservation, the country's first national wildlife refuge; (2) to advance commercial interests and bring money into the Treasury, it granted an exclusive private lease to the seal fishery from which the federal treasury was to receive annual rent and royalties; and (3) to provide for the Aleuts' comfort, maintenance, education, and protection, it created a government protectorate for the residents of the islands.[5] Money, seals, and Aleut welfare—these were the main goals of the federal program on the Pribilofs.

The lease required the Alaska Commercial Company to foster these aims. It granted the company exclusive property rights to seals for twenty

---

*Emphases here and throughout the book are added.

years in exchange for an annual rent to the Treasury of $55,000 and a royalty of $2.625 on every seal taken. It required the company to observe conservation regulations including a 100,000 annual limit on seal harvests,[6] and to provide for the physical and moral well-being of Aleuts by paying sealers a wage (to be determined by the company), establishing schools, and furnishing supplies—cordwood, salted salmon, and salt and barrels for preserving seal meat.[7] The company voluntarily assumed two additional obligations—rent-free houses and free medical care.[8]

The company administered the Pribilof operation from its San Francisco office. Its field manager on the Pribilofs, directly responsible to the San Francisco-based superintendent, had general charge of affairs on both islands including supervision of the other nine employees (teachers, physicians, cooks, carpenters). The company provided employees with very explicit, detailed rules and regulations about every phase of the enterprise. By and large, it adopted liberal labor-management policies. These were, of course, in management's interest since company profits hinged directly on an available and presumably satisfied Aleut work force. The company set the Aleuts' rate of pay at 40 cents per seal skin, similar to the rate in the immediately preceding period when Aleuts were selling skins competitively. It assumed support for widows and orphans. And most important, it protected Aleuts' political integrity by instructing its employees to observe the chief's authority in organizing work parties, use no coercion in getting people to labor, and refrain from interfering in the local government or domestic relations of the people.[9]

The Treasury Department administered the islands from Washington, D.C. Its field agents were directly responsible to the Secretary of the Treasury. Staff on the islands included an agent in charge and three assistant agents. The agent in charge was responsible for supervising the others as well as administering St. Paul. Another agent was in charge of St. George, and the rest assisted the administrators, taking over in their absences from the islands. In contrast to the company, the Treasury Secretary issued virtually no instructions to agents, especially about the human resource management aspects of the program. In the 1888 Congressional hearings, agents complained bitterly about this vacuum.

> A: I went there without instructions whatever with the exception of what Senator Voorhees gave me: "Determine to do your whole duty." That was all my instruction.
>
> Q: Did you get any from the Department?
>
> A: None whatever. The surrounding circumstances would dictate what a man's duty would be. . . .[10]

* * *

Q: Are there any regulations by the Treasury Department for the guidance of the Government agents on those islands?

A: I do not think there are. I never saw any.[11]

* * *

Q: Have you ever been furnished with regulations by the Secretary of the Treasury?

A: . . . the only instructions that I had while I was there was that of Secretary Boutwell, calling attention to the quass* business and to stop giving the natives sugar. . .

Q: This lease was entered into on the 3d of August, 1870, and I understood you to say you have no knowledge of any such rules or regulations made by the Secretary of the Treasury having been furnished?

A: No sir, *The rule is supposed to be made by his agents;* he has never made any.[12]

* * *

A: I landed on St. George Island first . . . remained there a short time . . . and then proceeded to St. Paul Island, and without any positive instructions from the Treasury Department, except in a general way . . . I did not know where the seal islands were . . . neither did I know what my duties would be.[13]

* * *

Q: Did you have any instructions from the Treasury Department?

A: No sir, I had none. When I left, I had some idea of matters up there and asked the Secretary about instructions, and *he asked me to write my own instructions.*[14]

This seems like shocking neglect of federal responsibility. Why, one wonders, did the Secretary not only fail to issue guidelines in the first place but turn a deaf ear when agents requested them? Aleut welfare was an explicit goal of the Pribilof program, and managers tended to see it as interdependent with the other two program objectives—money and seals.

In this matter all interests are identical. The government has its obligations to the people and desires also to continue its present revenue from the seal islands. The lessees need the help of the natives to properly prosecute their work according to the contract. The people need watchful care and guidance to strengthen them to resist temptations that assail a people just emerging from an inferior state.[15]

This sentiment, that each party depends on and benefits from the participation of the other, was expressed repeatedly in the 1888 Congressional hearings. One official even suggested that Aleuts would suffer from an insufficient supply of seal meat, their main staple, without the conservation and management efforts of the company and the government (and this was said at a time when the seals were in sharp decline).[16]

*Home-brewed beer and wine.

Yet, although recognizing the interdependence of their objectives, managers did not give them equal weight. Money and seals came first and were usually stated in that order.[17] This was not by accident. The Secretary of the Treasury in 1876 Congressional hearings went so far as to define the government's interests in the Pribilofs as distinct from the Aleuts' welfare.

> Q: You received the agents' reports?
>
> A: Yes, sir.
>
> Q: Were they satisfactory?
>
> A: I have no recollection to the contrary except in this one particular, some complaint about wood; and a complaint came to me in regard to one of their (company) men, Dr. McIntyre, that he was disposed not to concede to the natives. *It did not touch the interests of the government directly . . . but it touched the rights of the natives in some respects.*[18]

From the beginning, the prevailing sentiment in the Pribilof management system was clear. What was good for the company and the government was good for the Aleuts, and that, indeed, Aleuts' welfare directly depended on the profitability of the seal harvest. With this assumption, federal officials could, with a clear conscience, concentrate on the seals and forget about the people.

Furthermore, neglect of welfare responsibilities was not unusual in a period when social welfare ideas were poorly developed. For the most part, human welfare was equated with physical survival, and the lease assured that. Even in terms of prevailing ideas about Indian welfare, the Secretary probably believed he was fulfilling his obligation. In the conventional view, Indians were savages, uncivilized, "just emerging from an inferior state," and their only salvation lay in American education and conversion to Christianity. The Russians had already accomplished the religious conversion and the company was providing schools.

Another probable influence prompting the Secretary's inaction on guidelines was the very newness of the Pribilof management organization. Bureaucratic rules and routines evolve from experience, and new organizations characteristically adopt loose policies and structures to give managers time to become familiar with alternative strategies and tactics as they watch and assess the actions of front-line staff. A recent study of the careers of organizations showed that new organizations typically have a broad focus and undefined roles, functions, and lines of authority in addition to a general lack of predictability. As organizations orient to long-term goals and internal stability, they become increasingly structured and routinized.[19]

In any case, agents were given wide latitude to write their own rules, so it is important to know who these agents were, what backgrounds and qualifications they had. Curiously, though seal conservation was essential to the Department's main economic goal, it did not hire naturalists as agents. Judging by the diversity of agents' backgrounds, the Department specified no qualifications at all. A sample of early agents illustrates this: it includes a member of the Massachusetts legislature and former whaling captain, a Russian-speaking clerk in the Treasury Department, a physician, a judge, two army officers, a future editor of the Pittsburgh Press, a clerk in the Illinois legislature, and a former mayor of Indianapolis—a relatively eminent group.[20]

At first glance one wonders why these relatively high-status, well-trained persons would want jobs on the remote Pribilof Islands? Their high salary level suggests an answer. The agent in charge earned $10 a day; an assistant agent, $8; and the other two assistants, $6.[21] By contrast, the average income of United States workers (all industries) in 1870 was only $1.70 a day (for a five-and-a-half-day week).[22] The job was a political plum and undoubtedly was secured on that basis in a period when the patronage system was very popular. In addition to high wages, agents' jobs offered a singularly high level of power and responsibility.

And how did these agents view the Aleuts? Did they perceive them in stereotyped Indian terms as savages, as uncivilized, as inferior? Or did they see them as equals and citizens? The issue of Aleut citizenship was murky. The Russian government had distinguished between two groups of natives—dependent and independent tribes; it granted citizenship only to the former, which included the Aleuts. The treaty ceding the territory to the United States contained a similar distinction—all Russian subjects automatically became United States citizens except members of the uncivilized tribes, but the treaty did not define the uncivilized tribes or the implied category of civilized ones.[23] Most officials assumed that all Alaska natives, including the Aleuts, were uncivilized. There were a few exceptions to this interpretation: one by Vincent Colyer, special Indian Commissioner,[24] another by the first regular Treasury agent on the Pribilofs, Charles Bryant.

> I cannot refuse a dire share of praise to the natural gifts of the Aleutian race, and I beg leave to express here my earnest belief that the Aleutes might become as good American citizens as any admitted under the fifteenth amendment to the constitution.[25]

Bryant was impressed with the Aleuts' capabilities: "They have a well-organized system of government, under chiefs of their own selection, subject to removal at the will of the people. . . . Those now acting have done so for three years and are very efficient men."[26] Expressing his respect for the Aleuts, Bryant had all pertinent material translated into Russian so the Aleuts could read it. He agitated (without success) for the dismissal of a

St. George agent who abused the people.[27] And he fought, also in vain, to secure Aleuts' title to their houses. Before the Alaska Commercial Company era, Aleuts lived in their traditional *barabaras*—partially underground sod- and grass-covered houses.[28] The Russians considered the *barabaras* quite acceptable and made no effort to move Aleuts from them.[29] But the Americans, appalled at these "damp, insalubrious hovels," insisted that the Aleuts move to above-ground houses.[30] The Aleuts resisted. Their centuries-old underground houses had evolved as an adaptation to a cold, windy climate in a treeless environment; they were convinced that they would be cold in the above-ground houses.[31] But they had no choice. Company employees, with the support of Treasury agents, destroyed the *barabaras*. Though Bryant also favored the move to frame houses, he wanted Aleuts to have title to them, firmly convinced that the loss of home ownership would undermine their pride and independence. As the company planned to build the houses, Bryant asked its managers to give title to the Aleuts; the company refused outright. Then Bryant appealed to the Treasury Secretary to build the houses and arrange a form of repayment that would enable Aleuts to become home owners.[32] This plea also went unheard. The company furnished the materials for the houses, the Aleuts built them, and the company retained title. To this day Aleuts still don't own their homes although negotiations to transfer title to them are under way.

The image of Bryant advocating, supporting, and fighting for the Aleuts' causes differs strikingly from the authoritarian picture of agents presented earlier. And so it was at first, but in his six years as agent in charge of the islands, after repeated rejection of his efforts to help Aleuts, Bryant became discouraged and climbed on the bandwagon of agent suppression that apparently won Department approval. Bryant began to exercise increasing control over Aleuts' lives, even requiring them to report all community decisions to him for approval.[33]

Agents' increasing domination extended to all areas of Aleuts' lives—political, social, economic, and personal, but this did not seem to disturb federal officials who were preoccupied if not dazzled by the great financial returns from the seal industry.

The company's intensive promotion drive brought a substantial increase in the value of fur seal skins; the average price during the twenty years of its lease was three times greater than it had been in 1868. With a harvest of 100,000 seals a year selling at an average price of $14.67,[34] the company was making money hand over fist—an estimated $20 million gross and $18 million net in this twenty-year period.[35] The government's share was also impressive—a gross of $6 million and a net of over $5 million.[36] Henry Elliott, a conservationist and expert on the Pribilof Islands, noted in 1877 that the gross revenues to the Treasury not only covered all management costs but were six times greater than the federal government's total outlay for *all* services and programs in Alaska.[37]

Unusually high profits and revenues, these—and they could not be easily charged to overexploitation of the Pribilof Aleut workers whose income during this twenty-year period compared favorably with that of other industrial workers (male, non-farm). We use this standard of comparison (here and in subsequent analyses) because Pribilovians' work resembled that of other male nonfarm production workers. By the time of the transfer, the Aleuts were skilled in selecting, driving, slaughtering, and skinning the seals and had developed a division of labor accordingly. The harvest began very early in the day when, at the direction of the company supervisor, a few Aleut laborers would start the drive by running along the beach between the group of male seals and the sea. This served to isolate the seals, to awaken them, and to turn them away from escape to water. The workers then herded the seals slowly to convenient slaughter areas, and as they travelled, they allowed older seals and females to escape and return to the beach. Aleuts were especially skilled at recognizing the age and sex of seals. Next, Aleuts slaughtered the seals under direction of their chief, who was supervised by a company employee. At the killing ground, Aleuts clubbed seals in the head, stabbed them in the heart, and laid them out in order with the flippers cut loose for the skinner. Each operation was conducted by a different group of laborers, the clubbing and skinning by the most skilled and experienced, and the other jobs by the less skilled.

We estimated Aleuts' total income in terms of cash received for sealing, foxing, and occasional labor for the company and the government, as well as the goods and services provided by the company. Of all these sources, sealing was the major one, accounting for about 80 percent of Aleuts' total income.[38] In the first decade of this period, Aleuts' average annual income was somewhat less, about 20 percent, than that of other industrial workers. But in the second decade, it was substantially higher, about 40 percent.[39] The comparison is even more favorable if we consider that the Aleuts had access to subsistence products not available to most other workers. Elliott estimated an annual consumption of 600 pounds of seal meat per person on St. Paul.[40] The availability of seal meat and wages that compared to those of other workers do not bespeak affluence; however, the existence of savings accounts certainly suggests that Aleuts had surplus funds, funds not needed for basic necessities. The company paid Aleuts 4 percent interest on moneys deposited with it. By 1874 over half the Pribilof adults (over 17 years old) had savings accounts totalling more than $40,000, a considerable sum for that period.[41]

So the Aleuts were not impoverished in this period, furthermore, as the company paid them a competitive wage for labor performed, they enjoyed an economic status similar to that of other American workers. But that describes only part of the Aleuts' situation. Economic well-being involves more than physical survival and wage labor; it involves certain basic rights that were denied the Aleuts.

At first the company followed the Russians' practice of paying Aleuts' wages into a community fund to be distributed by the chief and priest (the priest was an Aleut) according to classifications which they determined.[42] Treasury agents very quickly altered this system by appropriating authority to assign classes. Their reason: concern about favoritism in the chief's and priest's classifications.[43] But more likely, as later events suggest, agents wanted the power to manipulate work classifications as a means of controlling Aleuts' work behavior. The power to lower a worker's class and wage is a compelling sanction.

Agents also violated Aleuts' freedom in the use of their money. The company did not pay sealing wages directly to the Aleuts. After the shares were announced, the company deposited the money with its cashier, designating the amount of credit due each hunter. When a hunter needed money, he presented his passbook to the cashier and received silver in payment. Agents soon placed restraints on the amount of money a sealer could withdraw. They rationalized this infringement in terms of the need to stretch Aleuts' wages until the next sealing division.[44] However, as with the work classifications, manipulation of Aleuts' access to their money proved to be another powerful weapon for controlling Aleuts' work behavior.

But why did agents need such control? Aleuts valued their sealing jobs and fought hard to perpetuate their monopoly on conducting the seal harvests (guaranteed in the 1870 legislation). Furthermore, there was no other significant source of employment on the islands. By and large, Aleuts worked willingly in the seal trade. They balked when it came to compulsory labor for government at no pay. Sealing took only a few months of the year. When the Aleuts were not sealing or working for the company, Treasury agents required them to work for the government. They paid them 10 cents an hour for construction and maintenance of government buildings, but this was an incidental part of Aleuts' labor for government. The major part, involving such things as rookery guarding, loading and unloading vessels, construction and maintenance of community facilities, was not paid.[45]

Agents were able to coerce Aleuts' labor by dint of their enormous sanctioning power extending beyond the manipulation of classifications and money withdrawals. When Aleuts refused to work, agents fined them, put them in irons, threatened them with exile, and in some cases, actually banished them from the islands. The daily logs of a St. Paul agent give a detailed account of the imposition of these sanctions.

> Yesterday ordered men to go to H.W.P. (Halfway Point) early this A.M. if good water, if not good water on foot across the island and pick up wood in piles. This A.M. the men did not go so I called Antone (the chief) and ordered him to get them off at once. I waited an hour and they did not start nor did Antone report. So I rang the bell and called the people together at the shop. I then called out the men mentioned. . . I ordered Karp Buterin, second chief, to take the men over to East Landing and get them off in the boat. He came forward and ordered them to come. They turned their faces to the crowd and appealed to them. The crowd told them not to go. As near as I could learn, they refused to obey and the crowd let out a shout and said they would not go after wood, to all go to their houses. I then ordered the chiefs to bring the men to the Government House. . . . They came. I requested Mr. Gray (cashier) to come and give them their books and to let me know the amount due the men from the company. He gave me the amounts. I then asked Martin Nederazoff if he was ready to go after wood and obey my order, and he said "no"; I fined him $15. I asked Stepan the same, and he answered "no"; I fined him $15. I asked Kerrick Terakanoff, he said "no"; I fined him $20. I asked Neon Tetoff, he said "yes"; I did not fine him . . . and said I would put them in irons if they did not dry up. . . I then stood them in a line on the floor and told them they had to obey me or I would fine them every dollar they had, besides I had given Mr. Allis orders not to sell them wood or coal, and the end would be they would have to leave the island. Victor called and requested permission to go to H.W.P. for wood and wanted, Peter, John and Nectary to go. I gave them permission and after some more talk the crowd in the Government House made up their minds better go. . . They all brought in large amounts of wood.[46]

In effect, while the company treated the Aleuts like other American workers, government agents treated them like Russian serfs in forcing them to labor without pay. It was the agents of a democratic government, not of a private profit-making company, that imposed this violation.

The government adopted other practices akin to serfdom, such as restricting Aleuts' movements to and from the islands. Technically, Aleuts were not confined to the islands, and the company observed a policy of offering free passage on its boats; but in practice, Aleuts could not leave or return to the islands without official permission. An agent's testimony on this issue is enlightening.

> I heard only one complaint, and that was the chief told me there was some money coming to the natives from some former year . . . and wanted to go to San Francisco and settle. I told him that as far as I was concerned I had no objection to it, but I had to report to my superior officer, and if he had no objection to it, he could go. I reported to Mr. Glidden at the time, and he said that he could not give him any permission then, as he would have to report to the Treasury Department and get the permit.[47]

After a trip to the Aleutians, Alaska's Governor Swineford gave further evidence of restrictions on Aleuts' travel. Aleuts told him, he wrote in his 1887 report, that no one could leave the Pribilofs without Treasury Department permission.[48] The use of this restriction soon became codified in administrative regulations and persisted until World War II.

Similar violations of rights occurred in the political arena. The respect Bryant accorded the Aleuts' indigenous political system died rather quickly. Agents wanted chiefs who could compel their people's labor, not chiefs who joined the people in rebellion. To this end, they soon began to remove elected chiefs from office and appoint substitutes much to the Aleuts' distress. A St. Paul agent vividly described the process of interference in chief selection.

> Anton Melovidov who was deprived of his office of first chief . . . having since then become a good and faithful man . . . in consideration of his good behavior and worth, appointed to their chief by the Treasury agent. The chiefs, Stephan and Volkoff were summoned to the company's office and with Mr. Gray for interpreter, were informed of Anton's appointment. They were instructed to inform him and the people that they might obey him as such. They both accepted the new appointee as satisfactory with them. Later in the day, however, Markel (Volkoff), the second chief, summoned the people together and posing as a champion of their rights, headed an opposition to Anton's appointment and asked for a pow-wow with the Treasury agents which was refused and the rule adopted to communicate with the people only through the chiefs was strictly enforced by the Treasury agents.
>
> Markel was spokesman and did all that he could to force the Treasury agents from their position and grant his request for a pow-wow, which he had promised the people . . . failing to accomplish his purpose he offered his resignation as second chief which was promptly accepted. And Anton Melovidov was promoted to the vacancy. Terentia Stephan followed with his resignation as first chief stating he regretted to do so but the people forced him to the step because Markel resigned . . . His resignation was accepted and Anton Melovidov again promoted and made first chief. He assumed the duties at once without hesitation or fear of the people, all of whom said they would not mind him. Markel was informed that any disobedience of the people would be severely punished, the opposition to Anton was worked up by Markel and the church party, who are constantly scheming to control everything pertaining to the business of the Islands and this disaffection if it may be called such is encouraged and doubtless suggested by the Rev. Paul Shaisnikoff's advice to his people. . . .[49]

By the end of the Alaska Commercial Company period, agents appropriated full authority to select chiefs: "Formerly the people elected (chiefs) but such abuses arose under the system that the government assumed the authority several years ago and has since continued to exercise it."[50] And thus the agents of government, not of the company, sounded the death knell for the Aleuts' ancient chief system.

In earlier times Aleut chiefs had been responsible not only for organizing work parties and village activities but also for administering justice, a function they continued to perform in modified form under Russian administration. Treasury agents quickly changed this practice, assuming authority not only to write the laws but to act as police, investigator, prosecutor, judge, and jury. They observed little distinction between legally defined crimes such as drunkenness and other behavior. Rather, they lumped all behavior they considered undesirable into a single category of punishable crime. They punished behavior as seemingly trivial as sauciness.

> Mr. Redpath (company manager) reported that Peter Krukoff was saucy to him. Peter was ordered to do some work and report to me.[51]
>
> * * *
>
> Complaint made about Widow Popoff being saucy to a passerby. I sent word to keep her mouth closed or I would let her live in some other part of town more out of the way.[52]

Alleged immorality was a constant concern of agents.

> Shortly after I got there . . . I called up the priest and the men and told them the state of affairs was very bad and they must correct it or that the government would send them to the Aleutian Islands to live on codfish; that this government could not afford to have such a black spot in existence.[53]
>
> * * *
>
> . . . I called his wife and she acknowledged she was bad and that he (husband) had told the truth and I got her to understand that she had got to do better if she remained upon this island, that this made three times her name appeared on the books. . . She laughed at me. I reached for the handcuffs and told her unless she was civil, I would iron her at once. . . I told her . . . and from now on until steamer St. Paul arrives she must be at her home at 8 p.m. every night and remain unless it was necessary to see the Doc that if she wanted to go and stay with neighbors, she must come with Metrofan and ask me. I have her to understand that she must obey me if she lives upon this island.[54]

Agents considered the manufacture and drinking of *quass* (home-brewed beer and wine) the most stubborn and frequent Aleut misbehavior. Although alcohol was unknown in the Aleutians before the Russians introduced it, Aleuts readily adopted its use. The Russian fur hunters, themselves topers, appeared to take no offense at Aleut drinking, nor did the priests; rather, Veniaminov was impressed that Aleut drinking was virtually never associated with crime or violence.

> Over the period of ten years which I spent in Unalaska (the Unalaska District included the Pribilofs), there was not a single case of homicide or criminal assault among the Aleuts, not even any brawl or significant quarrel despite the fact that many of them were often in an intoxicated condition.[55]

It was a different story when the Americans came. Drunken Indians were not to be tolerated—on this issue the Department was unequivocal. Prohibition of the sale or gift of liquor to Aleuts was a lease condition and one of the few clearly specified instructions to agents. At first, agents lectured Aleuts about the evils of drinking. Later they used more stringent measures. They conducted investigations.

> Mr. Gavitt (St. George agent) himself explained to me that he found the story of *quass* under the floor (of Aleuts' homes) was not true, by going to the houses and

tearing up the carpet and opening the trap-door where it was supposed to be stored, and he found none secreted there.[56]

They assigned work as punishment.

> The first disturbance that my attention has been called to on this island came this morning. Aga Kushing complained that Matfay Popoff came to his residence . . . drunk . . . and demanded of Kushing's wife some *quass*. She told him they had none, whereupon he struck her or at her, he then passed into the other room where Aga lay asleep. . . During the mellee they broke Aga's looking glass which cost $3.50. After hearing the case it was decided that Popof should pay for the looking glass . . . and in addition to that should bring ice from the lake to fill up the water (barrel) and tub at the Government house.[57]

They imposed fines.

> There had been one occasion when three of them went aboard a vessel and got some (alcohol) from a cook. . . We had them up to the police court and tried and fined them $10 apiece.[58]

They used irons.

> Kerric Tarakanoff on the street drunk. Called him to government house and put him in irons. . .[59]

They threatened and used exile.

> In connection with this subject, I beg to refer . . . to the removal from the island in June last of a young Russian named Nicholas Krukoff (Aleut from the Pribilofs). About that time a most disgraceful drunken debauche occurred on the island, which was participated in by as many as thirty persons, which finally led to a severe affray among the party of young men, with whom appeared said Krukoff. . . He was accordingly placed on board the revenue cutter June 11, and subsequently landed at Unalaska, where the agent of the Alaska Commercial Company directed provision to be made for his support until such time as it might be deemed advisable to permit him to return to the islands.[60]

Punishments for drinking involved individuals as well as the entire community. The agent in 1881 instituted a village-wide ban on the sale of sugar, the chief ingredient of *quass*.[61] Ten years later, there was also a community-wide prohibition against the sale of sugar; the agent pled for its removal because of the hardship it created for the families of drinkers.[62]

However severe the agents' punishments, the Aleuts refused to comply on this issue. It was as if they had to retain one area of life uncontaminated by agents' interference, one area where they could defy the encroaching power of agents. In recognition of the universality of this response among American Indians, anthropologist Nancy Lurie described Indian drinking as "the world's longest on-going protest demonstration."[63]

Like that of the Russian serf owners, agents' power was not limited to misbehavior and insubordination but extended to the Aleuts's private lives, to their very choice of marriage partners. The focus on promoting marriage sprang from Treasury administrators' concern about the rapidly declining population on the islands. From 1867 to 1889 the Pribilof Aleut population decreased by 28 percent.[64] Emigration was not a factor; there were twice as many moving to the community as leaving it in this period. The cause of the decline was the excess of deaths over births, not because the birth rate was low (it was considerably higher than that of the general population of the country) but because the death rate was alarmingly high, over three times the rate in Massachusetts (the only state that kept reliable death registration data at that time).[65] One wonders why the high death rate in a period when the Aleuts were not impoverished and had access to medical care? Was it a response to agent totalitarianism with its accompanying demoralization? It is said that when Aleuts want to die, they simply do so. Was it a response to living for the first time in insufficiently heated houses? The *barabaras* were heated by small stone lamps burning seal oil, while the above-ground houses into which they were moved required coal or cordwood for heating, items that were often in short supply.[66]

Whatever the cause, management focused on marriage as the solution to the population decline. Believing that church consanguinity regulations extending to the fourth and fifth degree of relationship reduced marriage chances on the islands, agents tried to convince the priest to liberalize these restrictions as one means of stimulating reproduction. In another effort agents, supported by the Washington office, induced men to go to other villages for wives, threatening punishments such as banishments if they refused to go. Listen to this entry in an agents' daily log.

> Alex Galaktionoff . . . goes to St. George to find a wife and with the distinct understanding that he is to find one before returning. If he gets married he is to return next spring —if not he is to seal over there.[67]

Agent coercion reared its head in the education area too. Aleuts had no formal system of education until the Russian Orthodox church organized schools. In the 1830s Father Veniaminov started schools for both boys and girls in the Pribilofs, teaching the Russian language to aid his conversion goals and also teaching the Aleut language, for which task he codified the language and composed a grammar, dictionary, primers, and other books.[68] Veniaminov admired the rapidity with which Aleuts became literate and bilingual.[69] They were quick learners in many areas. Some became noted as chess players, and some, educated in Russia, became doctors and navigators. Aleuts placed high value on the Russian Orthodox church, to which they converted en masse, and Russian education, both of which came to be vital symbols of their cultural identity.[70]

In conformity with the lease, the company started American schools in both villages.[71] Bryant was impressed with the St. Paul Aleuts' enthusiastic response: "all manifested great interest in learning the English language, and made good progress."[72] The St. George agent made a similar observation: "They are making rapid progress and feel anxious to learn the English language. Even men who have advanced to the age of 30 and 40 attend school."[73]

This educational honeymoon was short-lived. By 1873 agents began to complain about increasing Aleut resistance to the American schools, stemming from parents' fear that "in learning English their children will forget their Russian and weaken their attachment to the church."[74] Aleuts resisted not learning English per se but the low priority agents placed on Russian education. The priests were allowed to teach Russian school only after the eight-month American school session ended. By 1873 the school population had dwindled to just a few students.[75]

Education was one of the few areas of people management that commanded federal administrators' attention, even to the point of issuing explicit instructions to agents to compel Aleuts' school attendance. With this mandate, agents applied increasing pressure; they hit children and incarcerated both parents and children. An agents' daily log entry gives a vivid account of these pressures.

> On the fourth day after, he, Mr. McIntyre (Treasury agent), took him (a father who refused to send his son to the American school) from his house, put handcuffs on, and lodged him in the cellar of the company's house, a very cold, damp place, and kept him four days on bread and water, and during all this time the son had been confined in a dark closet in the company's house and kept on bread and water.[76]

These punishments, as humiliating and intimidating as they were, did not by themselves effect the Aleuts' compliance but the imposition of fines did. Agents began to fine parents for every day a child was absent. Continued resistence by Aleuts threatened their very livelihood and they submitted, but covert resistance to the schools, manifested in a refusal to learn, continued for many years.

Compulsory education was a liberal nineteenth-century reform. The irony was that so many working-class groups resisted it—European immigrants as well as Aleuts and Indians, and probably for the same reasons. Education is always a process of teaching a culture, of transmitting a language, values, and world view. To culturally alien groups, to the Aleuts as well as the immigrants, American education wrenched children from the language and influence of their parents; it was a threat to family and community continuity and solidarity. Enforcing school attendance was not always an issue. In a recent book on early school reform, Katz argues that enforcement became an issue in Massachusetts because industry needed a docile (immigrant) labor force.[77] The same could be argued in the Pribilof case.

We asked at the outset of this chapter how agents achieved sovereign power over the Pribilof Aleuts. They had a chance for despotic rule and they took it, with the support of the Washington office. Top managers' complicity cannot be excused on the basis of ignorance; they had access to the daily logs, correspondence, and reports that revealed agents' activities. By action or inaction, by silence or approval, by covert or overt means, managers supported the development of a politically repressive system on the Pribilofs, reflecting their dominant interest in economic, not humanitarian, goals. Moreover, they faced virtually no pressure to protect Aleuts' welfare and rights. Legislators certainly exerted none, although they were also aware of human abuses on the islands, abuses that were repeatedly mentioned in the 1876 and 1888 Congressional hearings. In response to most such revelations, legislators often changed the subject or called a recess;[78] they too seemed to consider the human condition peripheral to the Pribilof mission. Company managers also maintained silence about Treasury agents' excesses, probably because they did not want to hurt their chance for a lease renewal by offending government officials. Without counteracting pressure from any sources, agents, with the support of the federal government, could and did establish a form of totalitarian rule. It is important to underline that in a period of steamrolling exploitation of workers by private industry, it was the government, not the private company, that established the serf-like features of labor relations in the Pribilofs—restrictions on travel and forced labor; it was the government, not the private company, that promoted political domination of Aleuts; it was the government, not the private company, that supported and encouraged agent totalitarianism in the Pribilofs.

Endnotes

1. U.S. Congress, House, Fur Seal Fisheries of Alaska, H. Rpt. No. 3883, 50th Cong., 2nd sess., 1889, p. 153.
2. Ibid., p. 86.
3. Ibid., pp. 18-19.
4. 16 Stat. 180 (July 1, 1870).
5. Ibid.
6. Conservation regulations also prohibited the use of firearms, the taking of female seals, and the taking of male seals under one year of age.
7. U.S. Congress, House, Seal Fisheries of Alaska, H. Exec. Doc. No. 83, 44th Cong., 1st sess., 1875, pp. 21-22.
8. Ibid., p. 79.
9. Ibid., pp. 77-79.
10. Fur Seal Fisheries, H. Rpt. No. 3883, pp. 180-181.
11. Ibid., p. 227.

12. Ibid., p. 221.
13. Ibid., p. 42.
14. Ibid., p. 215.
15. Ibid., p. xxii.
16. Ibid., pp. xx, xxi.
17. Ibid., p. xxiii.
18. U.S. Congress, House, The Alaska Commercial Company, H. Rpt. No. 623, 44th Cong., 1st sess., 1876, p. 54.
19. William R. Rosengren, "The Careers of Clients and Organizations," in William R. Rosengren and Mark Lifton (eds.), Organizations and Clients: Essays in the Sociology of Service (Columbus, Ohio: Charles E. Merrill, 1970), pp. 117-135.
20. References to the identity of the Treasury agents are scattered throughout Fur Seal Fisheries, H. Rpt. No. 3883.
21. Ibid., p. 223; Seal Fisheries, H. Exec. Doc. No. 83, p. 68.
22. George Rogers, An Economics Analysis of the Pribilof Islands, 1870-1946. Prepared for the Indian Claims Commission, Docket Nos. 352 and 369 (Fairbanks: University of Alaska, Institute of Social, Economic and Government Research, 1976), p. 181, Table A-3.
23. Treaty of Cession, Article II, March 30, 1867. Copy appears in U.S. Congress, House, Russian America, H. Exec. Doc. No. 177, 40th Cong., 2nd sess., 1868, p. 5 ff.
24. Vincent Colyer, Report of the Honorable Vincent Colyer, United States Special Indian Commissioner, on the Indian Tribes and Their Surroundings in Alaska Territory, from Personal Observation and Inspection, 1869, H. Exec. Doc. No. 1414, 41st Cong., 2nd sess., 1869, p. 1032.
25. Seal Fisheries, H. Exec. Doc. No. 83, p. 40.
26. Ibid., pp. 61.
27. Ibid., pp. 132-133; The Alaska Commercial Company, H. Rpt. No. 623, pp. 101-103.
28. The Aleut *barabaras* housing single families, and *yurts*, housing several, were built close together. Around a shallow excavation, Aleuts built walls of stone or bone, banked on the outside with stones and matted grass. The *yurts* were entered through a hole in the top; and the *barabaras*, usually through a hole to one side. For warmth inside the dwellings, Aleuts stood or squatted over a small fire made of grass or over a bowl-shaped lamp in which the mossy wicks burned blubber. Aleš Hrdlička, The Aleutian and Commander Islands and their Inhabitants (Philadelphia: Wistar Institute, 1945), pp. 43-49.
29. Petr A. Tikhmenev, Historical Review of the Formation of the Russian-American Company and Its Activity up to the Present Time, Part I (St. Petersburg: St. Petersburg Printing Office of Edward Weimar, 1861), trans. Michael Dobrynin, p. 395. Available Bancroft Library, University of California, Berkeley.

30. Fur Seal Fisheries, H. Rpt. No. 3883, p. 5; Seal Fisheries, H. Exec. Doc. No. 83, pp. 62, 179; U.S. Treasury Department, Special Agents Division, Seal and Salmon Fisheries and General Resources of Alaska, 4 Vol. (Washington, D.C.: U.S. Government Printing Office, 1898, vol. I. Reports on the Condition of Seal Life on the Pribilof Islands by Special Treasury Agents in Charge, and Others, From 1868 to 1895, Inclusive, p. 68.
31. Charles Bryant, "On the Fur Seal Islands," The Century Illustrated Monthly Magazine, 39 (November 1889 to April 1890, Inclusive): 904.
32. Seal Fisheries, H. Exec. Doc. No. 83, pp. 62, 100.
33. The Alaska Commercial Company, H. Rpt. No. 623, p. 101.
34. "Mixed Fur Seal Records, Annual Reports, Pribilof Islands, 1786-1960," Alaska Division, Record Group 22, Item 420, National Archives, Washington, D.C.
35. A large part of the company's financial records was lost in the San Francisco fire. Source for these estimates in Henry W. Elliott, July 29, 1910, published in U.S. Congress, House, Hearing before the Committee on Expenditures in the Department of Commerce and Labor, House of Representatives, on House Resolution No. 73 to Investigate the Fur Seal Industry of Alaska, No. 14, 62nd Cong., 1st sess., 1911-1912, pp. 964-965.
36. Sources for these figures are: E.W. Sims, Report on Alaska Fur Seal Fisheries, H. Rpt. No. 251, 59th Cong., 2nd sess., 1906, p. 42; U.S. Congress, Senate, Fur-Seal Skin Sales, S. Doc. No. 213, 67th Cong., 2nd sess., April 20, 1922, p. 1; Fur Seal Fisheries, H. Rpt. No. 3883, p. 346; House Resolution No. 73, May 31, June 2, 1911, p. 964.
37. Article in Harper's Monthly, November 1877, quoted in Ernest Gruening, The State of Alaska (New York: Random House, 1968), pp. 511-512.
38. Rogers, An Economic Analysis, pp. 35-36; Seal and Salmon Fisheries (vol. 1), pp. 118, 261.
39. Because of a regulation of prices on goods in the company store (a maximum mark up of 25 percent), there does not appear to be need to adjust the United States and Pribilof data to arrive at comparative prices or equal dollars. Rogers, An Economic Analysis, p. 47.
40. Henry W. Elliott, The Seal Islands of Alaska, Section IX, Monograph A, Tenth Census of the United States (Washington, D.C.: Government Printing Office, 1881), p. 22.
41. Seal Fisheries, H. Exec. Doc. No. 83, p. 200.
42. Because of the decline in the Aleut population and work force and the company's need to secure a catch within the time allowed by law, the government imported workers from Unalaska to do work related to the seal harvest such as salting and loading the skins. The imported workers received no share of the Pribilof Aleuts' seal bonus. They were paid on a monthly rate ranging from $30 to $40 and received free board and room. Fur Seal Fisheries, H. Rpt. No. 3883, p. 156.
43. Ibid., pp. 22, 47, 253.
44. Ibid., p. xxvii.

45. Ibid., p. 47, 282; Pribilof Islands Daily Log, St. Paul, October 25, 1887.
46. Pribilof Islands Daily Log, St. Paul, October 12, 1888.
47. Fur Seal Fisheries, H. Rpt. No. 3883, p. 273.
48. Ibid., p. 410.
49. Pribilof Islands Daily Log, St. Paul, June 10, 1887.
50. Fur Seal Fisheries, H. Rpt. No. 3883, p. 335.
51. Pribilof Islands Daily Log, St. Paul, October 25, 1888.
52. Ibid., October 21, 1888.
53. Fur Seal Fisheries, H. Rpt. No. 3883, p. 214.
54. Pribilof Islands Daily Log, St. Paul, February 8, 1889.
55. Ivan E. Veniaminov, Notes on the Islands of the Unalaska District, Vol. 2 (St. Petersburg, 1840), trans. B. Keen and Assye Kardinelowska, pp. 54-55.
56. Fur Seal Fisheries, H. Rpt. No. 3883, p. 287.
57. Pribilof Islands Daily Log, St. George, October 31, 1877.
58. Fur Seal Fisheries, H. Rpt. No. 3883, p. 21.
59. Pribilof Islands Daily Log, St. Paul, July 27, 1889.
60. Seal and Salmon Fisheries, (Vol. 1), pp. 105-106.
61. Ibid., p. 147.
62. Ibid., p. 278.
63. Nancy O. Lurie, "The World's Longest On-Going Protest Demonstration," in Mac Marshall (ed.), Beliefs, Behaviors, Beverages: A Cross-Cultural Survey (Ann Arbor: The University of Michigan Press, 1979), pp. 127-144.
64. The population of the two communities was 422 in 1867 and 303 in 1889, a 28 percent decrease, and this in the face of a net migration gain of 53 persons. In 1887, a year death and birth figures are available, the crude birth rate for both villages was 49.3, while the crude death rate was 98.6. Dorothy Jones, A History of United States Administration in the Pribilof Islands, 1867-1946. Prepared for the Indian Claims Commission, Docket Nos. 352 and 369 (Fairbanks: University of Alaska, Institute of Social, Economic and Government Research, 1976), p. 47.
65. U.S. Department of Commerce, Bureau of Census, Statistical History of the United States, Colonial Times to the Present, 1965, Series B-163.
66. Seal and Salmon Fisheries, (Vol. 1), pp. 92, 99, 293.
67. Pribilof Islands Daily Log, St. Paul, September 1, 1889.
68. Peter Tikhmenev, Historical Review, Part I, p. 374; Helen Shenitz, "Alaska's Good Father," in Morgan Sherwood, ed., Alaska and its History (Seattle: University of Washington Press, 1967), pp. 39-41.
69. Veniaminov, Notes, trans., Richard Geogehan, p. 229.
70. Aleuts' attraction to the Russian Orthodox church appears to stem from several sources. Before 1788 when the Russians collected tribute from Aleuts, church membership exempted Aleuts from paying tribute for three years. Further, Aleuts found the rich ceremonial life of the church appealing. Finally, the success of the church may have been related to the church's adaptability to many Aleut customs and to conducting services in both Russian and Aleut.

In 1825 Ivan Veniaminov established the first Russian Orthodox church school in the Aleutians at Unalaska. His jurisdiction included the Pribilofs where schools were also established early in the century (Russian Orthodox churches were built at St. Paul in 1819 and St. George in 1833). Veniaminov emphasized training in the skills needed by the company as well as traditional Aleut interests such as art and music.

71. The year before the lease, a special Treasury agent who came from Russia, opened a school on St. George. Seal Fisheries, H. Exec. Doc. No. 83, p. 40.

72. Ibid., p. 51.

73. Ibid., p. 50.

74. Ibid., pp. 98-99.

75. Ibid., pp. 49, 99; Seal and Salmon Fisheries, (Vol. 1) p. 49; Fur Seal Fisheries, H. Rpt. No. 3883, pp. 252-253.

76. Seal Fisheries, H. Exec. Doc. No. 83, p. 133.

77. Michael B. Katz, The Irony of Early School Reform: Educational Innovation in Mid-Nineteenth Century Massachusetts (Cambridge: Harvard University Press, 1968).

78. Illustrations are scattered throughout Fur Seal Fisheries, H. Rpt. No. 3883, for example, pp. 153, 204.

CHAPTER 3

FROM WAGE EARNERS TO WARDS, 1890-1909

At the beginning of the second twenty-year lease, the Aleuts were wage earners. By its end they had become government wards supported by charity "hand-outs." A drastic change, yes?—brought about by the government's efforts to maintain its Pribilof priorities in the face of a changing external environment. The seal herd was in precipitous decline due to the growing popularity of pelagic (high seas) sealing, which is very wasteful.

However, before tracing these developments, I shall first describe the events leading to the dramatic demise of the Alaska Commercial Company in the seal islands. When it came time for the United States to grant the second lease in 1890, the Alaska Commercial Company's reputation was badly tarnished. In the early part of its lease, the company had faced continuous attacks by rival bidders and other San Francisco traders. In pursuit of their interests these free entrepreneurs organized the Alaska Trader's Protective Association, later renamed the Anti-Monopoly Association of the Pacific Coast. The Association vented its dissatisfactions in the Alaska Herald, a newspaper published in San Francisco between 1868 and 1876. Herald articles charged the company with mistreating Pribilof Aleuts and surreptitiously exceeding its annual seal quota. They also accused the government of suppressing a protest petition from the Aleuts. Allegedly, the Aleuts had given the petition to special Treasury agent Buynitsky in 1869, to another agent in 1870, and finally, in 1871, sent the petition directly to the Herald. The petition asserted that the Aleuts had been reduced to a state of slavery, compelled to labor, were at the mercy of the company, and were shut off from all intercourse with other portions of the public. Company spokesmen declared the petition a gross fabrication.[1]

These charges attracted nationwide attention. The virus of war and boom gave rise to rampant scandals involving both government and industry, and especially government corruption in relation to the great land steals. With growing public concern about the concentration of wealth and the alliance between government and big business, Congress in 1876 undertook an investigation of the Alaska Commercial Company.[2] The climax of the Congressional hearing was a retraction by Robert Desty, chief spokesman for the Association and journalist for the Herald. Desty confessed that he had been duped by the paper's publisher, Agapius Honcharenko.

> I have been part of a conspiracy to destroy the Alaska Commercial Company by persistent libel and I have been deceived, unwittingly and without the motive which actuated those who employed me. I have found that there is no reliable evidence to sustain a single charge that I have been induced to make against the Company.

Regarding the Aleuts' petition, Desty declared:

> He (Honcharenko) dictated it to me as a translation from the Russian. I corrected it for him and put in into shape for publication and affixed a list of names to it which he furnished me from a slip of paper, which names he informed me were those of residents of Alaska who intended to sign the petition, but which came down in this shape, as they were unacquainted with the mode and form of getting up petitions. He attached the names of five Aleuts who were actually dead before the date of the petition, which I subsequently learned.

Desty concluded his testimony with a full disavowal: "I now desire to retract all I have written against the company and this I do voluntarily without fear or compulsion of any sort." [3] No one knows what pressures were brought to bear to make Desty recant but we do know that he was an alien and at the hearing he announced that he was soon to return to France, his homeland. The hearing cleared the company of all charges;[4] nonetheless, attacks against it continued. One of the most damaging was by Alaska's territorial Governor Swineford who expressed alarm at the growing control the company exercised through its trading stations scattered across Alaska.[5]

With continuing attacks and the imminent need to renew the Pribilof lease, Congress again investigated the Alaska Commercial Company in 1888 and 1889; again it exonerated the company.[6] Nevertheless, sufficient doubt must have remained in officials' minds, for despite the company's experience and success in the fur seal trade, the Treasury Department granted the lease to another firm, the North American Commercial Company. The government had not felt impelled to grant the lease to the highest bidder in 1870. That it did so twenty years later suggests that it used the higher bid of the North American Commercial Company as a welcome excuse for terminating relations with the now-disreputable Alaska Commercial Company.

The second lease was more elaborate than the first. Accustomed to the services voluntarily provided by the Alaska Commercial Company, the department now required these from the new lessee: support for widows, orphans, and infirm; medical care; and rent-free houses, as well as construction of a church building. In addition, the lease increased the annual rent from $55,000 to $60,000 and the tax per skin from $2.625 to $7.625. Further, the government, not the company, was to set the Aleuts' pay scale.[7]

These requirements, however, were a minor burden to the company compared to the greatly restricted seal quotas, which reflected the decline in the seal population from an estimated 2 million in 1882 to 900,000 in 1890.[8] The increasing value of the skins was attracting a growing number of pelagic sealers, and open-sea sealing was extremely wasteful. Quite aside from the taking of seals that might otherwise have been harvested on the Pribilofs, pelagic sealing involved killing many females as the sex of the animal could not be determined on the high seas, and caused high losses in seals that could not be retrieved. Elliott estimated that approximately 55 percent of the seals taken by pelagic hunters were "mother seals" which meant that their pups were also destroyed.[9] A witness before the 1889 Congressional hearing testified that the average high seas hunter recovered only one in seven of the seals he killed—"the others sinking or getting away wounded."[10]

In an effort to control pelagic sealing, the United States seized and confiscated a number of sealing vessels operating in the Bering Sea. It justified these acts by claiming jurisdiction over Bering Sea seals. These confiscations led to conflict with Great Britain since the majority were Canadian vessels which sailed under the British flag. International negotiations, beginning in 1891 and continuing throughout the period of the second lease, were ineffective. Piecemeal measures such as prohibiting pelagic sealing during certain periods of the year and the use of firearms and explosives in seal hunting as well as limiting the Pribilof annual harvest for a few years to 7,500 seals for Aleuts' food failed to halt the seal decline.[11] Neither did a federal law prohibiting United States citizens from pelagic sealing.[12]

Anxiety about survival of the seals prompted the government to set very low seal quotas every year during the second lease. In contrast to the nearly two million seals taken by the Alaska Commercial Company, the new lessee was allowed to harvest a total of only 339,180.[13] The small trade in fox furs failed to compensate for this reduction.[14] Yet, even with the low seal harvests, the company realized a sizable profit—over five and one-half million dollars in the twenty-year period.[15] The company's favorable profit position was possible because of the increasing value of raw skins—worth $40 each in 1900—and also because it received a direct and indirect subsidy from the government in the form of management costs that were not reflected in the skin taxes, rent or the relief appropriation for the Pribilof Aleuts. Had the company been required to pay these costs, its net profit would have been reduced by more than half.[16]

Unlike the company, the government's surplus funds were wiped out; in fact, the government experienced a net loss of nearly two and one-half million dollars over the twenty years.[17]

There is nothing unusual about federal programs costing the government money. But in the Pribilof case, federal policy reflected a Congressional expectation that the program pay for itself at a minimum, or better yet, that it show a profit. The report of the 1876 Congressional hearings on the Alaska Commercial Company voiced this expectation.

> The contract, as made, was the best disposition of the interest that could have been made, for it is certain that it has resulted in the receipt of a very large revenue to the Treasury, and in the amelioration of the physical and moral condition of the natives.[18]

The report from the 1888 Congressional hearings expressed a similar expectation.

> That if the law protecting seal life is enforced the preservation of the rookeries will be assured, the revenue continued and increased, and the native inhabitants of the seal islands maintained *without cost to the Government*. . . That the fur seal industry will have paid into the Treasury over $9,000,000 (sic) during the period of the present lease. . . That the chief object of the purchase was the acquisition of the valuable products of the Bering Sea.[19]

In subsequent hearings, in fact, throughout the history of the Pribilof program, Congressional members and Pribilof managers repeatedly refer to its self-supporting and profitable character.

There is, of course, nothing out of the ordinary for government officials to express cost consciousness and embrace values of efficiency and economy. The point here is that from its origin, the Pribilof program, as a government enterprise, was held to private market-place standards of profitability that became deeply entrenched into the fabric of the management system. In effect, this gave rise to norms and attitudes that distinguish the Pribilof program from most other government activities, especially in the social welfare field.

Uncertainty about the future of the seals, the impasse in international negotiations, and the reality of a revenue loss made Washington policymakers frantic. They considered such desperate measures as destroying all the Pribilof seals and removing the Aleuts from the islands. In 1896, a bill in the House of Representatives stipulated that:

> if . . . the President finds himself unable to secure the cooperation of Great Britain . . . so as to protect and preserve the Alaskan seal herd for this year's sealing season, then the Secretary is authorized to take each and every fur seal on the Pribilof Islands and to sell the skins of said seals as he may elect.[20]

The House Committee on Foreign Relations unanimously recommended passage of the bill on the rationale of mercy, economy, and justice.

> If . . . we fail in this . . . notwithstanding we have been urging Great Britain for more than a year to unite with us in measures to preserve seal life, then considerations of mercy as well as of economy and justice demand that we should stop the further cruel starvation of thousands of seal pups by taking what seals are left and disposing of their skins and covering into the Treasury the proceeds which would probably reach $5,000,000.[21]

The bill did not pass, probably because of opposition from the company as well as the Senate.

In debate on the bill, Congressmen considered removing Aleuts from the Pribilofs since without seals the Aleuts would have no means of livelihood. An amendment to the relief appropriation bill for Aleuts in 1900 made the removal a possibility: "In the discretion of the Secretary of the Treasury any portion of this sum may be expended in transporting said native inhabitants to the mainland of Alaska."[22] This atmosphere of desperation, of dire threat to the Pribilof program, was the dominant force shaping Pribilof management policies in this period.

In the early 1890s, the Aleuts faced severe poverty. Though the government had raised their sealing rate from 40 to 50 cents a skin (75 cents in 1906), this in no way compensated for income lost from decreased seal harvests. The Aleuts worked at a piece rate and therefore sealing income declined in proportion to the reduction in harvests. The Aleuts' average annual income from all sources (including donor goods furnished by the company) in the 1890-1894 period was substantially below that of other United States production workers—one-third lower in St. Paul and 29 percent lower in St. George.[23]

Living side by side with the Aleuts, Treasury agents were keenly aware of their poverty and were especially concerned about it in view of their continued high death rate,[24] about three times higher than that in Massachusetts.[25] The St. Paul agent in 1890 noted in his daily log that "not one native was in good health."[26] Depopulation of the Aleuts was just as real a threat as the extinction of the seals. Still blaming the problem on low marriage rates, the Treasury Secretary established a policy designed to bring marriageable men into the village.

> The question of depopulation of the islands of St. Paul and St. George is a serious one and demands attention. . . You will therefore take into consideration the proposition to recruit the permanent inhabitants of the islands of St. Paul and St. George by placing upon them next year a small number (ten or twenty) of young men, or transferring to these islands several families in which are a number of young men.[27]

With this mandate, agents intensified efforts to promote marriage, using the same coercive tactics as in the preceding period: "Finally decided Neon Shabolin can marry Fecla Shane and Neon Mandregan can marry Mary Kotchootin. *Alex Melividov and one or two others to go to Unalaska or St. George and find wives or they can't come back.*"[28]

Apparently agents did not perceive coercion and exile as undermining the Aleuts' welfare. Like others in that day, they judged welfare in terms of physical well-being. Consequently, while they frightfully violated the Aleuts' rights, they also tried to protect the Aleuts from impoverishment. In the absence of government intervention, agents began to issue supplies of food and clothing on credit. Increasingly, they importuned the department to provide funds for the Aleuts' relief.

> The department will have to make some provision for the support and maintenance of these people, as their mode of making a living has been destroyed for the present, and the future is only what the charity of government will make it. There is utterly nothing here upon which they can depend for a livelihood until the much wished for return of seals takes place, an event too far in the future to give promise of better times to these unfortunate people.[29]

Appeals such as these came at a time when top management was reeling under the impact of the threatened destruction of its own mission in the Pribilofs. Cost considerations, important from the outset of the program, now became urgent—economy, belt tightening, these were the clamorous policy motifs. The Aleuts' poverty at a time like this apparently irked managers. As if swatting a pesky fly, their first reaction to agents' pleas for remedying poverty was an instruction to distribute among the Aleuts money they had collected for the church consistory in San Francisco. The agent in charge complied.

> In accordance with the instructions of May 2, the funds placed in the hands of the North American Commercial Company by the priest of the Greek church for transmission to the consistory at San Francisco was counted in the presence of the Government officer and the company official, and the amount was found to be $3,334.10.
>
> On June 26, a meeting of the priest and the chief men of the village was called, and they were informed that in view of the needy condition of the natives the Department deemed it wiser that these funds should be redistributed to them. The natives agreed that as the funds were to be distributed all those present in the village should be partakers of the benefits of it.[30]

Funds amounting to a little over $3,000—hardly a solution to a poverty problem. Moreover, this act antagonized church officials, and in response to their protests, the department returned the money several years later, although it repaid it from funds appropriated for the Aleuts' relief.[31]

But the Aleuts' poverty and high death rate and agents' alarm about them continued; the issue could no longer be avoided. Indian poverty, of course, was not unique to the Pribilofs. Deprived of a land base and subsistence resources, poverty was widespread among Indians in the reservations in the west, and federal relief for these tribes was common. In line with this practice, the department requested and was granted a Congressional relief appropriation for the Pribilof Aleuts. Beginning in 1894, Congress appropriated $19,500 annually for all but one year in the second lease period.[32]

The relief appropriation, intended as a poverty reduction measure, proved to be a turning point in labor relations on the Pribilofs as we shall soon see. It did, however, achieve its intended purpose. When calculated as income, the appropriation succeeded in bringing Aleuts' average annual income up to and in some years above that of the average United States production worker. St. George's income was even higher than St. Paul's due to the increase in fox skin sales.[33] One wonders if it were a coincidence or if the appropriation were designed to achieve parity with other workers.

On a per capita basis, though, because the Aleuts' families were larger than the national average, their income was below that of other workers. But this is a risky comparison, for the United States per capita figure includes all kinds of income—property, interest, profit. A better comparison is per capita personal consumption if we assume that Aleuts spent all their income on personal consumption (most of it was in the form of consumer goods in any case). This comparison shows that per capita consumption levels were 40.2 percent lower than national levels on St. Paul and 17.8 percent power on St. George. Thus, even with a comparable annual wage, the low per capita consumption level in the Pribilofs suggests that Aleuts faced greater poverty than other Americans.[34]

Because of the form by which it was administered, the relief appropriation presaged a major shift in the Aleuts' economic status. At first the department conceived the appropriation as a wage supplement, as payment for labor that formerly had been unpaid. Agents opened accounts for each sealer and made them debtors for the orders given them. At the same time agents credited sealers' accounts with the amounts earned doing labor for government, at the rate of 15 cents an hour, and included in the compensation plan work for which Aleuts had not been paid in the past, such as guarding the rookeries.[35]

This system seems reasonable. The Aleuts worked for the government for most of the year. Nonetheless, after a few years it ceased operating and was replaced by a system in which not only the appropriation but the sealing wage were distributed as charity. The St. Paul agent, Dr. Walter Lembkey, reminiscent of Bryant's vehement advocacy for Aleut autonomy in the earlier period, adamantly protested this change. His annual reports include page after page of objections.

> Heretofore the native could expend his earnings as he pleased. After the appropriation, however, the earnings were sequestered by the agents, and the natives had no voice whatever in the expenditure of the money for which they toiled. Each native was allotted articles of necessity to a certain amount each week payable from his wages and after the latter were expended the appropriation was drawn upon at the same rate until another sealing season intervened. . .
>
> This plan of compensation . . . is highly objectionable when considered from a sociological standpoint, its weakness being that it reduces all to a common level. It prevents the progress that accrues from the cultivation of superior skill or greater self-denial and makes a virtual almshouse of the Pribilof reservation by dealing with the inhabitants as indigents. It requires willing service of the native but takes from him his wage and expends it for his benefit without his consent. Incentive to increased individual efficiency is lacking because effort to that end is fruitless in bringing any

greater benefit than if it had not been made.

> It is reasonable to assume that the Government, while operating on the seal islands for its own profit, at the same time desires to better the condition of the native residents upon whose efforts it must depend for successful conduct of its business. The first step in that direction is to do away with the appropriation of Congress for their support and to increase the wage earned through the taking of skins to a sum at least equal to the amount necessary for their maintenance. This would at once eliminate the objectionable element of charity in the present system and allow each man to support himself and family from his own earnings . . . it would go far toward increasing the moral tone of the native, by making him more self-reliant and self-respecting. It can be taken without additional legislation, the Secretary of Commerce and Labor now having the power under existing law to fix the natives' compensation for taking skins.[36]

Lembkey was also indignant about the incredibly complicated system for administering the appropriation and the sealing wage.

> (1) From the whole amount appropriated by Congress a sum is deducted sufficient to pay for the annual supply of coal for both islands . . .
>
> (2) The remainder is apportioned between the two islands on a basis varying with the condition whether the natives' earnings from seal and fox skins . . . are greater or less than usual.
>
> (3) The amount apportioned for either island is then added to the amount realized from natives' earnings on that island and the total sum is allotted as follows:
>
> (a) An amount, say $1,000, is deducted for an "emergency fund" and the remainder is divided in 12 equal parts, representing months of the year, or for greater accuracy 52 equal parts, representing weeks. This determines the amount which may be expended each week or month . . . for the whole island.
>
> (b) The total number of natives to be supported by the Government is then ascertained from the census—two children being considered equal to one adult—and divided into weekly or monthly allotment for the whole island, thus establishing a per capita allowance for the week or month.
>
> (c) The number of natives in each family is then ascertained from the census, and the per capita amounts are combined to give a basis for the expenditure for each family for the week or month.
>
> (d) It having been demonstrated that a large family can live more cheaply per capita than a small one, a rearrangement of amounts is made, deducting a certain sum from the large family allotments and adding it to those for the small families, and a final adjustment is reached, giving—as in the fiscal year 1903—from about $5.50 per week for a family of two to about $8.50 or $9 a week for a family of seven.
>
> (e) Having thus established the amount to which each family is entitled, the issues of food and clothing are then made on Saturday of each week to the heads of families, each head being given an order for supplies . . . which is filled in the lessee's store. . .

(f) In case of sickness, death, childbirth, marriage, or other unusual conditions requiring an expenditure not contemplated in the regular allowance, the emergency fund is drawn upon.

(g) No expenditure from the appropriation has been allowed until the native head of family has expended his earnings from the taking of skins.

(h) Ledger accounts both of his earnings and the expenditures from the appropriation, are kept on the islands with each head of family, which is credited with his weekly allowance and debited with the amount of his weekly order.[37]

A bureaucratic labyrinth such as this doesn't spring spontaneously to life; its design must have taken considerable thought and planning. And what was behind the design? Cost considerations—plainly and simply. For one reason, Aleuts could and did use part of their cash earnings for purchases at Unalaska. Paying them in supplies eliminated this practice. For another reason, the government could, through manipulation of the quantity and quality of supplies, keep the costs of in kind payments at a bare minimum. Listen to the 1906 instructions to agents.

> Articles of strict necessity only should be issued. No expensive dress goods, boots, or other articles are to be provided. The native should be restricted to one pair of shoes each year and the women to one good dress. Ginghams, calicoes, muslins, and similar inexpensive dress goods may be issued in reasonable quantities.[38]

Agents' logs repeatedly reveal the inadequacy of government-issued supplies.

> Pribilof Islands Daily Log, St. George, August 27, 1898.
>
> Also informed the natives that I will have to reduce orders because of reduced money.

> Pribilof Islands Daily Log, St. Paul, January 25, 1896.
>
> It seems that neither milk nor lard is issued these people—which is not right.

> Pribilof Islands Daily Log, St. Paul, February 20, 1896.
>
> Owing to continued cold weather and scarcity of coal some of the widows agreed to double up temporarily.

> Pribilof Islands Daily Log, St. Paul, June 11, 1910.
>
> The natives came in this morning for their orders as usual but there was no such thing as filling their orders even though they are on short allowance.

Though the shortage of supplies in the above instance was due to the delayed arrival of the supply ship, agent Lembkey, a tireless champion of the Aleuts' welfare, argued that the supplies regularly furnished did not cover all necessities, such as candles, matches, stove repairs, cooking utensils, tableware, and furniture. He estimated the average annual costs of these other necessaries at $99.03 per family and showed that all men on St. George and thirteen men on St. Paul earned substantially less than that amount.[39]

Clearly, it was easier for managers to reduce costs by manipulating supplies than cash wages, and to accomplish this they instituted a system of payments in kind based on need rather than labor, a system that deprived Aleuts of their status as wage earners. If not wage earners, what was the Aleuts' economic status? They were not relief recipients; relief recipients are unemployed and the Aleuts labored. The Aleuts were wards of the government, a status that grew out of the protectorate relationship established in the 1870 Act. In our search of records, the first application of the term 'ward' to Pribilof Aleuts appeared in the Department's 1891 instructions to agents.[40] Thereafter, the Department routinely referred to the Aleuts as wards.

Precedents for the idea of wardship are embedded in the history of Indian policy in the United States, most of which concerned control over land. Early government policies toward Indians, based on recognition of their equal status, resulted in treaties that respected Indian property. But immigration and the demands of industrial development wrought profound changes in the relationship. Economic development and western expansion created a continuous demand for land, and Indians owned much of it. In 1830 Congress passed the Indian Removal Act which moved Indians from their land in the east to reservations in the west. This appeased but did not sate the land hunger. As western migration gathered momentum in the 1880s, there was a growing demand for access to the rest of the Indian lands. In 1887 Congress enacted the Indian Allotment Act (Dawes Act) which required Indians to divide their common lands into individual tracts. Ultimately, two-thirds of this land was sold to settlers.[41]

Removing Indians from their natural habitats and then breaking up their common lands which were the base of the economies, indeed, rendered Indians dependent on the government. In recognition of this dependency, Congress and the courts defined Indians as "domestic dependent nations" who were wards of the government. As used in common law, wardship refers to a relationship in which a guardian (a) has custody of the ward's person and can decide where the ward is to live, (b) is required to educate and maintain the ward out of the ward's estate, (c) is authorized to manage the ward's property for the benefit of the ward, (d) is precluded from profiting at the expense of the ward's estate, and (e) is accountable to the wards and the courts for its conduct toward the wards. Cohen, Ickes, and Margold, in a comprehensive review of federal Indian laws, asserted that the common law usage of wardship does not strictly characterize the relationship between the United States and Indians, but that there are enough similarities and parallels to account for its application in this country.[42]

One of the most salient features of wardship is the very broad and vaguely defined Congressional power exercised over Indians. By virtue of this broad power, legislation that would have been unconstitutional if applied to non-Indians was held to be constitutional when applied to Indians.[43] Inequality inheres in the exercise of such broad powers; in fact, court decisions gave official recognition to this inequality.

> *The recognized relationship between the parties to this controversy, therefore, is that between a superior and inferior*, whereby the latter is placed under the care and control of the former and which, while it authorized the adoption on the part of the United States of such policy as their own public interests may dictate, recognizes, on the other hand, such an interpretation of their acts and promises as justice and reason demand in all cases where power is exerted by the strong over those to whom they owe care and protection.[44]

These broad powers and the inequality embedded in them inevitably deprived Indians of the rights and privileges accorded other Americans. Even the citizenship rights of Indians were abrogated. Occasionally the courts confused the term 'wardship' with Indian noncitizenship. But Congressional acts and court decisions repeatedly show that the extent of Congressional power over Indians did not diminish when citizenship was granted. It remained in full force even after the passage of the Indian Citizenship Act in 1924. In the Pribilofs the wardship definition was established by a Treasury Secretary who himself believed Aleuts to be citizens.

> *1891 Instructions to Agents.*
>
> You will endeavor to secure the good will and confidence of the native inhabitants of the islands and advise them, whenever practicable, of their rights and duties as American citizens.[45]

Wardship laws distinguish between Congressional and administrative powers, limiting the latter to enforcing Congressional mandates; administrative agencies cannot issue and enforce their own regulations. But this distinction did not apply in the Pribilofs where the law gave the Secretary of the Treasury *carte blanche* in making rules and regulations related to the comfort, maintenance, education, and protection of the Aleuts. Incredibly broad administrative powers, these—they must represent a unique case in United States history.

While the Secretary of the Treasury was appointed protector of the Pribilof Aleuts, the Aleuts themselves were not legally defined as wards. Rather they became wards by administrative fiat. In 1929 the governor of Alaska asked the United States Department of Justice to clarify the political status of Alaska Indians—Indians was the generic term used for all Alaska natives. "In the opinion of this Department, Alaska Indians are not wards of government within the meaning of court cases applying to Indians in other parts of the United States," replied the United States attorney.[46] In recognition of the questionable legality or outright illegality of defining Pribilof Aleuts as wards, a high-ranking official in 1942 tried to cover the government's tracks.

> In correspondence and reports, we often have referred to the Pribilof natives as "virtual wards of the Government." This shows that technically or legally, we have

not considered them as wards of the Government though in effect they have been in that status.[47]

Curious, isn't it?—that after a practical, "dollars and cents" reason for denying Aleuts' status as wage earners arose, managers called on the ideology of wardship to explain it. In this case, certainly, ideology did not initiate policy, as scholars sometimes claim; it was brought into play to justify the policy. In any event, although managers probably considered the payment in kind an emergency measure during a period of economic depression in the islands, it came to be the defining feature of labor-management relations in the Pribilofs until quite recently.

The economic depression in the Pribilofs, although the dominant issue in this period, was not the sole management consideration. The Pribilof program was affected by a general trend toward greater elaboration of federal bureaucracies. In 1903, the government created a new department—Commerce and Labor to which it assigned administrative responsibility for the Pribilofs; in 1909, it established within the Department of Commerce and Labor, the Bureau of Fisheries which managed the Pribilofs thereafter. At the same time, the Pribilof program had to organize a more complex set of responsibilities than before due to expanded lease requirements, intensification of seal herd management, and administration of the Aleuts' relief appropriation. Relying on past experience in the Pribilofs, the new Department routinized its operation, and issued regular, detailed instructions which codified a number of practices that agents had informally established in the past. Obligatory labor was now official policy.

> . . . *You are directed to utilize their (the Aleuts') services* when not required by the company, in repairing roads, guarding the rookeries, and performing such other duties as seem desirable.

Interference in the Aleuts' political system was now officially sanctioned.

> No interference should be permitted in the selection of their chiefs by the native inhabitants of the islands. If it should transpire, however, that persons manifestly unsuitable for the position are chosen, *it will be your duty to interpose in the interests of good government and require the selection of proper persons,* but such action should be taken only in extreme cases.

The ban on sugar was now officially authorized.

> Should intoxication become so general among the people as to interfere with good government and jeopardize the peace, *you are authorized to discontinue altogether the sale of sugar and of other articles entering into the manufacture of intoxicants* for such length of time as may appear wise.

Exile was now officially condoned.

> Should natives or other persons become so unruly or immoral in conduct as to en-

danger the peace and good government of the people, *they should be removed from the islands* and the Revenue Cutter Service will be instructed to render such assistance as may be necessary for that purpose.

Secrecy about the Pribilof operation was now official policy.

> No information regarding the seals or as to any other matter pertaining to the seal islands is to be given out by you or by any of the assistant agents. All applications for such information should be referred to the department.[48]

These instruction remained in effect until after World War II.

And so the government, responsible for protecting Aleuts from potential abuse by a private company, itself created a system of political and economic domination and abuse, justified in terms that the Aleuts were wards of the government. And we see the forces that led the government to set up such a totalitarian system on the Pribilofs. The system grew from a set of priorities that placed economic incentives and market place standards first and the Aleuts' welfare last. Because Aleut labor was essential to its economic goals, the government assured the Aleuts' physical survival. But Aleut autonomy and freedom were not necessary to achieve its mission; in fact, officials saw them as a deterrent. More germane to bringing revenues into the treasury was forced labor, emasculation of the Aleuts' political authority, and punishments, including exile, for Aleut defiance. Nonetheless, in the economically prosperous years of the first lease, the government was satisfied that the Aleuts earned a reasonable wage and were paid in cash as were other American workers. In the years of the second lease, with the threatened extermination of the seals, a severe economic downturn, and an actual loss in federal revenues, cost considerations became the dominant concern. With a tradition of ignoring and even trampling on the Aleuts' rights, it was a simple short step to denying them their right to cash wages and to payment for labor performed. And given the times in which they lived, when the Indian wars were still in progress and when Indians were defined as wards with no civil rights, it was a simple step to justify any treatment of the Pribilof Aleuts in terms of Indian wardship status. When government agencies in general and the Pribilof management agency in particular became more beaucratically sophisticated, the Pribilof program routinized its operations and codified abusive practices that agents had informally introduced in the past and that Washington officials had implicitly blessed. Economic and political domination of the Pribilof Aleuts became official federal policy.

People considerations aside, by the end of the second lease, Pribilof managers still faced enormous anxiety about the future of the seals and of international negotiations to control pelagic sealing. Furthermore, there was talk that the North American Commercial Company was itself engaging in pelagic sealing. The department faced some hard decisions when it came time to consider a new lease.

Endnotes

1. U.S. Congress, House, Seal Fisheries of Alaska, H. Exec. Doc. No. 83, 44th Cong., 1st sess., 1876, pp. 152-171.
2. Conducted by the House Committee on Ways and Means.
3. U.S. Congress, House, The Alaska Commercial Company, H. Rpt. No. 623, 44th Cong., 1st sess., 1876, p. 143.
4. Ibid., p. 13.
5. U.S. Congress, House, Fur Seal Fisheries of Alaska, H. Rpt. No. 3883, 50th Cong., 2nd sess., 1889, p. xxviii.
6. Conducted by the House Committee on Merchant Marine and Fisheries. Fur Seal Fisheries, H. Rpt. No. 3883, p. vii.
7. U.S. Congress, Senate, Message from the President of the United States, S. Exec. Doc. No. 67, 53rd Cong., 3rd sess., 1895, pp. 34-36.
8. U.S. Treasury Department, Special Agents Division, Seal and Salmon Fisheries and General Resources of Alaska, 4 vol. (Washington, D.C.: Government Printing Office, 1898), Vol. 1: Reports on the Conditions of Seal Life on the Pribilof Islands by Special Treasury Agents in Charge, and Others, from 1865 to 1898, Both Inclusive, p. 188; Edwin W. Sims, Report on the Alaskan Fur-Seal Industry of Alaska, H. Rpt. No. 251, 59th Cong., 2nd sess., 1906, p. 41.
9. U.S. Congress, House, Hearings Before the Committee on Expenditures in the Department of Commerce and Labor, House of Representatives, on House Resolution No. 73, to Investigate the Fur-Seal Industry of Aaska, No. 14, 62nd Cong., 1st sess., 1911-1912, p. 967.
10. Fur Seal Fisheries, H. Rpt. No. 3883, p. 109.
11. In June 1891 the United States and Great Britain agreed upon a *modus vivendi* by which Great Britain was to prohibit seal killing until the following May in the Bering Sea eastward of the line of demarcation described in the Treaty of Cession, and the United States was to prohibit seal killing in the Pribilofs in excess of 7,500 seals to be taken for the subsistence of Aleuts. While the *modus vivendi* was to be effective for only one year, it was renewed in 1892 and 1893.

At the same time, the United States and Great Britain agreed to consign the seal controversy to a tribunal of arbitration. Meeting in Paris in 1894, the tribunal rejected the closed sea concept, required the United States to pay damages for seizing Canadian vessels, and agreed upon certain conservation measures—prohibitions against the use of firearms, nets, and explosives in hunting, and a closed season between May and September; however, it opened the season under certain restrictions in August, a time when the entire seal herd was in the Bering Sea. The above summarizes the negotiations contained in Message from the President, S. Exec. Doc. No. 67.
12. 30 Stat 226 (December 29, 1897).
13. U.S. Congress, Senate, Fur Seal Skin Sales, S. Doc. No. 213, 67th Cong.,

2nd sess., 1922, p. 1.

14. Gross revenues from the blue fox trade on the Pribilofs were only $235,258 over the twenty years of the lease. George Rogers, An Economic Analysis of the Pribilof Islands, 1870-1946. Prepared for the Indian Claims Commission, Docket Nos. 352 and 369 (Fairbanks: University of Alaska, Institute of Social, Economic and Government Research, 1976), p. 77.

Ownership of property rights to foxes became a hotly debated issue early in the second lease period. The company claimed that it had inherited property rights to foxes from the Alaska Commercial Company. The government agent in charge of the islands believed that the Treasury Department owned the foxes since they were on the islands in the Russian period. And free traders put in their bid to participate in the Pribilof fox trade. The department resolved these conflicting claims in favor of the company, giving it an exclusive lease to the Pribilof fox trade, although unlike the seal contract, the government received no revenues from it. This development, in essence, meant that the company had a monopoly of trade on the islands for fox and seal production and were the only industries. Seal and Salmon Fisheries, (Vol. 1), p. 281.

15. Rogers, An Economic Analysis, pp. 82-83.
16. Ibid., p. 78.
17. Ibid., p. 75.
18. The Alaska Commercial Company, H. Rpt. No. 623, p. 12.
19. Fur Seal Fisheries, H. Rpt. No. 3883, p. xxiii.
20. U.S. Congress, House, H. Rpt. No. 451, 54th Cong., 1st sess., 1896, p. 1.
21. Ibid., p. 2.
22. 30 Stat 1093 (March 3, 1899).
23. Rogers, An Economic Analysis, p. 96.
24. Pribilof Aleuts crude death rates exceeded birth rates nearly every year. In the 1890 to 1894 period, the average crude death rate was 61.2 in St. Paul and 49.2 in St. George compared to 18.2 for Massachusetts. Dorothy M. Jones, A History of United States Administration in the Pribilof Islands, 1867-1946. Prepared for the Indian Claims Commission, Dockets Nos. 352 and 369 (Fairbanks: University of Alaska, Institute of Social and Economic Research, 1976), p. 87.
25. U.S. Department of Commerce, Bureau of the Census, Statistical History of the United States, Colonial Times to the Present, 1965, Series B-163.
26. Pribilof Islands Daily Log, St. Paul, October 10, 1890.
27. Seal and Salmon Fisheries (Vol. 1), pp. 269-270.
28. Pribilof Islands Daily Log, St. Paul, August 2, 1892, September 1, 1892.
29. Seal and Salmon Fisheries (Vol. 1), p. 236.
30. Ibid., p. 331.
31. 28 Stat 391 (August 18, 1894). The appropriation for 1894 is stated as follows:

To enable the Secretary of the Treasury to furnish food, fuel, and clothing to the native inhabitants on the islands of St. Paul and St. George, Alaska, nineteen thousand five hundred dollars shall be appropriated and of the portion of said sum to be distributed to the inhabitants of St. Paul, three thousand three hundred and twenty-five dollars shall be paid to the bishop of the Greek Church, San Francisco, California, in full satisfaction of the amount contributed by members of said church of said island and placed in the hands of the agent of the North American Commercial Company for delivery to the bishop of said church, and afterwards, under instructions of the Treasury Department, expended in furnishing the natives of said island necessary supplies to prevent suffering and starvation, a prorata amount being allowed each of the families on the island.

32. The relief appropriation was dropped to $15,000 for the year 1904, 32 Stat 1111 (March 3, 1903).
33. Rogers, An Economic Analysis, p. 96.
34. Ibid., pp. 101, 102.
35. Seal and Salmon Fisheries (Vol. 1), p. 360.
36. U.S. Department of Commerce and Labor, Appendix A, to Hearings on House Resolution No. 73, 62nd Cong., 1st sess., 1911, pp. 1039-1041.
37. Ibid., pp. 22-23.
38. Ibid., p. 148.
39. Ibid., p. 216.
40. Seal and Salmon Fisheries (Vol. 1), p. 308. Agent Williams in 1891 referred to the department's definition of Pribilof Aleuts as wards of the government.
41. Theodore Haas, "The Legal Aspects of Indian Affairs from 1887-1957," The Annals of the American Academy of Political and Social Science: American Indians and Indian Life, May 1957, p. 15.
42. Felix S. Cohen, et. al., Handbook of Federal Indian Law (Washington, D.C.: U.S. Government Printing Office, 1942), p. 169.
43. Ibid., p. 170.
44. The Supreme Court of the United States in the case of Choctaw Nation versus United States, 1886.
45. Seal and Salmon Fisheries (Vol. 1), p. 270.
46. R.F. Roth, United States Attorney, to Governor Thomas Riggs (Alaska), May 13, 1921. Bureau of Fisheries Records, Federal Archives and Records Center, Seattle.
47. Ward T. Bower, Chief, Division of Alaska Fisheries, to Fredericka Martin, September 29, 1942. Fredericka Martin Records.
48. Appendix A to Hearings, 1911, pp. 41-42.

CHAPTER 4

SOLE FEDERAL JURISDICTION, 1910 to 1918

The Pribilof program was in trouble. The seal decline had reached crisis proportions—from an estimated two million animals in 1870 to only about 133,000 in 1910.[1] The program faced other threats to its stability in the 1910s such as continued revenue losses and a national scandal. Organizational survival preoccupied management and shaped its policies in this decade.

The crisis in seals could not be blamed on the private lease system but it came to be associated with it, especially in the face of mounting charges that the North American Commercial Company was engaging in illegal pelagic sealing—accusations soon confirmed by a Congressional investigation.[2] More important in discrediting the private lease system, however, was the emergence of a conservation lobby in the United States, activated by Theodore Roosevelt's succession to the Presidency in 1901. Before that, people had thought of natural resources primarily as a source for industrial exploitation. Roosevelt, however, popularized a conservation concept that stimulated the organization of national conservation groups, such as the Campfire Club of America. The Senate established a committee on conservation. And, in 1909, President Taft appointed a fur seal advisory board composed of prominent biologists, all but one of whom had visited the Pribilofs.[3] These groups clamored for an end to the private lease system and a moratorium on sealing in the Pribilofs to give the herd a chance to recover.

Congress responded to these pressures with the 1910 Fur Seal Act.[4] The Act ended the private lease system and assigned sole responsibility for the Pribilof program to the Department of Commerce and Labor. The Department and its Bureau of Fisheries were responsible not only for regulating the harvests and protecting the herd, but for harvesting and marketing the skins. Like its predecessor, the Act provided for the welfare of Aleuts. But additionally it required the Department to pay Aleut sealers fair compensation for their labor, though it offered no standards for determining what constituted fair compensation.

The Act, of course, did not resolve the seal crisis. That resolution depended on international negotiations; fortunately, these were nearing fruition. In 1911, the United States, Great Britain (representing Canada), Japan, and Russia signed a treaty—the North Pacific Fur Seal Convention—abolishing sealing on the high seas for fifteen years.[5] (The ban is still in effect; it was interrupted only once by Japan during World War II.) Japan and Russia were included in the treaty because the Japanese hunted seals that bred at the Russian-owned Commander Islands. In exchange for abstaining from pelagic sealing, Japan and Canada each were to receive 15 percent of the Russian and 15 percent of the United States' fur seal harvests.

Yes, two decades of struggle were at an end; the seal controversy was resolved. But the resolution created an additional strain for management, for now the program *had to* produce revenues to meet international obligations. Restoration of the herd became urgent. On the advice of Bureau of Fisheries biologists, Congress in 1912 declared a five-year moratorium on sealing in the Pribilofs, except for seals needed for the Aleuts' food.[6]

This respite gave the Bureau time to organize the seal business within the United States. In 1913 and 1914, probably because of the war in Europe, the Bureau sold the skins at auction in the United States. In 1915 it negotiated a contract with a St. Louis firm, Funsten and Brothers, to process and market the skins. Six years later, it signed a new contract with Funsten's successor, Fouke Fur Company (Fouke had been president of Funsten's),[7] which, aside from periodic supplements and one short interruption, is still in effect.

During the moratorium, revenues from the seal industry were very small; in the eight years 1911 to 1919, the government experienced a net loss of $755,947 in the Pribilof program.[8] If cost considerations were important in the past, they were paramount now.

The Congressional relief appropriation, which constituted the major portion of the Aleuts' livelihood, was no longer referred to as relief but as a wage supplement, undoubtedly because of the "fair compensation" clause in the 1910 Act. Pribilof management took pains to convey this change in concept to agents.

> **1911 Instructions to Agents**
> It is the purpose of this bureau not only to secure the comfort and maintenance of these people as required by law, but also, while doing so better their social and moral condition, by doing away with gratuities and furnishing them with the necessaries of life *only as a return for labor performed.*[9]

In line with this concept, management instructed agents to distribute the appropriation to the extent possible in the form of a wage payment rather than a gratuity. All of it was paid in supplies at the government store and in coal issues. This is how the system worked: each sealer received credit at the government store in varying amounts depending on work classifications; for example, the most skilled worker received an allowance of $5.00 a week, and the least skilled, $2.50.* The rest of the appropriation was distributed as

*The practice of paying wages in the form of store credit was not unique to the Pribilofs; it was also common practice in the fur trapping trade, especially when Indians were involved.

relief with fixed amounts assigned to widows, children, teenagers, and elderly.[10]

The Aleuts received no cash payments at all except negligible amounts for occasional labor for the naval radio station on St. Paul. At the outset of the new period, management directed agents to pay Aleuts in cash for labor on government property, but it soon eliminated funds for this purpose.[11]

In 1913 Congress increased the Aleuts' appropriation to $35,000; and in 1915, to $40,000.[12] When the appropriation is calculated as income along with services provided by the Bureau, such as free medical care and rent-free housing, and the small amount earned at miscellaneous labor, Aleuts' income matched that of other male production workers.[13] Yet, agents consistently complained about the Aleuts' poverty. Lembkey likened the Aleut's standard of living to that "of unskilled laborers of the poorer classes."[14] Agent Fassett who succeeded Lembkey also decried the low living standards: "Their children, in particular, are insufficiently nourished and clothed, and practically all the people are inadequately housed in old, dilapidated buildings now on the verge of collapse . . . and the allowance of fuel, which should have been more, has just been cut in half."[15] Physicians added their voices to the protest, especially when it came to milk for the children which was often unavailable.[16]

Yes, agents objected to the Aleuts' poverty. But more clamant was their outcry against the persistence of payments in kind. Lembkey railed against this injustice, claiming that it destroyed the Aleuts' incentives. In an effort to influence management, he tried a cash experiment in St. George for one year.

> In 1911 a plan was put in operation designed to induce the natives to save at least a small portion of their earnings. It was based upon the general principle that by reducing weekly and other issues of supplies to a minimum an unexpended balance would be created, which balance at the year's end was to be distributed in cash among the earners... If even from a weekly allowance the natives saved something, that saving was to be given him in cash at once. It was hoped he could be induced to open savings accounts with cash thus obtained, or at least to use it in purchasing some articles not otherwise obtainable that would increase his happiness and comfort . . .
>
> The results from a careful following of the plan are interesting. At the end of the first month in which the native men were informed that such savings as they made from their weekly allowances for family supplies would be paid in cash more than half the families in the village drew cash savings thus derived . . . They continued to do this during each remaining month of the year, almost every family saving something of the amount allowed for its support.
>
> Careful inquiries into the motives governing the making of these savings developed some interesting points. It seemed . . . that the main object of the native was not to hoard the cash thus obtained by saving but . . . to get possession of the cash itself,

> which in many instances he at once took to the store to expend for perhaps the very articles he had denied himself in order to make the saving. Some few, of course, used the cash to purchase in San Francisco articles which could not have been issued to them had they not the cash. No savings accounts were created. . .
>
> It is reported that the natives were greatly pleased with the plan as operated. . .
>
> The net result of this one year experiment is not large. It shows that the natives desire their earnings in cash. . . It shows also that if paid in cash for their labor in taking seal skins, etc., the greater portion . . . would be used for the same purposes for which the credit is used, namely, the purchase of the necessaries of life.[17]

Though Lembkey designed the experiment to induce Aleuts to save money, he quickly learned that savings had no meaning when there was nothing to purchase with them: "The reward of self-denial exists in the possibilities for greater enjoyment and comfort created as the result of self discipline. If the native has no use for this money, he will not save it; neither will anyone."[18] Lembkey concluded his report on the experiment with an impassioned plea to pay the Aleuts' wages in cash.[19]

With similar zeal, Agent Fassett lambasted the Bureau for paying the Aleuts in supplies.

> Although they themselves do not fully appreciate it, the fact cannot be denied that the people of St. Paul (and St. George as well) are living in actual slavery and that this condition exists and is maintained under the immediate control and direction of the United States government.
>
> Since 1911 heads of families have received one dollar in cash per year and their quota of the smallest and most restrictive stock of supplies furnished in many years.[20]

In much less sophisticated and vehement language, in the deferential tone often characteristic of subject people, the Aleuts also asked for some cash wages: "We feed foxes seven months and trap two months. We are willing to do the work but think we should get some cash. . . Respectfully ask that this petition be sent to the Commissioner."[21]

This modest demand and the more insistent ones by agents failed to move Washington officials—hardly surprising when it came to ignoring the Aleuts; that was customary. And such a lack of response was becoming increasingly customary in relation to agents. But why? Bureaucracies characteristically weigh and balance the demands of the interest groups that surround them. Agents' demands could hardly compete with those of Congress. The program had always faced Congressional expectations not only to be self-supporting, but to produce a revenue surplus. In this period, keenly aware of international obligations at a time of revenue losses, Congress had also posed a cost-cutting expectation. One way Congress expressed this expectation was to cut agents' salaries nearly in half and to reduce the administrative budget to the bone.[22] The Deputy Commissioner of Fisheries in 1914 considered the Pribilof budget "wholly inadequate to manage the business in an efficient manner."[23] Managers probably refused to consider restoring the Aleuts' cash wages because in those lean years they found it easier to manipulate supplies (for example reducing the coal allowance) than cash wages. Perhaps, too, sensitive to the "fair compensation" clause, they considered it less visibly a violation of fair compensation to reduce the amount of supplies than to lower cash wages.

With all the instability of this period, the Bureau of Fisheries also faced a national scandal. Since the beginning of sole federal jurisdiction, the record increasingly reveals instances of federal employee drunkenness and sexual abuse of Aleut women. In 1911 the St. George physician confessed to seduction of two girls who had come to his office for professional services. One of the girls became pregnant as a result and died in childbirth. The agent was irate.

> At 2 p.m., word was brought by that the Orloff infant had died and at 7 this evening Nadessa died having been unconscious about 36 hours.
>
> Nadessa was a beautiful girl, 19 years old, well behaved, modest and ladylike in every respect. Her downfall and subsequent death may be placed at the door of Dr. Morgan who was resident physician on this island. Nadessa concealed the fact of her condition until very recently when, under the seal of professional secrecy, she admitted to Dr. McGovern (St. Paul physician) that she was pregnant and stated to him that Dr. Morgan was responsible. Morgan himself informed Mr. Box last summer that he had sexual intercourse with both of the priest's daughters during the preceding winter, and in effect, he told Mr. Proctor the same thing. . . I will take this matter up with Mr. Lembkey on his arrival in June and see if something can be done toward bringing this brute of a Morgan to punishment.[24]

Lembkey must have summarily dismissed Morgan, for Morgan left St. George immediately after Lembkey arrived. Soon after that, Dr. McGovern became implicated in similar situations. "The entire cause of Dr. McGovern's demoralization and neglect of duty were his uncontrollable desire for and continuous indulgence in alcoholic liquors and his relations with some of the natives on the islands." wrote the agent when asking for the doctor's removal.[25] In 1914, a full-blown scandal involving five government employees on the islands erupted. It was front page news in the New York Times.

> Five American government agents were under arrest at their stations on the Pribilof Islands, better known as the Fur Seal Islands, in the Bering Sea, on charges of a serious nature affecting their conduct and treatment of the natives, men and women.
>
> Among the charges that have been lodged against the principal government agents

on the Pribilof Islands are debauching the wives of natives, terrorizing their husbands into silence, drunkenness and furnishing intoxicants to the natives, creating a condition in the community that has resulted in death and lawlessness. . .

> Pending the investigation, the inhabitants of the islands are being guarded by the vessels of the Bureau of Fisheries, the revenue cutter service, and the navy.

> The charges first reached Washington on June 30 in a communication to Secretary Redfield from Mr. and Mrs. Alvin D. Whitney, teachers on St. Paul Island. Mr. Redfield at once ordered Dr. Jones (Deputy Commissioner of Fisheries) to make the investigation... The Whitneys have submitted to Secretary Redfield a diary running from July, 1913 to May, 1914 reciting almost daily allegations of scandalous conduct on the part of officials. Reporting from St. George's Island, G. Dallas Hanna, a school teacher, said: "Morality among the natives is almost unknown." He added that conditions had grown worse since the government took over the fur seal fisheries in 1910.[26]

Those under accusation were P.R. Hatton, St. Paul agent; L.N. Tongue, St. Paul storekeeper; Dr. C.J. McGovern, St. Paul physician; A.H. Proctor, St. George agent; and P.L. McLenny, Navy wireless operator.

In making the investigation, Jones was appalled at the condition he found.

> It (the investigation) showed beyond a question of doubt that a deplorable condition has existed on these islands for years, and resulted in the dismissal from the service of both men on St. Paul Island. All government officials who have allowed the morals of the islands to be disturbed have violated their oath of office and are guilty of gross misconduct if not of criminal negligence.[27]

Information on the outcome of the charges against the five men is incomplete. The personnel record of the Navy employee could not be located. Dr. McGovern resigned his position before the arrests were made and his personnel file included no mention of the incident. The agent and the storekeeper at St. Paul were summarily fired from their jobs prior to their trial by the United States Department of Justice.[28] And the St. George agent must have been exonerated of all charges for he remained on his job and later became the first superintendent of the Pribilofs, a position that was established when the Bureau opened a Seattle office in 1920. His personnel file also contained no reference to the incident.

Sweeping out the malefactors was only part of the staff housecleaning on the Pribilofs. A new Bureau of Fisheries chief was appointed in 1914; shortly afterwards, except for Agent Proctor on St. George, there was a complete staff turnover including Lembkey. (We were unable to discover why, after ten years on the islands, Lembkey left; the Department of Labor could not locate his personnel file.) Why the turnover?—it appears to reflect the caretaking nature of management during this period and, therefore, the need for a different type of agent. Since there were no commercial harvests, agents' responsibilities were significantly reduced. The Congressional reduction in agents' salaries, from $3,650 in 1911 to $2,000 in 1913 was one reflection of this decrease in responsibilities.[29] Another was a change in agents' title from agent in charge to agent and caretaker. Furthermore, the Bureau hired less-qualified agents. Lembkey and the assistant agent on St. Paul had doctorates; none hired subsequently had this level of training. As caretakers, agents exercised far less authority than in the past; in fact, management eliminated agents' influence on policy by instructing them to keep their opinions to themselves.

> An examination of the recent report by Mr. Henry W. Elliot of his visit to the Seal Islands in the summer of 1913 shows a number of extracts from the island logs. It is observed that the agents . . . making entries into the logs have not confined themselves to statements of facts. They have apparently felt free to incorporate into the logs personal opinions and comments. Matters of these kinds have no legitimate place in the official log.
>
> You are directed hereafter to record in the log all important facts as to the daily occurrences on the islands, *omitting expressions of opinion and personal comments.*[30]

Agents must have received similar instructions regarding annual reports, for these became increasingly routine, divested of the rich comments and descriptions in earlier reports and confined to such pedestrian matters as records of harvests and payments to Aleut sealers.

This change in agents' role may have sprung from an additional source. Now that the federal government was solely responsible and accountable for the Pribilof program, managers wanted tighter control over agents; they wanted, not agent independence as in the past, but agent loyalty, reliability of response, and obedience to rules and regulations issued from above. Whatever motivated these changes, the upshot was to silence agents and divest them of most of their power.

While this was a dark period in the Pribilof history, the Bureau of Fisheries adopted what appeared to be an enlightened policy toward higher education of Aleuts. Until 1910, the private lessees had provided education only through the fourth or fifth grade. But when the government became fully responsible for the program, management suggested training "a number of the brighter girls and boys to do a part of the clerical work incident to the administration of the service,"[31] (training that would entail attendance at high schools outside the Pribilofs). What accounts for this change? Did the assumption of greater responsibility spark managers' consciences? Did it make them more sensitive to demands of the Indian rights movement which crusaded for education as the chief means for assimilating Indians? Perhaps, but there appears to be a more clamant motivation—to train Aleuts for middle-level jobs in these cost-cutting years. The hiring of Aleut clerks, bookkeepers, and storekeepers could effect a considerable savings in labor costs since the Bureau had to provide transportation and room and board for imported employees.

The Bureau faced an immediate obstacle in implementing the new policy—the Aleuts had not yet mastered the English language. The agent in 1910 asserted that only a few Aleuts had an adequate grasp of English.[32] Members of a special government investigating committee in 1913 came to a similar conclusion: "About half the population can answer simple English questions, and five or six speak English well."[33] Agents and teachers blamed this learning failure on the persistence of the Russian school, the priest's refusal to conduct the church service in English, and parents' insistence on speaking Aleut in the home. Lembkey advanced a different hypothesis; he attributed the failure to the low caliber of the schools.

> The teachers supplied by those companies were usually, if not always, selected with reference to their ability to perform clerical or other duties rather than for their fitness as teachers. The companies seemed to regard the schools as a matter of secondary importance and required the teachers to devote most of their time to work bearing no relation to the education of native children. As a result, with a few notable exceptions, the persons who performed the duties of teacher had no special fitness or training for those duties. . . It is not surprising, therefore, that no rational system of education has been worked out to meet the needs of those people and that so little progress has been made.[34]

In response to Lembkey's explanation, the Bureau immediately hired trained teachers. But still its major thrust was to suppress the Aleut language. Managers directed teachers to forbid the use of the Aleut tongue in the school and playground. They prohibited the Russian school, which was again operating, from holding classes during the eight-month American school session. They banned the use of interpreters. And they instructed agents "in all the relations of the Government with the natives and the natives with the Government, only the English language shall be employed, and you will discourage in every possible way the use of any other language."[35] Agents forbade the use of the Aleut language in public recreation places and enjoined the priests to conduct at least part of the church service in English.

Undoubtedly, the Bureau justified these suppressions in humanitarian terms. Education was a privilege, and the Bureau was providing the Aleuts opportunities for growth and development. But, as Michael Katz stoutly asserts in his study of nineteenth century school reform:

> We have still to see a movement driven by a desire to bring joy and delight to the life of the individual, to enrich experience solely for the purpose of making life more full and lovely. The goals...quite the contrary, have been extrinsic; they have stressed the needs of societv and the economy.[36]

Katz argues that educational reform was imposed on an unwilling working class in the name of humanitarian ideals by middle-class persons concerned about political and economic imperatives. Furthermore, he points out that despite educational reformers' rhetoric about cultural relativity, a mentality of cultural absolutism dominated the schools and thereby alienated working class populations.

And so in the Pribilofs, Aleuts were alienated by the cultural suppressions that were embedded in their education. Yes, some probably aspired to high school training, but as an option rather than a substitute for their cultural institutions. They were intent on guarding and nourishing what little remained of their culture. Listen to this moving defense of their cultural institutions that were under attack.

> We gathered and talked and they all agreed and writing to Washington, D.C., this is what we are asking for. . .
>
> Second in this business we are told not to talk in our own language, and not to have our own interpreter . . . and, in this case, our agent want us to talk just one language, and it is pretty hard from them older men, and for this case we want the interpreter, and the community chief, besides the government foreman like we used to have before so as to know what they are talking about and tell what they are saying. . .
>
> Fifth, we are keeping our religion in good order, and think it's higher above all things and we want our children to be good, for that case we are asking you for our school (the Russian school) to be here, open four times a week, from 4:00 o'clock P.M. to 6:00 o'clock P.M. and also on Saturdays, and we know the public school up here is pretty good and our children are getting along very good in English language and we want those other school hours to be going on after the children goes out from the public school to their home.[37]

In characteristic fashion, the Commissioner stubbornly rejected the Aleuts' appeal: "The Bureau can make no modification in its present rule in regard to the use of the native language . . . (and) the Bureau cannot consent to the reestablishment of the independent native school."[38]

Suppression of the native language was one facet of the campaign to educate Aleuts, another was attendance at the Chemawa Indian school in Salem, Oregon. One might pause for a moment and think, wait a minute, this was a belt-tightening, cost-conscious period—why was the Bureau assuming additional expenses to educate Aleuts? Would the return from their clerical services adequately compensate for the expenditures? There was virtually no expense involved in the education venture. The Bureau of Fisheries provided transportation on its vessels which sailed whether or not they transported students. And the Bureau of Indian Affairs in the Department of Interior covered the boarding and tuition costs. So, beginning in 1911, Pribilof students (mostly from St. Paul since vessels called so infrequently at St. George) began to attend high school in Oregon.

The education plan, however, backfired. While it provided the anticipated training, it also threatened to reduce the size of the sealing labor force because some Chemawa students did not want to return to the islands. The Bureau expected high school training to produce a pool of potential clerical workers from which it could draw several employees, with the rest returning to sealing work. When students refused to return home or developed ambitions that might produce dissatisfaction with sealing work, officials and agents expressed apprehension. Apparently in an effort to discover conditions that would justify terminating the high school program, the Commissioner of Fisheries in 1919 directed St. George agent Crompton to investigate the Chemawa school. Crompton gave the school a clean bill of health.

> During the day all of the Pribilof boys were separately questioned regarding their comforts and treatment. They were informed that my visit was for the purpose of hearing their grievances if they had any, but they were unanimous in their praise of their treatment and in addition seemed to have a strong "school spirit" of pride in the institution. . . Though I observed closely, nothing seems to indicate that the children were not well cared for in all respects. The food was inspected and the dormitories seen, and all was on an equal with conditions found in the first class boarding schools.[39]

Nonetheless, Crompton strongly recommended discontinuing the Chemawa program in the Pribilofs.

> The question of sending Pribilof Island native children to Chemawa, then, becomes one of policy rather than of doubt regarding the care they might receive while there. It is the writer's opinion that it is not in the interests of the United States to send the children to outside schools and I doubt that it adds to the ultimate happiness of the individuals.
>
> Boys who have attended the school at Chemawa return to the islands in a dissatisfied frame of mind. They have had just sufficient education to see the contrast between a life on the Islands and one in the states and not enough education or experience to see clearly the reasons for the difference. For example, one boy . . . who has spent nearly six years at the school informed me that after he had finished high school (in approximately two more years), it was his intention to go to work and buy his parents a home in Oregon. While this is a praiseworthy ambition, it is quite apparent that unless he is a very unusual boy, it will never materialize. . . He added that he would like to return to St. George Island if he were given a "position" with the Bureau. While the agents always desire to encourage the brighter boys by giving them work which calls for intelligence, it is evident that *the latter ambition of this boy will not be realized under the present system of payments.* In short, after seeing the environment of Americans of moderate or ample means in a country and climate much more pleasant than the Pribilof Islands, *they return with an unexpressed feeling of discontent with the Island conditions. . .*
>
> It is recommended that no more children be sent to the Chemawa school at the instigation of the Bureau.[40]

The superintendent of the Pribilofs agreed with the agent's recommendation but for a different reason.

> The advisability of sending children from these islands to the Chemawa school has been for some time a matter of doubt with me and for that reason I have ceased in my efforts to interest the children. The chief objection is the short time which most of them are willing to remain at this school coupled with the fact that it has generally been the custom to send only those of the best intelligence, *some few of whom have elected to remain away permanently*, and to this extent the government's interests on the Islands, as well as the best interest of the remaining population, have suffered.[41]

The Commissioner of Fisheries finally resolved the issue with a new policy terminating the Chemawa school program in the Pribilofs.

> After careful consideration of your report and recommendations, you are informed that until otherwise advised, the policy of the Bureau will be to send no more native children to the Chemawa school unless specific request to do so is made by the parents or guardian. It is realized that occasionally natives may desire to go to Chemawa, but it does not seem the course of wisdom for the Bureau to urge or instigate such attendance.[42]

Of course, if the Bureau didn't approve these occasional applications there was no way the Aleuts could attend; they had no funds for transportation. Even this occasional option was denied them several years later by a stipulation in the Office of Indian Affairs' budget prohibiting the use of its funds for the support or education of *any* Alaska native pupil except upon the individual order of the Secretary of the Interior.[43] And thus ended the brief experiment in high school education for the Aleuts.

Curiously, those who had graduated from Chemawa were not hired for Bureau positions when they returned to the islands. One wonders why, when the purpose of the plan was to train Aleuts for middle-level jobs. Crompton suggested an answer when he acknowledged the incompatibility between holding a Bureau position and the system of payment in kind. The hiring of Aleut employees would have called that system into question. Would Aleuts employed in Bureau jobs be paid in supplies? That would have been difficult to justify. But if they were paid in cash like other federal employees, it would have introduced a double standard in the family and community. For example, how would the agent have determined the allowance for an Aleut family? Yes, the Bureau undoubtedly had second thoughts about the wisdom of training and hiring Aleuts when it might threaten the foundation of labor-management relations on the islands.

In sum, serious threats to the Pribilof program in this first decade of sole federal jurisdiction riveted management's attention to survival needs, and Congressional pressure and budgetary constraints focused management's eye on cost considerations. These were the pressures shaping policy and practices. But by 1918 the seal herd was in healthy condition and commercial sealing was about to resume, promising a return to the halcyon days of revenue surplus. Would these new conditions prompt management to restore agents' former powers or liberalize its labor policies? Would management reinstate cash wages to Aleuts? Would it provide them the same economic benefits that became available to other American workers? How would the situation of the Aleuts in 1935 compare to that of their parents of 1915?

Endnotes

1. U.S. Congress, House, The Fur Seal Industry of Alaska. H. Rpt. No. 1425, 62nd Cong., 3rd sess., 1913, p.2; National Resource Committee, Regional Planning, Part VII, Alaska, Its Resources and Development. No. I. Report of the Alaska Resources Committee (Washington, D.C.: Government Printing Office, 1937), p. 66.
2. The Fur Seal Industry of Alaska, H. Rpt. No. 1425, pp. 2-3.
3. Members of the advisory board were: Dr. David Starr Jordan, president of Standford University; Dr. Leonard Stejneger, head curator of biology, United States National Museum; Dr. C. Hart Merriam, chief of the Biological Survey; Dr. Frederick A. Lucas, Director of the American Museum of Natural History; Dr. Charles H. Townsend, director of the New York Aquarium; Mr. Edwin W. Sims, former solicitor for the Department of Commerce and Labor; and Mr. Frank H. Hitchcock, Postmaster General and formerly chief clerk of the Department of Commerce and Labor. U.S. Congress, House, Hearings Before the Committee on Expenditures in the Department of Commerce and Labor, House of Representatives, on House Resolution No. 73 to Investigate the Fur Seal Industry of Alaska, No. I, 62nd Cong., 1st sess., 1911, p. 109; U.S. Congress, Senate, Hearings Before the Committee on Conservation of Natural Resources on Bill S. 7242 entitled "An Act to Protect the Seal Fisheries of Alaska and for Other Purposes," S. Doc. 605, 61st Cong., 2nd sess., 1910, pp. 25-27.
4. Public Law 146 (April 21, 1910).
5. Only Indians of the Northwest Coast were allowed to continue pelagic sealing provided they used no firearms.
6. 37 Stat 499 (August 24, 1912).
7. For the contract and supplements, see U.S. Congress, Senate, Fur Skin Sales, S. Doc. 213, 67th Cong., 2nd sess., 1922, pp. 31-43.
8. George Rogers, An Economic Analysis of the Pribilof Islands, 1870-1946. Prepared for Indian Claims Commission Docket Nos. 352 and 369 (Fairbanks: University of Alaska, Institute of Social, Economic and Government Research, 1976), p. 124.
9. U.S. Congress, House, Appendix A to Hearings Before the Committee on Expenditures in the Department of Commerce and Labor, House of Repre-

sentatives, on House Resolution No. 73 to Investigate the Fur Seal Industry of Alaska, 62nd Cong., 1st sess., 1911, p. 1187.

10. The 1915 schedule was as follows:

Classification	Weekly Reward
Seal clubber	$ 5.00
Seal skinner, first class	5.00
Seal skinner, second class	4.50
Mechanic, first class	4.50
Mechanic, second class	4.00
Laborer, first class	3.50
Laborer, second class	3.00
Laborer, third class	2.50
Boy, first class	1.00
Boy, second class	.75
Boy, third class	.50

Widows as heads of families $3.50 a week. Other adults 16 years of age and over, if male, and 18 years if female, are allowed $1.00 each for their support. All others irrespective of age and sex received $.50.

H.C. Fassett, Agent and Caretaker, to Commissioner of Fisheries, January 30, 1915, Bureau of Fisheries Records, St. Paul Island.

11. H.C. Fassett, to Commissioner of Fisheries, February 10, 1915, Bureau Records, St. Paul.

12. 38 Stat. 475 (August 12, 1912); 38 Stat. 664 (August 1, 1914).

13. Rogers, An Economic Analysis, p. 159.

14. Memorandum re Remuneration of Natives on St. Paul Island, March 10, 1915, Bureau Records, St. Paul.

15. H.C. Fassett to Commissioner of Fisheries, October 20, 1916, Bureau Records, St. Paul.

16. W. Byrd Hunt to St. Paul agent, August 16, 1916, Bureau Records, St. Paul.

17. Wilfred E. Osgood, et al., The Fur Seal and Other Life of the Pribilof Islands, Alaska in 1914, (Washington, D.C.: Government Printing Office, 1915), pp. 136-137. Also issued as U.S. Congress, S. Doc. 980, 63rd Cong., 3rd sess.; and Bureau of Fisheries Doc. No. 820, 1915.

18. Ibid., p. 137.

19. Ibid., pp. 137-138.

20. H.C. Fassett to Commissioner of Fisheries, October 20, 1916, Bureau Records, St. Paul.

21. A.H. Proctor to Commissioner of Fisheries, September 28, 1913, Bureau Records, St. Paul.

22. 36 Stat. 1441 (March 4, 1911).

23. Osgood, The Fur Seal and Other Life, p. 141.

24. Pribilof Islands Daily Log, St. Paul, December 16, 1911.

25. P.R. Hatton, Agent and Caretaker, to Commissioner of Fisheries, June

23, 1914, Bureau Records, St. Paul.
26. New York Times, July 20, 1914, p. 1.
27. E. Lester Jones, Report of Alaska Investigations in 1914 (Washington, D.C.: Government Printing Office, 1915), p. 126.
28. Secretary of Commerce and Labor to Honorable Blair Lee, U.S. Senate, July 29, 1914, in personnel file of L.M. Tongue.
29. 36 Stat. 1441 (March 4, 1911).
30. H.W. Smith, Commissioner of Fisheries, to Phillip R. Hatton, St. Paul Agent and Caretaker, November 10, 1913, Bureau Records, St. Paul.
31. Appendix A to Hearings, 1911, p. 1195.
32. Ibid., p. 983.
33. Osgood, The Fur Seals and Other Life, 146.
34. U.S. Department of Commerce, Bureau of Fisheries, Alaska Fisheries and Fur Industries in 1912, Doc. No. 780, 1913, p. 78.
35. Commissioner of Fisheries to H.C. Fassett, August 8, 1914, Bureau Records, St. Paul.
36. Michael B. Katz, The Irony of Early School Reform: Educational Innovation in Mid-Nineteenth Century Massachusetts (Cambridge, Mass.: Harvard University Press, 1968), p. 214.
37. St. Paul Community to Commissioner of Fisheries, October 10, 1916, Bureau Records, St. Paul.
38. Notice to Natives, July 17, 1917, signed by H.C. Fassett, Bureau Records, St. Paul.
39. C.E. Crompton, St. George Agent and Caretaker, to Commissioner of Fisheries, January 19, 1920, Bureau Records, St. Paul.
40. Ibid.
41. A.H. Proctor, Superintendent, to C.E. Crompton, St. George Island, September 2, 1920, Bureau Records, St. Paul.
42. Commissioner H.M. Smith to C.E. Crompton, St. George Island, January 20, 1921, Bureau Records, St. Paul.
43. Hubert Work, Superintendent, Chemawa Indian Training School, to Secretary of Commerce, August 7, 1924, Bureau Records, St. Paul.

CHAPTER 5

A COLONIAL REGIME, 1918-1942

> One day I picked up my bag of groceries. We got only two cans of tuna fish, number 2 size, that was our whole supply of meat for the week. It was my wife's birthday. So I thought, what the heck, we'll have a party and use both cans. We ate potatoes and rice for the rest of the week.[1]

Forty years after the event, this old Aleuts' words still echo with anguish.

Dramatic economic and social reforms swept the nation in the 1930s—collective bargaining rights; wages and hours legislation; social security benefits; welfare benefits that, among other things, replaced relief baskets with cash; and an enlightened Indian Reorganization Act. Indeed, the future looked brighter to the average American; it retained a dismal hue in the Pribilofs.

The Pribilof management system had become set in concrete. Social systems tend to develop a life of their own, a set of attitudes, norms, and practices that, although originally adopted as means to an end, become ends in themselves; they become comfortable, familiar, automatic sets of responses. How often managers explained their practices by saying, "but that is the way it has always been done."

By the 1920s this familiar, comfortable system in the Pribilofs had the earmarks of a typical colonialism. In part, this reflected national attitudes toward Alaska—the pioneer philosophy of grabbing what was available and getting out fast. Alaska was a highly specialized source of raw materials and products for the home country. A federal government-private corporate regime for the control and exploitation of these resources dominated Alaska's development at least until World War II. Prior to that time, white Alaskans' efforts to control their resources and destinies and achieve political independence met with indifference.[2]

This colonialist attitude obviously influenced the evolution of the Pribilof management system. But that system was not simply a subset of the broader Alaska pattern; it was a different variety of colonialism because Aleuts are a racial minority whom government subjected to far more blatant domination than Alaska whites ever experienced. The Aleuts could not, as the whites did, move freely, marry whom they pleased, organize to promote their interests, engage in free trade, or receive New Deal benefits. Furthermore, while few interest groups protested Alaska colonialism, none expressed concern about that on the Pribilofs. Remember, the Pribilofs were extremely isolated, especially prior to air service. The government allowed few visitors and maintained a policy of secrecy about its operations. The only outside group with knowledge of events on the islands, the Russian Orthodox church, remained silent because the church discouraged secular activities. The Pribilof situation was simply hidden from public view. Without visibility, insulated from interest-group pressures, a far more extreme form of colonialism developed in the Pribilofs, closely resembling that of European nations in Africa and South America.

The colonial concept is useful in explaining why in the 1920s and 1930s the Aleuts' situation worsened as that of other Americans improved. A colonial relationship characteristically involves a developed industrial nation (1) appropriating and exploiting the resources of an underdeveloped one, (2) using the labor power of workers in that nation to develop the resource, (3) paying the workers near-starvation wages buttressed by special goods and services to keep them alive and functioning, (4) undermining them psychologically to keep them abject and thus available for such exploitation, and (5) dominating their political life to assure access to the human and natural resources.[3]

The United States, of course, was not a foreign government, but the Pribilofs was a case of internal colonialism. The issue of resource appropriation in the Pribilofs is not clear cut. The government's right to claim ownership of a wildlife resource for conservation purposes is well established, but not the right to own the resource for commercial development and profit making. Aside from these unique attributes, the government's relationship with Pribilovians was typically colonial—in paying near-starvation wages supplemented by goods and services, in political and economic domination, and in psychological debasement.

Colonialist structures are accompanied by an ideology that depicts the colonized as less than human, as bereft of ordinary human feelings, and therefore undeserving of human rights. If colonial administrators perceived their subjects as fully human, they would lack the justification and perhaps the will to keep them oppressed. With this mentality, administrators perpetrate indignities on the colonized that they would consider outrageous if anyone directed the same behavior toward them.[4] This ideological dehumanization inevitably leads to blaming the victims for their condition. One wonders, how, when colonialist ideologies and practices conflict with the values of the home country, administrator loyalty is maintained. It is bought by special rewards in money, status, prestige, and privilege, rewards symbolizing a superior status by dint of class, race, and occupational position.

With this framework in mind we return to the promising days of 1918 in the Pribilofs when conditions favored a resumption of commercial sealing. The seal herd again thrived, estimated at nearly one-half million animals.[5] In the interests of conservation, Bureau of Fisheries biologists urged the reopening of commercial sealing. Without harvests the seals might run out of food. Furthermore, unlimited by harvests the seals could, by their eating habits, substantially reduce other commercially valuable fisheries. Assured of the compatibility between profits and conservation, the government resumed seal harvests in 1918. At first, management set low seal quotas, but gradually it increased the size to a peak of about 95,000 in 1941.[6]

Net revenues from the seal industry again refreshed the federal treasury—over three and one-half million dollars in the period 1918 to 1942.[7] A favorable circumstance, this, for improving the economic situation of the Aleuts. But it didn't.

The Bureau of Fisheries restored the sealing and foxing bonuses in 1918, but continued to compensate Aleuts for labor in the non-sealing season, the major portion of the year, with supplies and services. In absolute terms, Aleuts' average annual income from all sources—bonuses, supplies, and services—remained stationary or decreased. Minor ups and downs occurred, but the trend was downward. For example, the average income in St. Paul was $1,443 in 1919; $1,070 in 1929; and only $753 in 1939.[8] In relative terms their income situation was even worse. Since 1923 the gap in income between Aleut and United States production workers ever widened. In 1925 Aleuts' income represented 76 percent that of the average production worker; in 1930 it was 67 percent; and in 1940 it was only one-half.[9] The fair-compensation clause in the 1910 Fur Seal Act apparently had no impact at all; no one questioned the adequacy of Aleuts' compensation, and consequently, management had no need to account for it.

The inadequacy of the Aleuts' income was but one aspect of their economic deprivation. In kind wage payments was another. Aleuts had always received a portion of their income in supplies and services. But during the first private lease, they earned an adequate cash income—in kind payments constituted a minor portion of their total income. Then, during the lean years and the moratorium on commercial sealing, management supported Aleuts with supplies—cash earnings were negligible. With the resumption of sealing, management restored the bonus system but failed to acknowledge a significant change in circumstances. Seal rates (ranging between 50 cents and $1.20 in this period) and harvests were too low to provide a semblance of an adequate cash wage.[10] In the 1920s and 1930s Aleuts' cash earnings usually represented less than half of their total income. In other words, at least half and in some years the major part of their income, was paid in goods and services.[11] Furthermore, unlike earlier periods when management maintained a somewhat loose arrangement regarding the Aleuts' work obligations, it now obliged them by contract to work year-round, a 44-hour week.[12] These significantly altered circumstances failed to generate new policy; in fact, management stubbornly refused to consider any change in the balance between in kind and cash compensation.

The new brand of agents, by this time effectively silenced by top management, no longer protested the in kind wage. One lone administrator's voice in 1921 appealed for a small increase in cash for several categories of workers. The Commissioner of Fisheries dismissed the request out of hand: "You are advised that other more important demands upon available funds precludes, for the present, favorable consideration for payments in cash . . ."[13] The Commissioner's opposition to this particular request foreshadowed what became a hard and fast policy for the next three decades.

But why the resistance to compensating Aleuts like other American workers? Was it simply a question of bureaucratic lethargy, of thoughtlessly continuing a traditional practice? In part it was both, especially in the context of management's entrenched colonialist mentality. Listen to the superintendent's view of Aleuts in 1936.

> . . . it is true that the natives will spend their money for luxuries instead of necessities. It would not be so bad if they would look after their luxuries, but we all know that they won't.
>
> It is going to still take years of training before the natives will understand the value of either money or merchandise, and they never will unless we train them to do so and make them suffer when they waste their funds.[14]

Why should managers concern themselves with paying Aleuts in cash when they were convinced Aleuts were incapable of managing it?

But pause a moment. Bureaucratic habits and regressive attitudes often persist precisely because they serve a purpose; in this case, the purpose had to do not just with the in kind payments but a combined system of in kind and bonus payments. Because Aleuts were totally dependent on the bonuses as the only source for cash, managers' manipulation of the bonus was a powerful means of control. A high-ranking official in 1941 openly acknowledged this function of the bonus.

> An interesting feature of the Sealing and Foxing Division is that at times *it is very valuable from the standpoint of administration and maintaining control over the natives.* Upon several occasions when infractions of the rules have occurred, the agent demoted a man from one sealing class to a lower class, thus reducing the amount of his income. The possibility of such action has been a strong deterrent to violation of the rules.[15]

The most compelling incentive to retaining in kind compensation, however, was still its cost-saving value. The presence of surplus federal revenues from the seal industry did not relieve Congressional pressures on the program to make money. On the contrary, this expectation intensified in this period because of the losses suffered during the lean years and the moratorium on commercial harvests;[16] the new international obligations; and the Great Depression, during which Congress at times impounded the Pribilof budget.[17]

These pressures embroiled the Bureau in cost considerations. And managers well appreciated the cost-saving value of the in kind wage payments. The Pribilof superintendent in 1925 cast light on how this process worked, how the supplies could be manipulated to effect wage reductions and regulate Aleuts' cash expenditures.

> We are now paying the natives a considerable amount of money each season in cash. In a great many instances, in fact in most cases, a large proportion of this money is being spent for items which are not of any real value, and are not essential . . .
>
> There are, however, a great many items in the schedule which the natives should not be supplied free of charge, but they should purchase them with their own funds. It will therefore be necessary to make reductions in the number of absolutely unessential items heretofore furnished.[18]

These "absolutely inessential items" probably referred to such goods as a pair of dress shoes, a second dress, candles, matches, kitchenware, bedding—little else was available in the government store. But the point is, by manipulating these supplies, management effectively reduced wages and accomplished this in a less visible manner than would have been possible had Aleuts received a full cash wage. Yes, economic incentives played a powerful role in management's determination to retain the system of in kind and bonus wages, a system which it justified in terms of Aleuts' inability to handle money.

Top managers persisted in conveying the notion that goods and services represented wages for labor performed. For example, in the 1922 Congressional appropriation hearings, when asked if Aleuts received compensation for their labor, a top official replied: "Their chief compensation is food, fuel, and clothing."[19] Throughout this period, managers referred to the supplies as payment for labor.[20] Nonetheless, they distributed the supplies as if they were gratuities, substituting family requirements for labor force participation and work classifications as a basis for determining the amounts to be distributed.

To compound the economic discrimination, the very manner of distributing supplies degraded Aleuts. Early in this period, Aleut heads of household could still order food from available supplies in the store. But this practice soon ended and the storekeeper, instructed by the agent, filled the grocery bags. Every Saturday morning the household head picked up the bag. Only the head could go to the store, not the women who did the cooking (unless they were themselves heads of households). In cases where married brothers lived in the same house, a relatively common arrangement because there was a continual housing shortage, the younger brother was not allowed to go to the store. "I couldn't even bring food to my family; they had to eat my brother's food; it was humiliating," opined a St. George man.[21] Collecting the pre-selected bags demoralized people; "Every week they threw a bag of groceries at us, that was our pay," a St. Paul man painfully recalled.[22]

As if this weren't indignity enough, the contents of the bags caused anguish. While the Bureau provided schedules of the particular foods and amounts to be distributed, these were merely guides and were not necessarily followed. The Bureau could and did reduce supplies when it saw fit. For example, the following caveat accompanied the 1930 schedule:

> The schedule contains a number of increases in issues on important items. It will be impossible to increase such items this year. . . The schedule also contains a number of important decreases. . . .
>
> It is desired that where practical, decreases in issues be carried into effect at an early date.[23]

Even if the schedule had been followed, it was deficient in important items—milk (although agents distributed small amounts of canned milk), eggs (which the 1941 agents said were distributed only on Easter), fresh meat, fresh fruit, and fresh leafy vegetables. Physicians' reports repeatedly referred to these nutritional deficits. Furthermore, supplies of canned meat and fish were discontinued when seal meat or other locally caught products were available.

In response to a questionnaire survey by the 1941 Pribilof physician that contained not a single question about the food supplies, virtually every respondent complained about the food.[24] We found a similar response in interviews with Aleuts. Regardless of the subject of the interview, nearly every person referred to the abominably inadequate supplies.

> The government store carried the worst brands of canned goods, no popular brands like Libby's or Hunt's. The cans had no brand names at all. And the clothes were picked for us. We weren't allowed to pick colors, just take what they gave us. They just threw the clothes at you. Sometimes they didn't fit. They carried only two sizes—small and large.
>
> * * *
>
> We got three pairs of shoes a year. They were like made out of paper. When we needed a new pair we had to take the old one to the store. Agent would say, have to wear them two more weeks, no matter if the soles were worn through and flapping.
>
> * * *
>
> They just gave us work shoes. Nothing to dress the children up in. Two cans of milk a week. that's all, even if you had babies.
>
> * * *
>
> I start working for the government 1937 only cash compensation we used to get was from the seal harvest . . . for the rest of the year we used to work for our food which was to be issued from the government store once a week which by no means

was satisfactory or enough for a week, one can salmon or one can corned beef . . . each week . . . no fresh meat at all, they used to discontinue the can meat when the sealing starts so we can eat only seal meat. Good thing we had sea lions and ducks and sea gulls around the island, otherwise we would starve. The Bureau staff employees used to have their own food storage room . . . with a lot of fancy canned goods, eggs, and fresh meat for their own use. They used to issue us eggs occasionally when they were no longer edible.[25]

* * *

My kids were hungry a lot. Some days we had only bread and oatmeal or oatmeal and potatoes for the children.

* * *

I kept a diary about what we were given to eat. This was in 1947 but it was the same in earlier years.

April 23
Breakfast: Coffee and bread
Lunch: Tea and bread
Dinner: Fried potatoes

April 24
Breakfast: Coffee and bread
Lunch: Tea and bread
Dinner: Duck

April 25
Breakfast: Coffee and bread
Lunch: Duck soup
Dinner: Duck soup

March 18 This is what I wrote down: Don't know what we're going to have for dinner. Last week we didn't have any meat, only coffee, bread, and potatoes. Today is my birthday.
Lunch: Spam and rice
Dinner: Corned flakes, puffed wheat

In 1941 the mess hall cook told a nurse that he enjoyed living at St. Paul in the summer when people had some money from the seal division, "but I couldn't stay here all winter with the hungry kids coming around for dry bread and hawk eyes (agent) watching from the office to be sure I didn't give them a crust."[26] That year the nurse, Fredericka Martin, decided to test the Aleut diet to see if she could eat just what a sealer did and still have energy to do her work.

I planned to limit us to the experiment for a week. One day was enough. Or, rather, too much. We had to calm our surprised, protesting, neglected stomachs before we could go to sleep. It was not only the kind of food but the small quantity which ended our test. I no longer wondered why the kids sneaked around the garbage cans and ate some filthy refuse. I started trying to fill some of these small, two-legged bottomless pits that I had seen gathering in raids on the garbage cans behind the house. I had to limit my generosity. Each youngster brought his friend to be fed. Though I decreased my gifts, they still hovered around the house for handouts.[27]

On such niggardly rations how did the Aleuts stay alive and healthy? And, indeed, the population increased steadily in this period, not from immigration but from a net natural gain. The birthrate, though lower than in the past, far outstripped the death rate, which had taken a sharp drop (although it was still double that for the general population at the end of this period).[28] Does this mean that the government food issues were sufficient to maintain rising levels of health? The Aleut people claim that their survival would have been threatened had they been solely dependent on the supplies issued, had they not supplemented the supplies with locally caught products and their own cash purchases. But even with the supplements, they often went hungry: "The sealers were so weak from hunger at times. They got tired. Agents said they were lazy. They weren't, just didn't have anything in their system," explained an old-timer.[29]

Keeping people on the edge of hunger and denying them the smallest consumer pleasure reflects the dehumanizing process in the colonial relationship; it demoralizes people and demoralization renders them abject and dependent on whatever crumbs are thrown their way.

To plunge the sword of debasement yet deeper, management discriminated against Aleuts even in the distribution of domestic animals—reindeer, sheep, and cows.

The government had cows but they gave the meat to the white people. We only got beef on Christmas and Easter.

* * *

They didn't give the people beef until after the war. Before that it went to Bureau employees.

* * *

We had sheep on the islands all my life. But I never tasted sheep meat until I was thirty-seven years old. Most of the fresh meat went to the whites.

* * *

We got cow's milk only when the mess hall cook had leftovers.[30]

The official record confirms the Aleuts' allegations.

1935 Annual Report

We have a small dairy herd on the islands which furnishes a good supply of raw milk for the white employees and some for the natives.[31]

A later report specified the distribution of cow's milk for three months in 1944 and 1945. In October 1944, for example, Aleuts received only 19 percent of the 267 gallons distributed, while four white employees alone received 36 percent. A similar disproportion characterized the other months.[32]

One might explain the minimal supplies in terms of managers' cost consciousness, but how can one explain depriving Aleuts of a proportionate share of locally grown products which entailed insignificant costs? Was this another feature of the dehumanizing process? Perhaps, but there seems to be an additional reason. Maintaining a colonial system also requires special rewards to employees—why else would they do such "dirty work?" Rewards in reindeer and cow meat, of course, are insubstantial in themselves, but they symbolize a superior status, one of the rewards by which management won staff commitment.

Other staff privileges reinforced this special status, such as strikingly better houses and facilities. While Aleuts had no electricity until the late 1920s and had no running water, indoor plumbing, refrigeration, or furnace systems until after World War II, bureau employees had all these facilities by 1918 save refrigeration which they secured in 1929.[33] Even some facilities that were available to both Aleuts and whites were distributed in a discriminatory fashion. In a 1926 communication from the St. Paul agent to the superintendent, the agent advised: "Whenever it is necessary to order a new range for any of the natives . . . it should be one for the white cottages and the old one given to the native."[34]

Social segregation, pervasive in the Pribilofs, was one of the chief means of conveying staff superiority over the Aleuts. Race segregation was, in fact, official policy.

> Superintendent to St. Paul Agent, November 14, 1924
>
> Will you kindly notify all of the employees of the Bureau of Fisheries that hereafter no employees will be permitted to play cards with natives at the Pribilof Islands. Any person found guilty of playing cards will be discharged from the service without granting of leave of absense.[35]

* * *

> Superintendent to Radioman-in-charge, August 23, 1927
>
> In order that there may be no misunderstanding regarding their actions, no white person should visit native houses after dark and we hope that white persons will find it advisable to refrain from entertaining natives at any time, except on business. I am instructing the agent to record and report any occurrences where white persons are present at native parties or visiting natives after dark.[36]

* * *

Superintendent to St. Paul Agent, March 30, 1937

Please advise all new employees especially those to be quartered in the Fouke bunkhouse that *the Bureau does not approve of employees associating with natives in a social way.* Employees are not to enter native houses except on official business and natives are not to be permitted to remain in the bunkhouse except when they come there on business.[37]

* * *

Notice by Agent, June 9, 1938

The Recreation Hall has been set aside by the Bureau of Fisheries for the benefit of white employees.[38]

Aleuts had to sit in the balcony of the movie house; the whites sat downstairs. Aleuts recount incidents when the Bureau threatened teachers who visited them with immediate discharge unless the visits stopped. The Bureau even prohibited sailors on supply ships from visiting them.

Racism wasn't news in America. But this was not informal discrimination; these were official acts by a department of government. Nurse Martin was indignant at the pervasive racist attitudes of Bureau officials.

This attitude, so ingrained, mingled with the conviction that the Aleuts were barely above the animals, inferior in every way to the whites. "Treat them like thoroughbred animals," the agent told Dr. Berenberg and his wife, "and you'll get along alright."[39]

The system of racial segregation persisted with the same strength even after the war against fascism. Describing her 1957 visit to the Pribilofs, the late Helen Shenitz, an Alaskan historian as well as member of the Russian Orthodox church, expressed indignation and outrage about the racism.

By the time we arrived at St. Paul it became obvious to me that I have encountered something that was unbelievable to me; Aleuts, the peons, and whites, the lords . . .

My first encounter with . . . race discrimination took place in the evening of the day of my arrival on St. Paul. My hostess informed me that on St. Paul there was a tradition that the first evening after arrival of the Penguin, a reception was held for the newly arrived. Besides myself there were newly arrived, a carpenter and a cook. So, came the evening and to the reception we went. After being introduced to everyone I looked around and then most naively asked: Where are (the) Aleuts? The woman whom I asked just froze, and after staring at me for a few seconds, in an icy cold voice, she said: "We do not mingle with the natives." That was my first lesson. . .

When I came back to the priest's house a group of whites were there. Enthused by my conversation with the Aleut woman I told the group about it, told them what a charming hostess that woman was. Immediately I knew that I said or did something wrong. Well, I most certainly have found what I did wrong in a hurry. One of the whites took me aside and said: "We do not associate with the natives and you made a mistake by going to that woman's house."[40]

Racism and segregation are bedrocks of a colonial system, serving several functions—keeping the oppressed demoralized and without spirit, rewarding managers with symbols of superiority, and most importantly, keeping staff and victims separated lest association breed empathy—sympathetic employees might speak out, protest, cause an investigation, and thereby threaten the system. Better to encourage employees to think of the Aleuts as "thorough-bred animals."

The tale of social and economic injustice in the Pribilofs goes on. The first half of the twentieth century saw tremendous gains for the citizenry, reaching a climax in the reforms of the 1930s. These reforms produced virtually no impact in the Pribilofs. Wages and hours laws and the Social Security Act with unemployment, retirement, and disability benefits for non-federal employees were not available. Aleuts were judged ineligible not because management defined them as federal employees, but because it defined them as wards of the government. As early as 1918, the Secretary of Commerce asked the Solicitor of the United States for an opinion on the application of Alaska's eight-hour law to Pribilof Aleuts. "You are accordingly advised that the Act of the Alaska legislature above quoted has no application to those persons employed by the U.S. on the Pribilof Islands."[41] The Solicitor's opinion apparently legitimized federal policy because Pribilof Aleuts received no Social Security benefits until the 1960s.

Neither did they receive benefits for federal workers—workmen's compensation in 1916, retirement in 1920, and paid annual leave in 1936, among others. For this purpose, the Bureau distinguished between natives (sealers) and employees (agents, storekeepers, teachers, etc.). Only employees received civil service status. The Bureau failed to recognize Aleuts as civil servants until 1950 (and then it was in unclassified status). Thus, Pribilof Aleuts occupied an undefined work status, not federal and not non-federal. This undefined status gave the Bureau the advantage of not having to contribute social security and retirement taxes.

The St. George community tried to compensate for the absence of retirement benefits. Mutual aid, an ancient Aleut institution, remained more viable in St. George than St. Paul probably because white contact there was less intensive. A St. George Aleut recounted the community's response to his father's retirement problem.

> When he retired, he didn't have any money at all, not even for tobacco. He didn't go sealing or foxing so he got no cash. The community worried about him. They got together and decided to give him a second class share in the sealing division. Agent said, "no, sealing division belongs to the people who work." The community gave him some money from their shares but it wasn't much. I guess it wasn't enough. He died a year later, just a year after retiring. The community got together and said, no matter what, everyone who retires gets a second class share.[42]

This event occurred in the 1920s. St. Paul Aleuts remember no similar community effort.

Collective bargaining rights, a national norm by the 1930s, was not even a faint possibility on the Pribilofs. Aleuts were a captive labor force and therefore could not threaten to or actually leave their jobs, which is, after all, the fundamental means for bargaining. The Bureau could and did prevent Aleuts from departing the islands.

> Commissioner to Superintendent, January 11, 1921
>
> Mr. Christoffers has forwarded to this office a copy of his letter of the 5th instant to you stating that he does not consider it advisable to have Pribilof Natives proceed to Seattle for the winter, as in the recent case of Paul Merculieff. The Bureau concurs fully in the sentiments expressed by Mr. Christoffers. You will be guided accordingly.[43]

Even if sealers could support themselves outside the Pribilofs, the Bureau still had to feed their families, and therefore managers tried to keep sealers on the islands throughout the year. For the most part, however, Aleuts didn't ask to leave the village. Their testimony on this issue is illuminating.

> I was afraid to leave. They could give your house away.
>
> * * *
>
> They discouraged our going off the islands. We expected to be told, no, if we asked to go out of the Aleutians so we didn't ask.
>
> * * *
>
> We always used to have permission to leave and they used to threaten us, if we didn't come back on time, they would say we might lose our houses or our jobs. So people didn't leave.
>
> * * *
>
> If you got out without permission, they reduced your sealing division. They threatened not to give food to your family. They said they wouldn't take care of our families.[44]

The awful fear that management would deny their right to return further deterred Aleuts from leaving the islands. This fear was grounded in reality. For instance, women who married men from other places faced virtual exile. As the government prohibited outsiders from Pribilof residence, the women had to move to their husbands' villages, and they could never again live in the Pribilofs even if widowed or divorced, except if it were to marry a Pribilof man. Men who left might also lose residency rights, especially if managers considered them undesirable. Here are some examples from the 1930s.

Superintendent to Agent, March 16, 1936

It is desirous that Gavril Stepetin Kochergin be employed at Unalaska as a temporary native this season . . . Gavril is a former resident of St. Paul. He has made application to return permanently to the islands and whether or not his application is approved depends on how he makes out this summer.[45]

* * *

St. Paul Agent to Francis Mandregan, March 4, 1939

The question of your return to St. Paul has been brought up several times but in the last such instance the superintendent made it plain that he considered it poor policy, in view of your past record of bad conduct . . . we feel that your past improper conduct now makes it impossible to permit you to return to St. Paul. . .

However, if you are not satisfied with our decision, you have the right to appeal to Superintendent Christoffers in Seattle.[46]

Since the agent was simply conveying Christoffers' decision, it seems academic to propose appealing to Christoffers. In any event, it takes only a few exiles, a few instances where emigrants were refused permission to return, to instill terror in the hearts of the others.

Thus, Aleuts were a captive labor force either because they were denied permission to leave or because they were afraid to ask for it. Consequently, few left the village. Between 1925 and 1940 only thirty-three Aleuts permanently left St. Paul, and the majority of these were women who married men from other villages.[47] Dependent on a single industry for survival, Aleuts lacked the choice to give or withhold their labor. Even if the bolder among them spoke up, they faced sanctions such as work demotions. A further deterrent to bargaining was the Aleuts' lack of awareness of labor unions: "We didn't know about labor unions because we were stuck here. We didn't learn about unions until the evacuation when we met people in southeastern Alaska."[48]

So far, we've talked about the economic situation of Aleut men. Women were excluded simply because they were not part of the Pribilof work force. The sealing and foxing enterprises employed only men. Jobs for women were limited to midwifery at $5 per delivery, nurse's assistant at the hospital for an incredible 35 cents for a twelve-hour day (in 1937),[49] and occasionally housework in the homes of whites. This latter opportunity was infrequent because of resistance by management and the white women themselves. The 1924 superintendent outlawed the hiring of Aleut maids.

I do not consider (that) the families of permanent white residents require native janitress services for making up beds, cleaning personally occupied rooms, etc. When the new houses for white families are completed it will be necessary for the families occupying them to do their own work.[50]

Martin pointed out that the white women themselves often hesitated to hire

Aleut women because they didn't want them to touch their food. How many ramifications of the colonial mentality—the Aleuts were seen as unfit to touch the clothes and food of the superiors. In any case, there was virtually no employment for the Aleut women.

As in the past, economic control was accompanied by political domination, even in the face of radically changing times. The 1924 Indian Citizenship Act had no bearing in the Pribilofs. Bureau officials stubbornly held to the belief that their Aleut wards were noncitizens. Martin described managers' attitudes on this subject.

> I held many discussions with Fish and Wildlife Service officials about the status of Aleuts. All insisted they were not citizens—even when I showed them a copy of the U.S.—Russian Treaty of Transfer and told them of the post-war legislation in the 20s giving all native Americans citizenship. . . . the Aleuts were longer in learning about that legislation, because they were so isolated—by geography, naturally, but more so by official policy.[51]

Under the circumstances, Aleuts couldn't vote or exercise any other citizenship rights—for example, the right to local self-government.

Local self-government at the least means that people (1) have some degree of autonomy in organizing local political affairs and participating in important community decisions, (2) are treated as equal to other groups in the political decision-making process, and (3) have their interests represented in larger groups. In native American communities, local self government also means that people exercise some control over the substance of their society.[52] None of these attributes any longer characterized local organization and decision-making in the Pribilofs. The Bureau actively discouraged and interfered with the Aleuts' indigenous political authority until it faded into oblivion. Contemporary Aleuts in St. Paul have no recollection of a chief. Their St. George counterparts recall a chief as late as 1938 but also remember that he was divested of power. The last reference we found to a chief in the official record was in a 1916 petition to the Commissioner of Fisheries.[53]

And what replaced the indigenous political system? Nothing really, although several community organizations did emerge—native canteens in the mid-1920s and community clubs in the 1930s. Management's support of these developments probably reflected sensitivity to the national movement for an enlightened Indian policy, culminating in the 1934 Indian Reorganization Act (Wheeler-Howard Act). But these community organizations resembled local self-governance in form only. In substance, the community clubs were subject to the ultimate authority of the agents. The clubs, limited primarily to recreational activities, operated through three committees: civic, recreation,and hobby. The club presidents organized community work, such as maintaining the church and cemetery. Even with these narrow functions, agents had veto power over all club decisions. Contemporary old-timers say that since the government owned all the tools, equipment, and buildings, they could not even hold a dance without the agents' permission, and that approval hinged on the mood of the agent. Thus, the community clubs were not fertile ground for relearning the art of self-government.

The same held true for the native canteens. The initiative for the canteens came from the Aleuts, from their desperation for a source to supplement the scant supplies in the government store. And, indeed, the canteens carried such luxury items as photographic equipment, musical instruments, cookies and candies, and packaged meat.[54] Initially, the Aleuts capitalized the canteens from their small cash earnings; later, the canteens became self-sustaining. Agents supported the canteens, but again were unwilling to relinquish the reins of control. The canteen policy board, on which agents sat, determined margins of profit and the uses to which profits would be put. The profits belonged to the Aleut community and could be used for projects such as construction of a church or recreational facility. All board decisions, however, depended on agents' approval. Even in managing the enterprise, agents controlled policy and finances. Canteen managers' responsibilities were limited to keeping accounts, maintaining stock, and serving customers, while agents were in charge of purchasing, disbursement of funds, general supervision, credit policy, weekly allowances to Aleuts, and the right to restrict purchases, such as the amount of sugar and tobacco an individual could purchase in a year.[55] As if the Aleuts were children, management let them play at community organization while preventing their political development.

As in the past, agents continued to dominate the administration of justice—in assuming authority to investigate and prosecute crimes and determine punishments which still included deportation. A few changes occurred in the structure of the justice system, but these did not alter the agents' role. United States Commissioners were appointed to both islands, in 1918 on St. Paul and several years later on St. George. But Commissioners' duties were limited to recording births, deaths, and marriages and approving adoptions. Furthermore, the agents often doubled as Commissioners, even as late as 1945.[56] Early in this period, floating courts operated in Alaska, but the evidence at hand indicates that agents rarely sent cases to them, probably because of a Bureau practice of referring cases only when a conviction seemed certain. The St. Paul agent in 1940 told of having received verbal instructions from top management to handle cases himself unless he had *positive* proof for a conviction.[57] This meant that agents also acted as courts for preliminary hearings in serious cases.

Drunkenness persisted as the major justice problem of concern to agents, because it kept sealers from their jobs. Undaunted by the ineffectiveness of measures they had used in the past, agents continued to demote and even exile people for drunkenness. With suppression of so many of their cultural institutions, Pribilof Aleuts seemed to cling to this one collective expression of abandon and defiance.

One of the Aleuts' most keenly felt cultural devastations was the continuing attack on the Russian-Aleut school and language. Management had succeeded in suppressing the Russian school and the Russian language. Also, it instructed teachers to wipe out the use of the Aleut tongue. Nearly every annual school report stressed suppression of the Aleut language.

And how did teachers effect this suppression? Grimacing as if nauseated and in pain, a St. George woman described the teachers' methods.

> The teachers used to put medicine, I can still taste that vile stuff, in our mouth if we spoke Aleut. They said not to do any Aleut crafts. They told our parents not to talk Aleut. We kids were afraid to speak Aleut even in our homes; we were afraid the teacher would find out and put that terrible tasting medicine in our mouths.[58]

Paradoxically, while the ostensible reason for discouraging Aleut culture and language was to facilitate students' progress in the American school, the Bureau of Fisheries provided a very limited educational experience. High school education was becoming the norm in the United States, but in St. George only five grades were offered; in St. Paul, six. Furthermore, whatever the student's progress through these grades, school was arbitrarily terminated at age sixteen when boys were required to enter the sealing gang.

> When we got to the end, at sixteen, they told us that was enough schooling for sealers. Said you go to work now. We were like slaves. They don't want to teach us nothing too much.

* * *

> At sixteen they made us go to work. Further schooling wasn't allowed, not even for the girls though they didn't have to work. The agent wouldn't let us go.
>
> How did they stop you?
>
> They threatened us, and then we had no way of transportation unless they transported us. You had to have government permission to go out on their boats.[59]

Aleuts felt insulted by the low caliber of American education offered.

> The teachers were told in Seattle, don't teach the Aleuts anything. Just teach them to say, yes sir, and sign their names.

* * *

I think the teachers were instructed not to teach us anything, to keep us ignorant. When I started school, they had only one book—Pinochio—that everyone would take turns looking at. We just played in school. They didn't teach anything thoroughly.

* * *

They told me I was in the fifth grade but I noticed they gave me the same books I used in the fourth grade.[60]

What does it mean for the Bureau to insist on American education and then provide such a grossly inadequate one? Again it reflects the colonialist nature of the system on the Pribilofs. The Bureau needed not educated Aleuts but work horses who knew enough English and arithmetic to manage their jobs. And specifically, the Bureau did not want enlightened Aleuts who might organize around their dissatisfactions or take Bureau positions, acts that could threaten the underpinnings of the segregated system.

With this deficient education, Aleut learning was probably unremarkable. Teachers certainly thought so. But as in most explanations of Aleut capabilities, the whites in charge tended to question not the adequacy of the programs they introduced but of the Aleuts. The 1927 head teacher at St. Paul explained the low levels of Aleut learning in the following terms:

That the pupils are retarded is beyond a doubt. This is charged to:

1. Innate lack of mental ability.
2. Use of the Aleut language.
3. General inertness and irresponsibility.[61]

With its low priority on humanism, Pribilof management created intense pain for Aleuts by destroying an age-old welfare custom. Informal adoptions were common practice in Aleut villages and an important source of cultural pride, for this custom symbolized some of the Aleuts' most sacred values—communality, sharing, and care for all members. The Bureau approved adoptions only when they involved Pribilof children. When they concerned children from other villages, the Bureau generally opposed them because it did not want an additional mouth to feed.

Commissioner of Fisheries to Superintendent, January 22, 1924

Reference is made to your letter of January 15, 1924 in regard to the desire of Solomonia Melovidov . . . a native woman of St. Paul Island . . . to bring to St. Paul a child adopted by her. In the meantime permission will not be given to bring the child to St. Paul Island. The adopting mother is herself a ward of the government and is in no position to assume the responsibility involved. . .

The Bureau is not entirely satisfied as to the facts in the case, the only representation of which appears to be in a telegram sent to Mr. Proctor (superintendent) by Solomonia Melovidov herself. This woman is not deemed capable of deciding for herself whether she has legally adopted the child or not.

The laws of Alaska . . . seem to make it incumbent upon the (United States) Commissioner who orders an adoption to satisfy himself that the person who adopts a child is of sufficient ability and in all respects a proper person to bring up the child and furnish suitable nurturance and education. It is difficult to see how a Commissioner could have satisfied himself affirmatively on these matters in respect to Solomonia Melovidov, who is herself, as stated above, a ward of the Government . . .[62]

* * *

St. Paul Agent to Superintendent, February 2, 1924

To have taken the matter up with Mr. Bolshanin (U.S. Commissioner in Unalaska) would doubtless have raised fairly a legal question as to the wardship which the U.S. Government may or may not exercise over the native residents of the Pribilof Islands, which I am not in a position to answer . . .

Whatever the status of these people may be, one point is absolutely clear and that is that the Department has every right to restrict landing upon the Pribilof Islands and in exercising that authority could no doubt prevent unauthorized adoptions . . .

This is the first instance in which a native of the Pribilof Islands has adopted a child not already resident on the Islands. If the precedent thus established is followed out to its logical conclusion, any native of the Islands may go to Unalaska or elsewhere and by legally adopting one or any number of native children, can bring them to the Pribilof Islands where they will be supported. . .

With the view of protecting the interests of the Government as well as the interests of the Seal Island Natives, it is suggested that a suitable regulation covering this matter is made by proper authority.[63]

Ultimately, the Bureau granted permission to bring the adopted child to the Pribilofs, probably for the reason the agent suggested, to avoid stirring up questions about the legality of Aleut wardship. The following year two St. Paul women made application to adopt their younger sisters from another village. This time the Bureau refused.

St. Paul Agent to Superintendent, January 21, 1925

Last season Mrs. Alexandria Bourdukofsky and Nellie Krukof made a request to adopt two of their sisters now at Ikatan (an Aleut village). It is not considered desirable to grant their request . . . The Government cannot undertake to furnish food and subsistence to all of the natives of the Aleutian Islands who would really desire to go to the Pribilofs. No general rule can, however, be made as there might be instances where it would be desirable to permit natives from the Aleutian Islands to make their homes at the Pribilofs. This would probably be only in the case where grown boys desire to make the Pribilofs their home. Such boys could no doubt be worked to advantage by the Government in each instance.[64]

In 1933 the Bureau established a firm policy opposing adoption of children from other villages.

I wish to advise that the Bureau will not approve at this time of any Pribilof inhabitants adopting natives from villages other than the Pribilof Islands. It is especially necessary at this time to reduce expenses.[65]

Four years later the Office of Indian Affairs appealed to the Bureau to allow a St. George woman to adopt her younger sister in Unalaska because the sister's home life was very damaging. The Bureau flatly refused.

> The Bureau of Fisheries appropriations are provided for maintenance and support of the Pribilof island natives only, and I do not see at present where we would have the right to permit natives not born on the islands to become permanent residents, except when they marry Pribilof natives.[66]

In essence, Bureau policy on this issue arbitrarily limited family size as a means of keeping costs down. This meant that the Bureau was not conceiving the goods and services by which it paid Aleuts as wages at all, for wages imply that workers control the use of their earnings. Furthermore, this policy involved a larger issue, for it struck a blow at the heart of a central Aleut cultural institution.

The long arm of Bureau control reached into the most intimate, personal aspects of Aleuts' lives. The Bureau still tried to regulate Aleuts' choice of marriage partners.

> Superintendent to St. Paul Agent, December 3, 1935
>
> The Bureau does not particularly approve of natives of the Pribilof Islands marrying Aleutian natives and bringing them to the islands as there are so many marriageable natives of both sexes at the islands.
>
> In many cases where Pribilof natives have married Aleutian women and brought them to the Islands we have had considerable trouble with them on account of the fact that they are not good housekeepers or as cleanly as the Pribilof natives . . . For this reason I would suggest that you attempt to talk John Fratis out of his intended trip to secure a wife.[67]

In the ideology of Bureau officials, what's the difference who an Aleut marries? Isn't a Pribilof maiden as good as one from elsewhere? This typical colonial mentality denies that Aleuts might want to search for love as much as anyone. Furthermore, this policy must have been very confusing to Aleuts when several decades earlier management followed an opposite one by coercing men to go outside the islands to find wives. In any case, this dehumanizing attitude combined with the Bureau's power to keep people from leaving the islands resulted in regulating Aleuts in the most fateful of life choices.

The Bureau even invaded the sanctuary of the family home.

> August 22, 1927
>
> Leonty Philemenof and his wife are having family quarrels. It was found necessary to separate them temporarily . . .[68]

August 25, 1938—St. Paul Island

ALL NATIVES TAKE NOTICE

> **Beginning today all card playing will terminate promptly at 10:45 p.m. There will be no card playing, or the playing of any other games, in native houses or in any other place after that hour. The recent epidemic of sickness has been attributed directly to loss of rest resulting from late card games. In the event the above orders are disregarded, card playing at night will be prohibited entirely.**[69]

With all the other indignities heaped on them, Aleuts faced regulation in their private family hours.

In sum, this dramatic case of hidden, internal colonialism in the democratic United States evolved from national colonialist attitudes toward Alaska, deeply embedded racist attitudes, and the particular mission and pattern of the Pribilof management institution. Its goals were seals and profits; the Aleut sealers were secondary, instrumental to an end rather than an end in themselves. It involved only one short step from treatment as instruments to treatment as commodities, to be managed in the cheapest possible manner.

The colonial relationship found expression not only in economic exploitation and political domination but in a many-faceted process of dehumanization to socialize Aleuts for their role as commodities. Management gained staff cooperation in this process with rewards symbolizing superior status. And it justified its exploitation by pointing the finger of blame at its victims.

The powerful progressive reforms of the 1930s failed to dent this oppressive system. Management succeeded in perpetuating it, first because it wanted to, second because it was able to. The isolation of the islands and secrecy of the federal operation there hid the Pribilof situation from public view; management was virtually insulated from interest groups, within or outside the islands. Then came World War II, a war against the most terrible totalitarianism known to humankind. How did Pribilof colonialism fare in these circumstances?

Endnotes

1. Field Notes, St. Paul, Alaska, October 1975.
2. For an excellent discussion of Alaska colonialism, see George W. Rogers, The Future of Alaska: Economic Consequences of Statehood (Baltimore: The Johns Hopkins Press, 1962), pp. 80-92.
3. Paul A. Baran, The Political Economy of Growth (New York: Monthly Review Press, 1957), pp. 201-205; Albert Memmi, The Colonizer and The

Colonized (Boston: Beacon Press, 1965).
4. Memmi, The Colonizer and the Colonized, Introduction by Jean-Paul Sartre.
5. George Rogers, An Economic Analysis of the Pribilof Islands, 1870-1946, Prepared for the Indian Claims Commission Dockets Nos. 352 and 369 (Fairbanks: University of Alaska, Institute of Social, Economic and Government Research, 1976), p. 117.
6. Ibid.
7. Ibid., p. 124.
8. Ibid., p. 159.
9. Ibid., computed from Table 36, p. 199.
10. In the 1920s, harvests ranged from about 15,000 to 40,000. In the 1930s they increased to peak of about 65,000. 1941 saw the highest harvest in this period of 95,013. Rogers, An Economic Analysis, p. 117.
11. Ibid., pp. 138-141.
12. Order, by H.C. Fassett, Agent and Caretaker, St. Paul Island, February 7, 1917. Bureau of Fisheries Records, St. Paul Island.
13. H.L. Smith, Commissioner of Fisheries, to A.H. Proctor, Superintendent, June 6, 1921. Bureau Records, St. Paul.
14. H.J. Christoffers, Superintendent, to L.C. McMillin, Agent and Caretaker, St. George Island, April 20, 1936. Bureau Records, Federal Archives and Records Center, Seattle.
15. Ralph Baker, Junior Administrative Assistant, Division of Alaska Fisheries, "Native Canteens of the Pribilof Islands, Alaska," October 20, 1941. p. 4, Bureau Records, Federal Archives.
16. Between 1913 and 1917 the government suffered a net loss of nearly $600,000. U.S. General Services Administration, Office of Finance, Accounting Division, Accounting Report on Pribilof Islands: Aleut Community of St. Paul Island and Aleut Tribe v. United States, Docket Nos. 352 and 369 1977), p. 20.
17. U.S. Department of Commerce, Appropriation Bill for 1935, Hearing Before the Subcommittee of U.S. Congress, House Committee on Appropriations, 73rd Cong., 2nd sess., 1934, p. 265.
18. H.J. Christoffers, Superintendent, to St. Paul and St. George Agents, January 21, 1925. Bureau Records, St. Paul.
19. U.S. Department of Commerce and Labor, Appropriation Bill for 1923, Hearing Before the Subcommittee of House Committee on Appropriations, 67th Cong., 2nd sess., 1922, p. 653.
20. See, for example, U.S. Department of Commerce, Bureau of Fisheries, Alaska Fishery and Fur-Seal Industries in 1935, Administrative Report No. 23, p. 47.
21. Field Notes, St. Paul, October 1975.
22. Ibid.
23. Superintendent to A.J. Messner, Acting Agent and Caretaker, Octo-

ber 15, 1930. Bureau Records, Federal Archives.
24. Samuel R. Berenberg, M.D., "Annual Medical Report, 1941-42," Medical Department, Fish and Wildlife Service, St. Paul Island, Alaska, pp. 49-50. (This is a draft copy of the report furnished by Fredericka Martin who was Dr. Berenberg's wife at the time the report was written.)
25. Written statement by St. Paul Aleut, prepared for Hearings on Violation of the Fair and Honorable Dealings Clause of the Indian Claims Commission Act, circa 1969.
26. Fredericka Martin, "The Wind is No River," unpublished manuscript, p. 194. Fredericka Martin Records.
27. Ibid., p. 461.
28. Dorothy M. Jones, A History of United States Administration in the Pribilof Islands, 1867-1946, Prepared for the Indian Claims Commission Docket Nos. 352 and 369 (Fairbanks: University of Alaska, Institute of Social, Economic and Government Research, 1976), p. 119.
29. Field notes, St. Paul, October 1975.
30. Field notes, St. George and St. Paul, October 1975.
31. "Agents' Annual Report," St. Paul Island, April 15, 1935. Bureau Records, St. Paul.
32. "Agents' Annual Report," St. Paul Island, 1945. Bureau Records, St. Paul.
33. H.J. Christoffers, Superintendent, to Commissioner of Fisheries, March 6, 1928. Bureau Records, St. Paul.
34. St. Paul Agent to H.J. Christoffers, January 27, 1926. Bureau Records, St. Paul.
35. Bureau Records, St. Paul.
36. Bureau Records, Federal Archives.
37. Bureau Records, St. Paul.
38. Bureau Records, St. Paul.
39. Fredericka Martin, "Recapitulation of Errors of Administration and Abuse and Exploitation of Pribilof American Aleuts by the United States Government, 1867 to 1946," unpublished. Fredericka Martin Records.
40. Helen A. Shenitz, "Pribilovians, the Forgotten People of Alaska." Paper presented at the Alaska Science Conference, Fairbanks, Alaska, August 3, 1965, pp. 10-12.
41. A.L. Thurman, Solicitor, to Secretary of Commerce, February 15, 1918, Bureau Records, St. Paul.
42. Field notes, St. Paul, October 1975.
43. Bureau Records, St. Paul.
44. Field notes, St. George and St. Paul, October, 1975.
45. Bureau Records, St. Paul.
46. Bureau Records, St. Paul.
47. Don C. Foote, Victor Fischer, and George W. Rogers, St. Paul Community Study: An Economic and Social Analysis of St. Paul, Pribilof Islands, Alaska (Fairbanks: University of Alaska, Institute of Social, Economic and

Government Research, 1968), pp. 30-31, 34.
48. Field notes, St. Paul, October 1975.
49. St. Paul Physician to Superintendent, October 13, 1937. Bureau Records, St. Paul.
50. H.J. Christoffers, Superintendent, to J.W. Lipke, Agent and Caretaker, April 28, 1924. Bureau Records, St. Paul.
51. Fredericka Martin to Dorothy Jones, February 12, 1976.
52. For a thoughtful definition of self-government, see Gerald A. McBeath and Thomas A. Morehouse, Alaska Native Self-Government (Anchorage: University of Alaska, Institute of Social and Economic Research, 1978), p. 3. Soon to be published as The Dynamics of Alaska Native Self-Government (Lanham, Maryland: University Press of America, 1980).
53. St. Paul Community to Commissioner of Fisheries, October 10, 1916, Bureau Records, St. Paul.
54. Ralph Baker, "Native Canteens of the Pribilof Islands," October 20, 1941, p. 1, Bureau Records, Federal Archives.
55. "St. Paul Island Native Canteen," May 6, 1927; "Regulations Regarding Handling of Native Canteens on the Pribilófs," April 20, 1928, Bureau Records, St. Paul.
56. For example, Agent Daniel Benson also doubled as the U.S. Commissioner in the Pribilofs in 1945. Jack Martin, U.S. Commissioner, to Daniel Benson, U.S. Commissioner, St. George, July 27, 1940. Bureau Records, St. Paul.
57. St. Paul Agent and Caretaker to T.H. Erickson, Jr., Administrative Assistant, March 13, 1940, Bureau Records, Federal Archives.
58. Field notes, St. George, October 1975.
59. Field notes, St. Paul, October 1975.
60. Field notes, St. George and St. Paul, October 1975.
61. School Report, signed by Hubert G. Armstrong, teacher, contained in letter, E.C. Johnston, Agent and Caretaker, St. Paul, to Superintendent, May 27, 1927. Bureau Records, St. Paul.
62. Henry O'Malley, Commissioner, to H.J. Christoffers, Superintendent, January 22, 1924, Bureau Records, St. Paul.
63. A.H. Proctor to H.J. Christoffers, February 2, 1924, Bureau Records, St. Paul.
64. H.J. Christoffers to H.H. Hungerford, Agent and Caretaker, St. Paul, January 21, 1925, Bureau Records, St. Paul.
65. Superintendent to H.A. Peterson, St. Paul Island, January 24, 1933, Bureau Records, Federal Archives.
66. H.J. Christoffers to George C. Penny, Office of Indian Affairs, Juneau, January 5, 1937, Bureau Records, Federal Archives.
67. H.J. Christoffers, Superintendent, to J.W. Lipke, Agent, December 3, 1935, Bureau Records, St. Paul.
68. Pribilof Islands Daily Log, St. George, August 22, 1927.
69. Notice, signed by John Lipke, Agent and Caretaker, and George Roger Chute, Assistant Agent, August 25, 1938, Bureau Records, St. Paul.

St. George Island. Circa 1915.

(This and subsequent photos, pages 88 through 106, are from The William R. Browne Collection.)

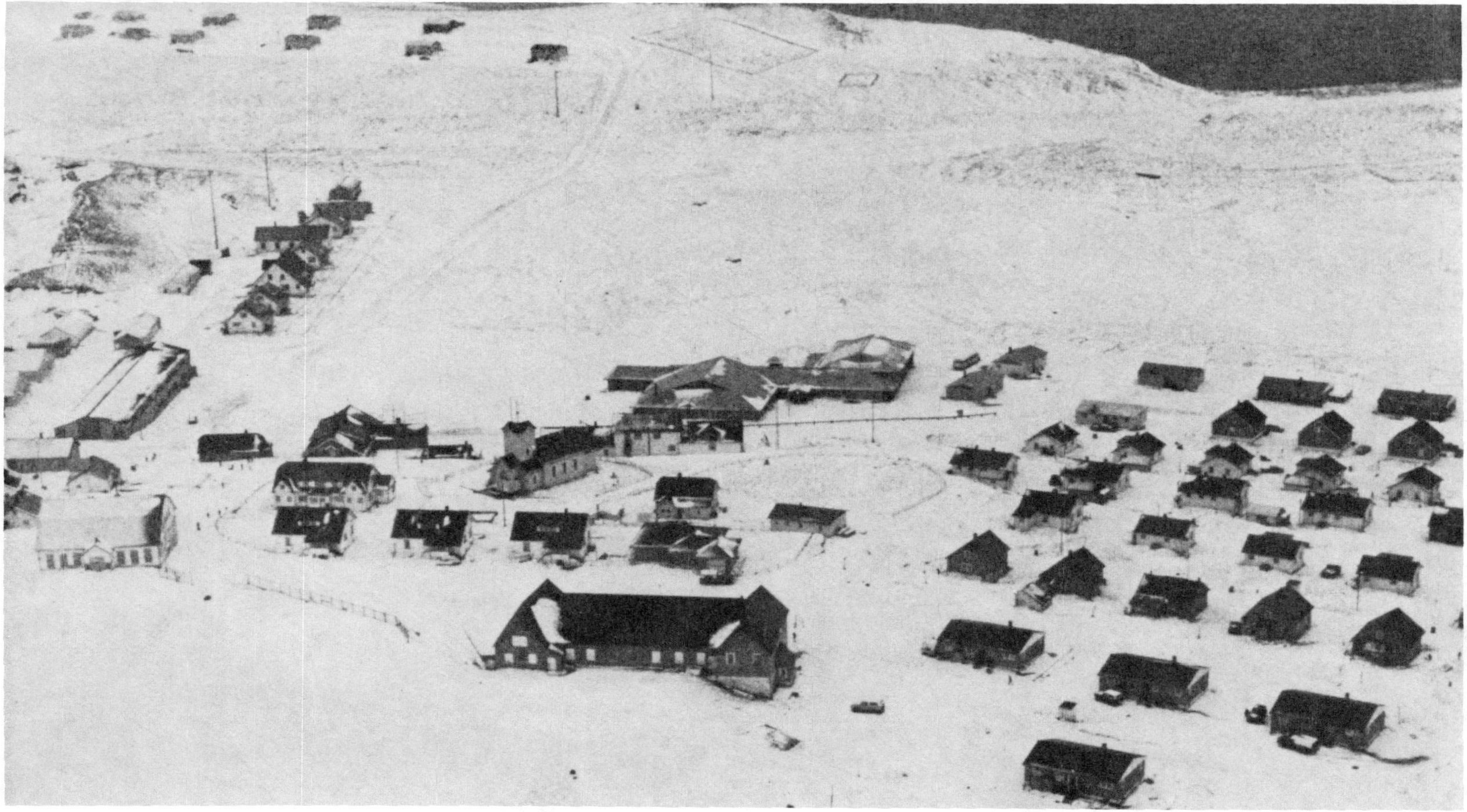

St. Paul, Winter 1974.

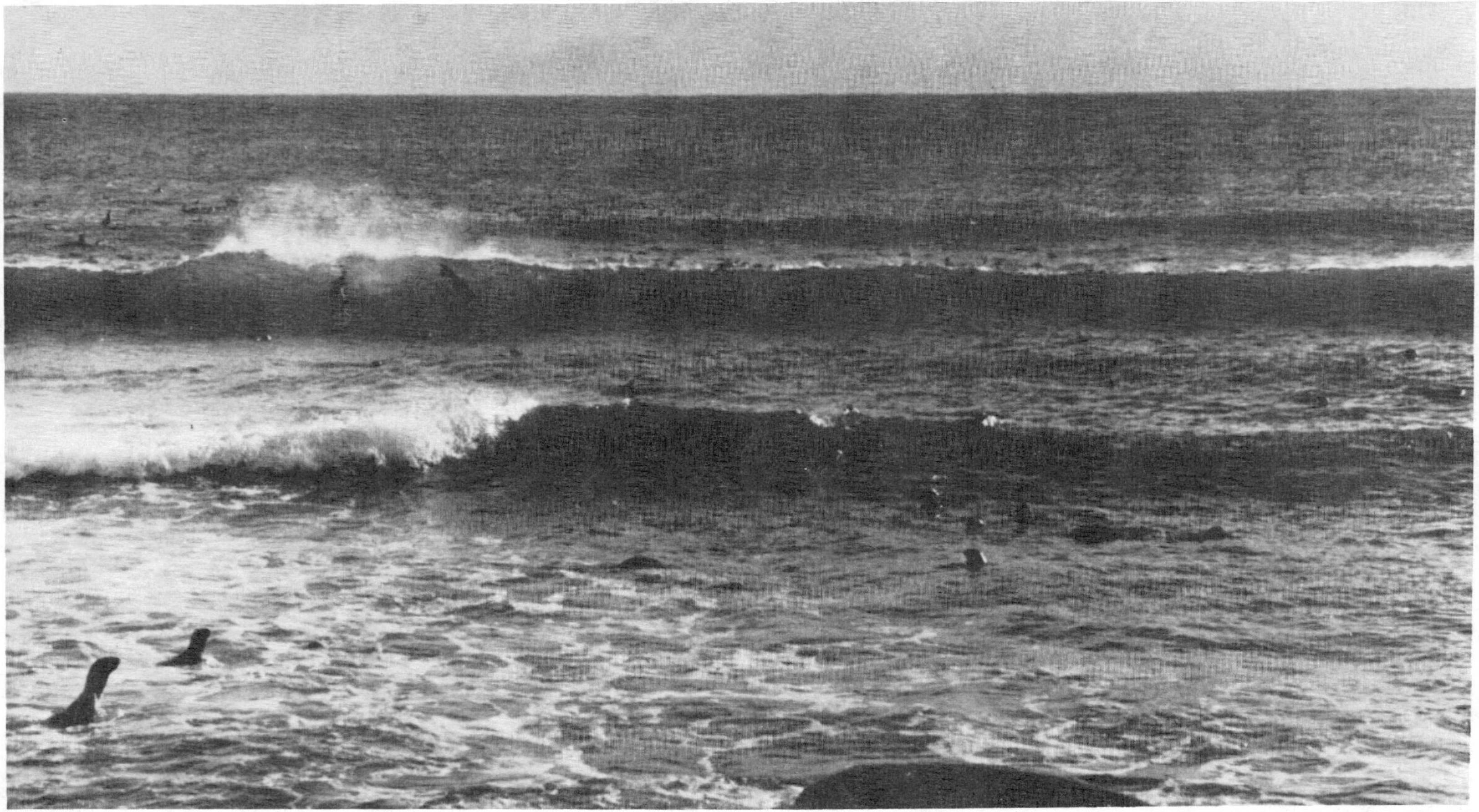

Seals in the Bering Sea off St. Paul Island.

Seals on the Beach and in the Water of Lukanin Bay. St. Paul Village is in the background.

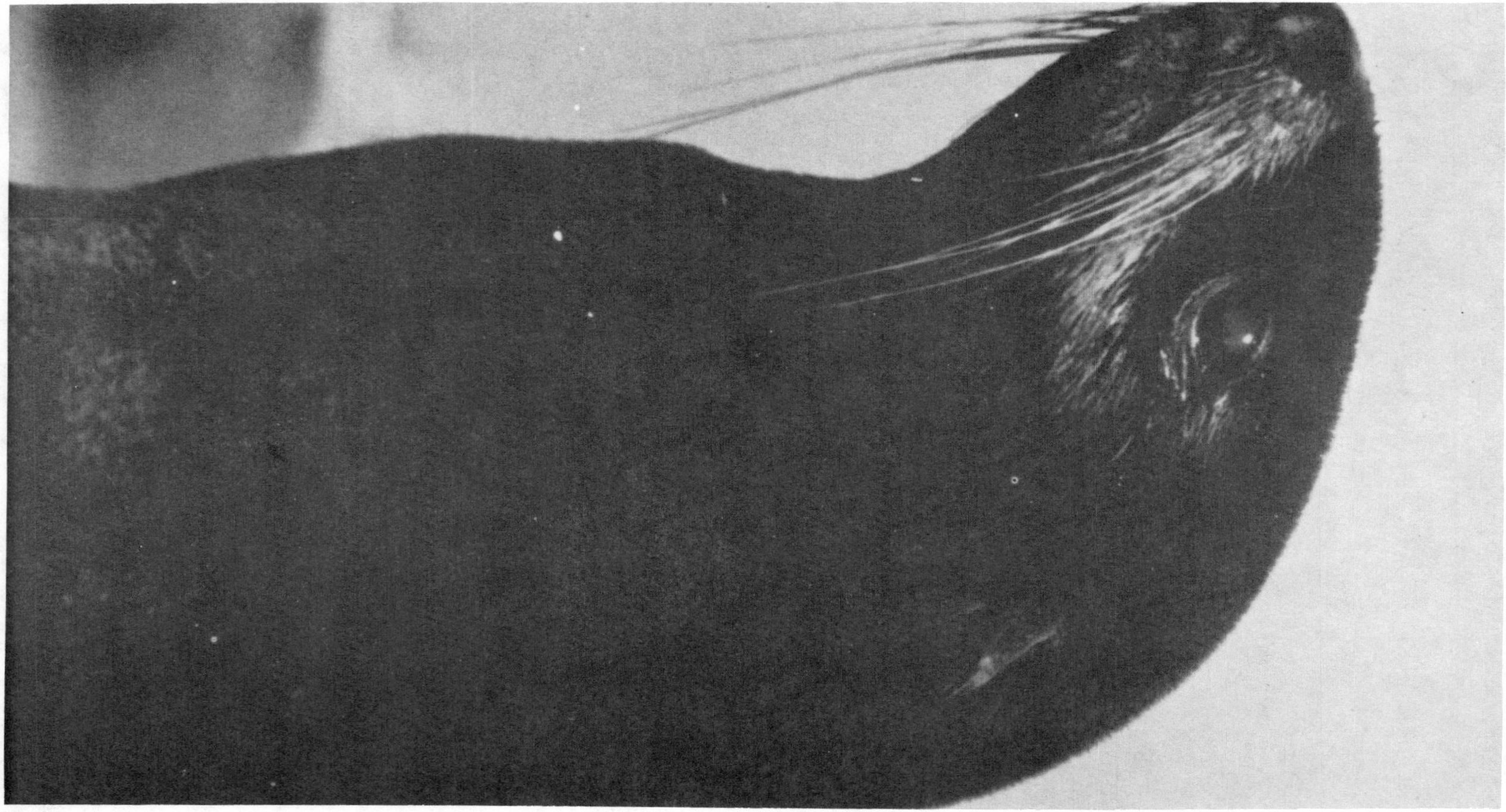

A Young Female Seal.

St. Paul Woman. Circa 1910.

St. Paul Sealer. Circa 1910.

Boat Builders—Who are also the Crew. St. George Aleuts pose in their motor launch "Ulakaia." Powered by a two-cycle gasoline engine, the craft was used for towing *bidars* (large skin boats) and for halibut fishing. Pre-World War I.

Lightering Supplies to Shore. Since neither St. Paul nor St. George possesses a natural harbor, supplies must be carried from ship to shore in small boats. The large skin boat on the right of the motor launch is a *bidar*.

The Native Brotherhood on St. Paul. Circa 1910.

St. George Family, Circa 1920.

St. George Junior High School and Aleut Students. Circa 1922.

Intérior of St. George School. Circa 1922.

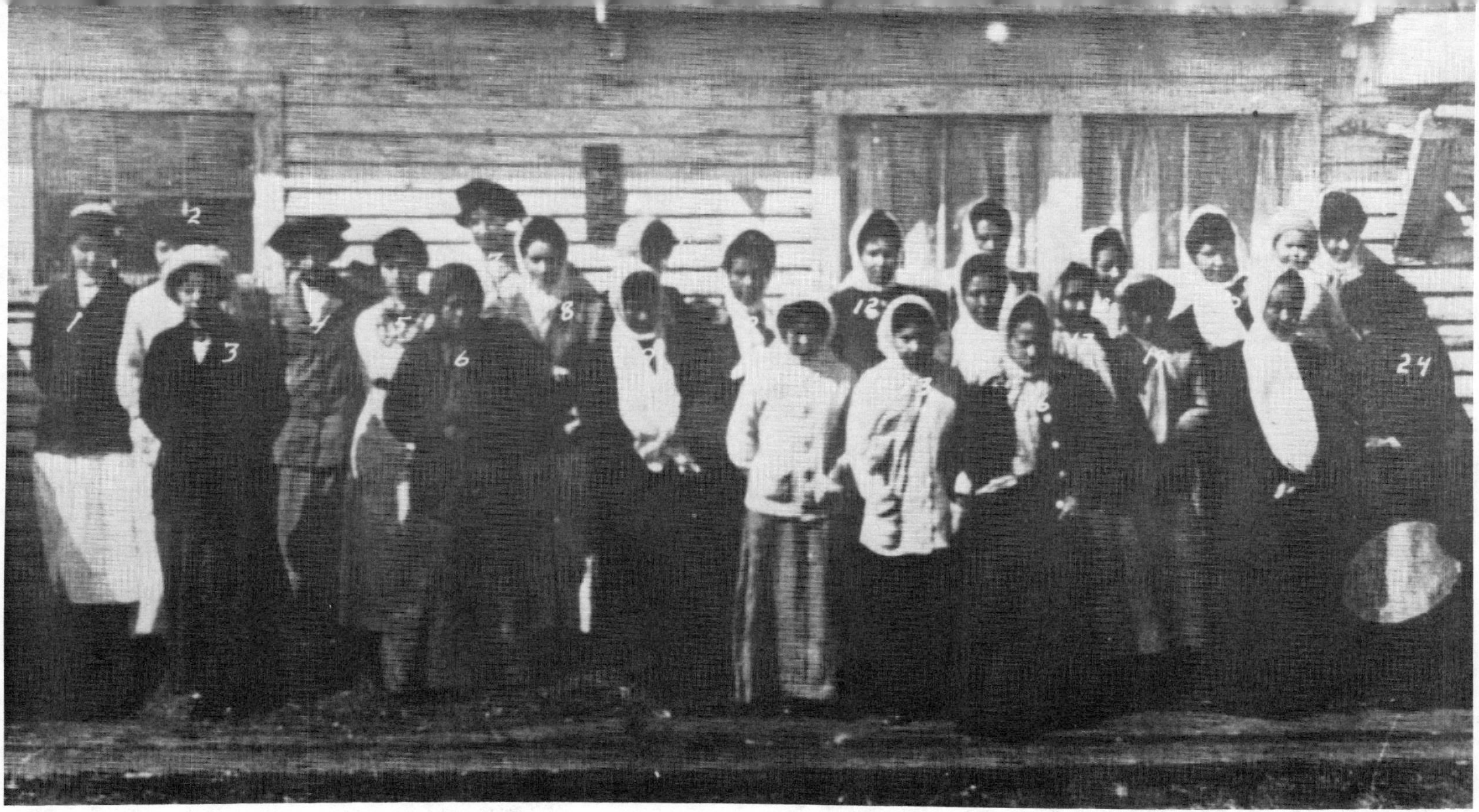

Aleut Women in Front of the Old Company House on St. George. Circa 1921.

Interior of Russian Orthodox Church on St. Paul Island. The Priest is Father John Orloff. Circa 1910.

An Aleut Wedding Party on the Steps of the St. Paul Church. (Number 14 to the right of the bride is Treasury agent Dr. Walter Lembkey, early champion of Aleuts' welfare. Circa 1910.

A Procession Celebrating St. Paul's Day Enters the St. Paul Church. Circa 1907.

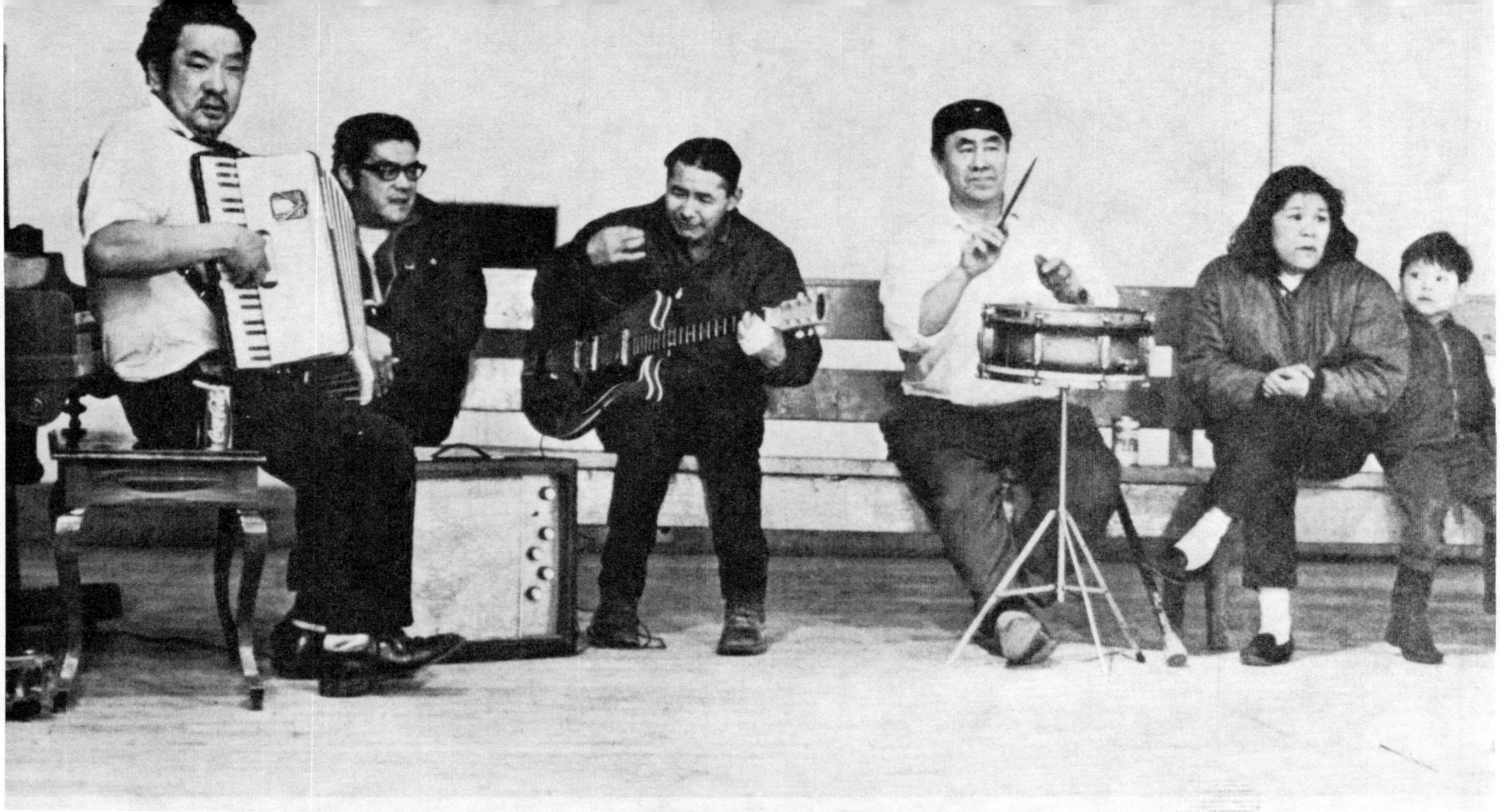

A Three-Piece Aleut Band Entertains During a Party on St. Paul. Circa 1968.

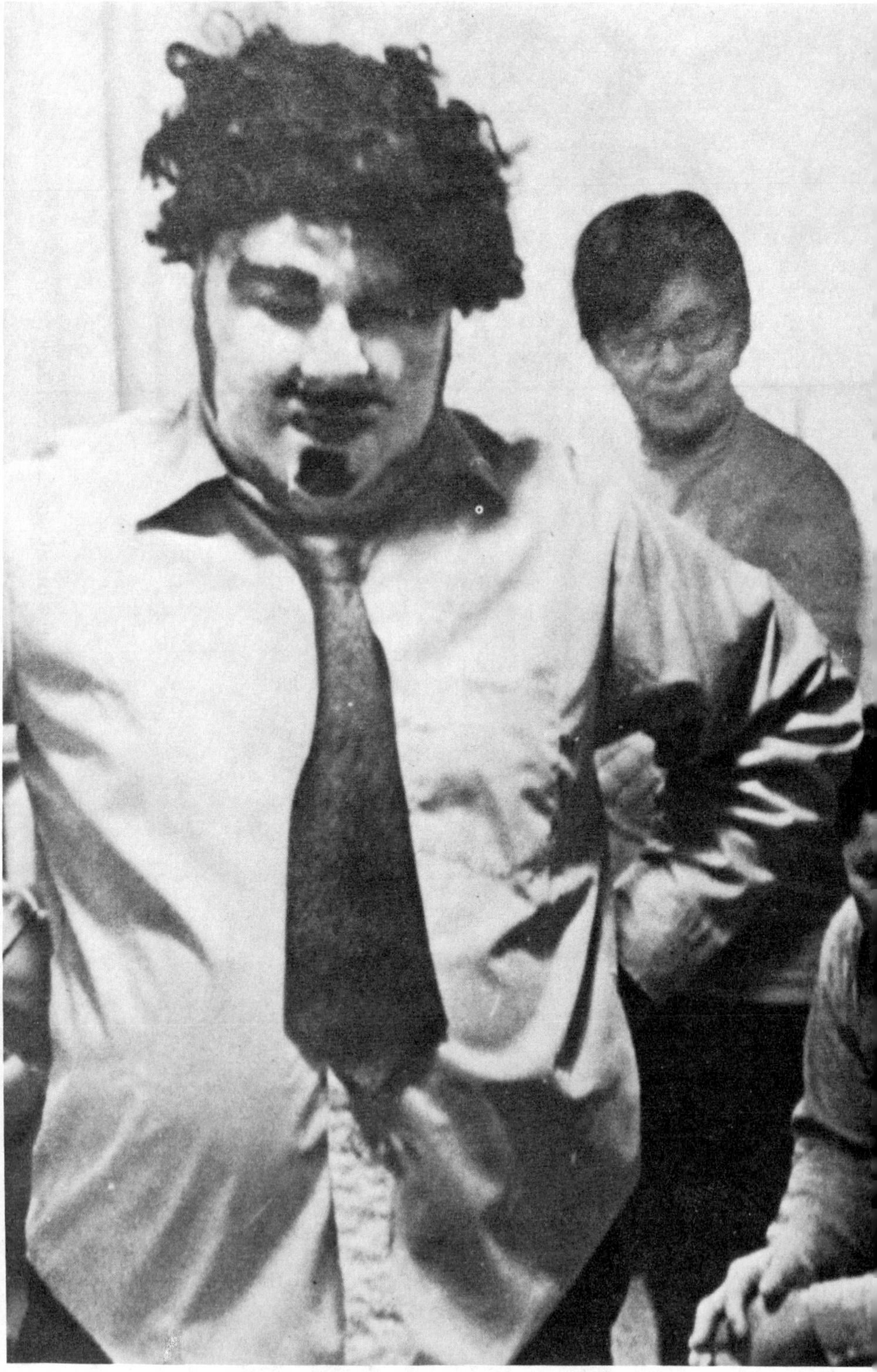
Masking at an Aleut Ceremony. Circa 1968.

CHAPTER 6

REFUGEES

On February 19, 1942 President Roosevelt issued an executive order calling for the confinement of enemy aliens—Germans, Italians, and Japanese—with the assurance that no group would be condemned wholesale. The people of the West Coast adamantly protested the round-up of Germans and Italians, but not of the Japanese who, unlike the others, were not white and were legally barred from naturalized citizenship. Between March and August 1942, the War Department herded 110,000 West Coast Japanese, by birth or ancestry, into barbed wire enclosures.[1] The living conditions were execrable. In one camp, for example, the government housed the Japanese in horse stalls. The government impounded the internees' money and paid them in scrip good only at the camps.* In a diary of his experiences, a camp resident described the daily horror of being stared at by a steady deluge of visitors—7,000 in a three-month period—"as if we were some caged monstrosity."[2] This outrage is probably unparalleled in United States history. What occurred on the Pribilofs was a microcosmic repetition.

On June 3 and 4, 1942 the Japanese bombed Dutch Harbor and Unalaska. On June 7 Japanese troops landed on the Aleutian Islands of Kiska and Attu. One week later a U.S. Naval vessel arrived at St. Paul; the captain announced plans for the immediate evacuation of the entire population of both islands. Hastily boarding up their houses and packing the few belongings they were allowed to take, the Pribilof people left their islands two days later, for an unknown destination.

Aleuts from the western and central Aleutians were also evacuated, but that was more clearly for protection than it was on the distant northerly Pribilofs; in fact, the military suggested another motivation for the Pribilof evacuation—the Navy needed the St. Paul houses and facilities.[3] The Navy failed to inform the Bureau of Fisheries of the evacuation until it dumped the Aleuts at Funter Bay in southeastern Alaska. Though the Pribilof Aleuts were now 1,500 miles from their home base, the government continued to manage them.[4]

Conditions at the camps matched those the Japanese-Americans experienced. Funter Bay on Admirality Island, about sixty miles from Juneau, was the site of an abandoned cannery in which the St. Paul evacuees were housed. The St. George camp was across the bay at an old mine site. Living conditions on the Pribilofs seemed like paradise when compared to the camps. Even the agent was aghast.

---

*Later, the government liberalized this restraint.

Most of the buildings at the cannery have been unused for 12 years or more and are all dry-rotted. . .

All the cooking for the entire village was accomplished on two old stoves, and it was a miracle how the natives could get the meals for some 290 people on such small cooking space. . .

The Territorial Department of Health officers visited the camps and declared them both very much unsanitary. .

Pipes around the cannery are laid helter skelter on top of the ground, patched with rubber hose, and will soon have to be discontinued on account of cold weather. . .

All the water for washing clothing is now heated on the cook stove. . .

Many of the people are sleeping so many in a room that they have to sleep in relays as there is not sufficient room for them to all lay down at the same time in their cramped stuffy quarters—no bunks, no mattresses.[5]

By September camp accommodations remained unimproved: "Many natives are still sleeping on the floor with only a blanket under them. Others pile all the bedding on the children and wear stocking caps, coats, or anything they have to keep warm at night."[6] A month later, the St. Paul agent resigned in protest: "I wish to submit my resignation as agent and caretaker of the Pribilof Islands . . . I feel I cannot stay and watch a people I have grown somewhat attached to . . . through a time of which I sincerely believe only a miracle can prevent a tragedy of sickness and cause extreme suffering to them."[7]

A year later a physician's report indicated that the camp situation was even worse:

As we entered the first bunkhouse, the odor of human excreta and waste was so pungent that I could hardly make the grade. . . The buildings were in total darkness except for a few candles here and there which I considered distinct fire hazards since the partitions between rooms were made mostly by hangings of wool blankets. The overcrowded housing condition is really beyond description since a mother and as many as three or four children were found in several beds and two or three children in one bunk.[8]

The Aleut women expressed their gnawing anguish in a petition to the government.

We the people of this place wants a better place than this to live. This place is no place for a living creature. We drink impure water and then get sick (and) the children's get skin diseases even the grown ups are sick from cold.

We ate from the mess house and it is near the toilet only a few yards away. We eat the filth that is flying around.

We got no place to take a bath and no place to wash our clothes or dry them when

> it rains. We women are always lugging water up stairs and take turns warming it up and the stove is small.
>
> We live in a room with our children just enough to turn around in; we used blankets for walls just to live in private. . .
>
> We all have rights to speak for ourselves.[9]

The persistence of such a state took its toll. For the first time in decades, the Pribilof Aleuts' death rate outstripped the birth rate.[10] And we found the first official record of madness among Pribilof Aleuts.[11]

What was going on in the Pribilof program to tolerate and condone such human outrage? The Department of Commerce was no longer in charge of the program; administrative responsibility was transferred in 1940 to the newly created Fish and Wildlife Service (a merger of the Bureau of Fisheries and Bureau of Biological Survey) in the Department of Interior. The line of of command was similar to that in the past, from the Director of the Fish and Wildlife Service (based in Chicago during the war years) to the Chief of Alaska Fisheries, to the Seattle-based superintendent, to the agents in the field.

What pressures influenced Pribilof management policy during these war years? For one thing, because of the wartime inflation, the price of seal skins leaped; it nearly doubled between 1939 and 1941.[12] Management still gauged its success as it had in the past, on bringing surplus revenues into the Treasury. Furthermore, the military considered marine oils produced on the Pribilofs important to the war effort. With these considerations in mind, Pribilof management adhered to a single goal—to get the seal show back on the road as quickly as possible.

Several months after the evacuation, Secretary of Interior Harold Ickes sought War Department approval for the resumption of sealing in the 1943 season.

> This action (the evacuation) caused great inconvenience and hardship, and resulted in the loss of more than a million dollars by reason of the discontinuance of operations at the Pribilof Islands. . .
>
> I urge that arrangements be made to return the natives and supervisory personnel by Naval transport to the Pribilof Islands next April or May to resume sealing and other operations.[13]

Secretary of War Stimson had different priorities:

> Occupation of the Pribilof Islands was made possible by using the housing of the former occupants, and insufficient housing exists for both troops and the native population. Furthermore, the return of the native civilians would incur an additional burden on our already overtaxed shipping facilities in that area.[14]

It is not known why Stimson shortly reversed himself. Less than a month after writing the above letter, although the Japanese were still in the Aleutians. Stimson agreed to repatriate the residents of St. George, where no troops were stationed, and temporarily return St. Paul Aleuts for the 1943 sealing season.[15]

The return of the natives—yes—that was critical to the planned resumption of sealing. To this end managers tried to exercise strict control over the Aleuts' movements. As the draft threatened to disperse the Aleuts, managers resisted their registration, claiming the exemption on the basis of Aleuts' wardship status.

Fisheries Management Supervisor to Pribilof Supervisor, September 8, 1942

> Draft board in Juneau is becoming insistant on registration of our natives STOP Am awaiting your answer to letter July eleventh as to whether instructions issued at islands hold here for no registration account their being wards of Government STOP.[16]

The draft board dismissed this logic out of hand and required all eligible Funter Bay evacuees to register under the Selective Service Act.[17] Losing this round, managers then appealed to the Commanding General of the Army to assign inducted Alaska natives to the Pribilofs for summer sealing work; this request was granted for the 1944 season.[18]

But the draft was only one obstacle to keeping the Aleut group intact; another was the lure of high-paying jobs in Juneau. With the acute labor shortage at that time, the United States Employment Service campaigned in the camps for recruits: "We state that these Pribilof people, or at least the able-bodied men among them, are needed in the labor market in southeastern Alaska and that we have made plans to, and are ready to interview, classify, and place them." [19] Eager for such jobs and for opportunities to learn the mysteries of that larger world from which they had always been isolated, Aleuts increasingly asked the superindendent for permission to leave the camps. At first the superintendent flatly refused, arguing that ". . . to allow them to roam at will would mean an enormous task to collect them when return to the islands is possible. . . . The best workmen would be the ones best able to compete with outside labor and least willing to return to their homes."[20] Hard to believe, isn't it?—as if Aleuts were cattle that needed to be herded and rounded up. In the meantime, higher-level managers, those accountable for the treatment of Aleuts, were becoming uneasy about this blatant confinement. After all, Aleuts had been arbitrarily evacuated because of a national emergency. By no standards could they be considered enemy aliens. And the country was engaged in an all-out war against totalitarianism. Under these conditions how could management justify incarcerating Aleuts in camps? The chief of Alaska Fisheries cautioned the superintendent to at least liberalize his rhetoric about Aleuts' freedom of movement:

> As stated . . . by Mr. Moores yesterday, we have no definite hold on Pribilof natives who are evacuated to Funter Bay. . . If they go away from Funter Bay to engage in other work, there is nothing we can do to stop them. . .
>
> To hold the natives together it is the opinion here that an outstanding feature is to develop local work programs at Funter Bay.[21]

Yes, the chief proposed a new tactic; it boiled down to replacing forced confinement with covert means for holding onto the Aleuts.

But this was a stopgap measure. Recognizing the inevitability of the men eventually leaving the camps for jobs in Juneau, the superintendent tried to establish a plan for controlling their living arrangement. He appealed to the Director of the United States Employment Service to place the Pribilof men in groups in isolated places where they could easily be recalled, and to give their wages to the agents.

> It is our desire to keep our native organization as nearly intact as possible . . .
>
> In placing the men, it is desired that units at any one place be as large as possible. We believe that we can keep better control over the natives if we had 15 men at one location rather than 3 men at each of 5 locations. . .
>
> As you know, the importation of liquor is not permitted on the Pribilof Islands. Consequently, the more isolated the locations where our men are placed, the easier it will be to control its use. . .
>
> In selecting working units . . . Mr. Lee C. McMillin, for the St. Paul Island natives, and Mr. Benson, for the St. George Island natives should be consulted. . .
>
> While final decision has not been made as to the method of payment of wages to Pribilof workmen, it is desired that payments be made in a lump sum through the Agents in charge of each island contingent. It is planned to pool the total amount earned in the same manner as we have previously done on the Islands.[22]

Apparently shocked at this request, the Employment Service manager righteously refused: "The United States Employment Service cannot treat the Aleuts any differently than any other group of persons . . . and it is our policy to try to place any registrant on some job that he is suited for."[23]

Now it was no longer a question of simple dependence on the Aleuts' skills in the seal industry. Their skills were no longer exclusive. The introduction of blubbering machines in the 1930s rendered that process mechanical and made the skinning process far simpler. The Fish and Wildlife Service recognized the less skilled nature of sealing work when it planned to use natives from other parts of Alaska for the 1943 sealing season, and after the war when management considered using imported labor for a seasonal operation on the islands. Rather it seems that managers were reluctant to yield any part of their Pribilof jurisdiction which included control over both seals and the Aleut people.

In any event official policy now declared Aleuts free to work in southeastern Alaska. (The Fish and Wildlife Service still prohibited them from leaving the state.)[24] Aleuts responded enthusiastically to this newly won freedom: "It went through the population like wildfire . . . the best workmen are now leaving at every opportunity," wrote the agent.[25] Policy is one thing but its implementation can take the form of support or subversion. This agent chose to subvert it: "Have had several meetings with the natives and have convinced some that they have a duty with their families and to stay here . . . ten men have left the St. Paul group . . . and we have double who want to go. Have practically refused any more until the Penguin arrives."[26]

With these pressures against leaving the camps and with staff keeping close tabs on those who did, the agents succeeded in organizing sealing gangs for the 1943 season. Remember, the plan was to repatriate St. George and take St. Paul sealers to the islands only for the sealing season. The Aleuts objected to the plan. Emboldened by the contacts they made in Juneau, some openly resisted: "The native gang here at Funter wish for me to notify you that they do not want to make the trip to the Islands until the war is over. Some here and one I know in Juneau say they will not return while the war lasts. Others say they will go only if ordered to do so."[27]

Only if ordered to do so—why that condition? Because assertiveness does not mean emancipation, and so long as the government controlled access to the islands, the Aleuts had to comply or face banishment. And, indeed, agents threatened to refuse permission to return if they did not comply with the 1943 sealing plan. The superintendent supported this practice:

> If any workman remains in Juneau or deserts his post during the summer . . . (he) will forfeit any share of the sealing division. Also I will seriously consider recommending that he be denied return to St. Paul for residence. As St. George is being rehabilitated, any workman who refuses to return this spring will not share in the sealing division and will not be allowed to return at any later date if I can help it. This will include his immediate family.[28]

In response to the superintendent's report of this action, the Chief of Alaska Fisheries alerted him to the problems such open discrimination was creating at higher levels of the organization.

> It is believed . . . it would be unwise to arrive at a definite, binding conclusion with respect to the problem outlined by you at this time . . . The question of right to occupancy of the islands by the natives has not been studied exhaustively. . .

The extent to which the Government is legally obligated to maintain the natives is not defined in any existing law, but rather is a matter for administrative determination by the Secretary and has been handled in the past by policy built up over the years. . .

Mr. Chaney (legal counsel) is inclined to discourage any thought of bringing this entire matter into the open for legal opinion at the present time. He believes that individual cases should be evaluated and treated separately instead of formulating a decisive, all-inclusive policy which may not hold up under legal assault later.[29]

The message seems clear enough. Violations of Aleuts' legal rights that no one questioned before were now under scrutiny.

Objections and questions came from an expanding number of sources. In the spring of 1943, agents in Juneau to collect the Aleuts, ran into immediate opposition from the Corps of Engineers:

McMillin in Juneau attempting to organize natives for coming expedition STOP U.S. Engineers by letter protest withdrawal of Pribilof workmen from defense construction STOP many of these men have worked into skilled capacities and engineers say quote crews cannot spare a man at the present unquote. Engineers also verbally advise a protest being filed through official channels STOP.[30]

Apparently unruffled by this development, the superintendent simply informed the engineers that the Aleuts had been only loaned to them,[31] as if negotiating some piece of property.

Never mind defense needs; never mind the wishes of the Aleuts; management's myopic eye was firmly fixed on sealing. According to the Aleuts, agents applied unceasing pressure to convince them to return. As the Aleuts feared further resistance might jeopardize their occupancy rights, they finally acceded, except at first for the St. George people who refused to be repatriated while the Japanese remained in the Aleutians. Management vacillated, first acceding to their demand, then denying it. Their spirit broken, the St. George people also surrendered. The plan was to return the St. George men at the beginning of the sealing season and their families at its end. However, when their wives had a change of heart and refused to return as planned, the St. George men insisted on leaving the islands, and the Bureau acquiesced.

Customarily, management ignored Aleuts' demands, but times were changing. The interest groups to which management had to respond were enlarging and diversifying. Visitors to the camps, appalled at what they saw and learned, increasingly threatened to expose the government's mistreatment of the Aleuts. The assistant supervisor jolted the Fish and Wildlife Service into equating with this reality.

Scarcely a day passes that some well meaning person does not descend upon us with recriminations for our heartless methods. Censorship has kept the press off our necks thus far but this line of defense is weakening rapidly. A few days ago we were advised by one of the physicians who had inspected the camps and aided in emergency work there, that he was preparing a report to the Surgeon General of the U.S. and also to Secretary Ickes and has no intention of "pulling any punches." He warned that it was only a question of time until some publication . . . would get hold of the story and play it up, much to the disadvantage of the Service and the Department of the Interior as a whole. He pointed out that the value of this year's fur seal take from the Pribilofs would nearly equal the original purchase price of Alaska, yet the people who made it possible are being herded into quarters unfit for pigs; denied adequate medical attention; lack of healthful diet and even facilities to keep warm and are virtually prisoners of the Government, though theoretically possessing the status of citizenship. He paints a dark picture but there is plenty of food for thought in his observations and one can easily visualize what a story a sensational publication could make out of the situation. . .

In considering the entire situation we believe it would be a great advantage to concentrate on and improve the Funter problems rather than to create new ones which would arise in attempting to rehabilitate St. George Island at this time.[32]

The letter sent a shockwave through the Fish and Wildlife Service. The Chief of Alaska Fisheries reversed policy and assigned top priority to improving conditions at the camps: "I am glad Mr. Hynes wrote this letter as I feel he has drawn the picture correctly, and as a result, further efforts should be made to sharply improve the housing and health conditions of our people at Funter . . . it is essential that you make this your number one task."[33]

It had taken one and a half years after the evacuation for public opinion to force management to improve the camps. But it was nearly too late. Five months later, in May 1944, with the Japanese routed from the Aleutians, the government repatriated St. Paul and St. George Aleuts. The large majority of Pribilovians returned immediately, most because of desire and some because of agents' threats that failure to return would result in loss of their homes or occupancy rights.

The repatriates found their villages in shambles—looted and damaged. The agent vividly described the scene.

Inspection of St. Paul village disclosed conditions which were difficult to believe. . . Most of the buildings, including the native houses, bore evidence of having been ransacked. . . Doors had been left open and windows were broken, and snow drifts were still piled high inside these openings. Snow which had drifted through and melted had flooded the basements of various buildings. . . Plumbing, water lines and tanks were broken in all parts of the village . . .

In many buildings losses could be attributed to actual looting or vandalism. Boxes and chests of personal belongings had been opened by prying off locks and other fastenings, and contents were scattered in the search for things of value. Furniture was marred or broken, overstuffed pieces were torn or rendered unserviceable, and household fixtures had been removed or damaged.

Warehouses and storerooms showed that there had been complete disregard for the value of stores. . . The carpenter shop did not contain any tools, and a survey of machine shop and garage showed that a large proportion of valuable tools had disappeared.[34]

As if this weren't shock enough, the Aleuts faced a reversion to pre-evacuation policies as management tried to restore colonial control over them. A first step was to eliminate the Aleuts' assertive and defiant attitudes learned during the evacuation. Even before the repatriation, managers called attention to this need.

Chief of Alaska Fisheries to Superintendent, November 3, 1943

The time has come to deal more severely with those of the Pribilof natives who need such action. In this connection, Dr. Gabrielson (Director, Fish and Wildlife Service) told me that when at Funter in September he learned of how a native refused to obey a reasonable, simple order of Mr. Merriott, or was otherwise impudent, whereupon Mr. Merriott laid hold of him and shook him up, with the result that thereafter he behaved himself. Dr. Gabrielson was very favorably impressed by the action thus taken by Mr. Merriott.[35]

The St. Paul agent believed these defiant attitudes could be easily corrected after the repatriation.

They have accumulated many ideas and thoughts, many of which are not the best for themselves or for the Bureau. Their attitudes, in many respects, have changed for the worse, but it is believed this will all be rectified in short order upon return to the Island.[36]

Back on the islands, agents took vigorous steps to subdue the Aleuts.

I am not surprised that Mr. Benson has had to jail several of the natives, or even threaten to send some off the islands, in order to quiet them down. . . I think the situation might have been worse following the sojourn of the natives in southeastern Alaska when some of them acquired habits and notions that will take time to eradicate.[37]

Yes, again protected by the isolation of the islands, management firmly believed that it could restore the former colonial relationship.

In reviewing the few excruciating years of the evacuation, we see that the type of outrage committed against the Japanese-Americans in World War II was enacted in microcosm against the Pribilof Aleuts, possible in both cases because of pervasive racist attitudes that condone inhumanity when perpetrated on people with colored skins. At Funter Bay, horrendous camp conditions persisted because management, fighting for its survival, kept a single-minded eye on restoring the seal harvests as quickly as possible—the conditions of the Aleuts be damned. However, given the pressure of a war against fascism and increasing surveillance by outsiders, management had to make some changes. It sought to change the form rather than the substance of its relationship with the Aleut people by replacing overt, blatant discrimination with more subtle, less visible tactics for control. After the repatriation, when managers felt protected by the isolation of the islands, they renewed efforts to restore the colonial-type relationship, unaware as they were that, indeed, a new era was dawning in the Pribilofs.

Endnotes

1. Edward H. Spicer, Asaek T. Hansen, Katherine Luomala, Martin K. Opler, Impounded People, Japanese Americans in the Relocation Centers (Tucson: University of Arizona Press, 1969); Roger Daniels, The Decision to Relocate the Japanese Americans (Philadelphia: J.B. Lippincott, 1975).
2. Charles Kikuchi, The Kikuchi Diary (Urbana, Illinois: University of Illinois Press, 1973), p. 157.
3. Henry L. Stimson, Secretary of War, to Harold L. Ickes, Secretary of the Interior, December 4, 1942. U.S. Fish and Wildlife Service Records, Federal Archives and Records Center, Seattle.
4. Funds for the support of the evacuees came from the Supplemental Appropriation Act of December 23, 1941 which provided for the relief and civilian defense of the populations of Alaska, Puerto Rico, and the Virgin Islands.
5. Agent and Caretaker to E.C. Johnston, Superintendent, August 5, 1942. Fish and Wildlife Service Records, Federal Archives.
6. L.C. McMillin, Agent, to E.C. Johnston, September 12, 1942, p. 3., Fish and Wildlife Service Records, Federal Archives.
7. Agent and Caretaker to E.C. Johnston, October 7, 1942. Fish and Wildlife Service Records, St. Paul.
8. N. Berneta Block, M.D., Director, Division of Maternal and Child Health and Crippled Children's Services, Alaska Division of Health, "Report of Trip to Funter Bay, October 2-6, 1943," Fish and Wildlife Service Records, Federal Archives.
9. Petition contained in communication from E.C. Johnston, to Ward T. Bower, Chief of Alaska Fisheries, October 10, 1942. Fish and Wildlife Service Records, Federal Archives.
10. U.S. Department of Interior, Fish and Wildlife Service, Alaska Fishery and Fur-Seal Industries in 1942, p. 41; . . . in 1943, p. 42.
11. H.O. Bauer, M.D., to J.P. Eberhardt, M.D:, Office of Indian Affairs, November 30, 1943. Fish and Wildlife Service Records, Federal Archives.
12. Computed from Table 28 in George Rogers, An Economic Analysis of the Pribilof Islands, 1870-1946. Prepared for Indian Claims Commission Docket Nos. 352 and 369 (Fairbanks: University of Alaska, Institute of Social, Economic and Government Research, 1976), p. 128.

13. Harold L. Ickes, Secretary of Interior, to Henry L. Stimson, Secretary of War, November 23, 1942. Fish and Wildlife Service Records, Federal Archives.
14. Henry M. Stimson to Harold L. Ickes, December 4, 1942. Fish and Wildlife Service Records, Federal Archives.
15. Henry M. Stimson to Harold L. Ickes, January 2, 1943. Fish and Wildlife Service Records, Federal Archives.
16. Clarence Olson, Fishery Management Supervisor, to E.C. Johnston, September 8, 1942. Fish and Wildlife Service Records, St. Paul.
17. Bess O'Neil, Principal Clerk, to Captain Collins, Fish and Wildlife Service, September 26, 1942, Fish and Wildlife Service Records, St. Paul.
18. E.C. Johnston to Commanding General, Alaska Defense, November 9, 1943; S.B. Buckner, Jr., Lieutenant General, U.S. Army, to E.C. Johnston, November 9, 1942; S.B. Buckner, Jr., Lieutenant General, U.S. Army, to E.C. Johnston, November 27, 1943, Fish and Wildlife Service Records, Federal Archives.
19. R.E. Barnes, Acting Director, United States Employment Service, Alaska, to E.C. Johnston, June 29, 1942. Fish and Wildlife Service Records, Federal Archives.
20. E.C. Johnston to Ward T. Bower, Chief, Division of Alaska Fisheries, July 15, 1942. Fish and Wildlife Service Records, Federal Archives.
21. Ward T. Bower to E.C. Johnston, July 31, 1942. Fish and Wildlife Service Records, St. Paul.
22. E.C. Johnston to R.E. Barnes, July 7, 1942, Fish and Wildlife Service Records, Federal Archives; see also L.C. McMillin, St. Paul agent, to R.E. Barnes, July 13, 1942, Fish and Wildlife Service Records, St. Paul.
23. Everett Smith, Local Manager, United States Employment Service, to L.C. McMillin, September 19, 1942. Fish and Wildlife Service Records, St. Paul.
24. E.C. Johnston to Mrs. Mildred Greenhagen (potential employer in Seattle), November 2, 1942. Fish and Wildlife Service Records, Federal Archives.
25. L.C. McMillin to E.C. Johnston, September 12, 1942. Fish and Wildlife Service Records, Federal Archives.
26. Ibid.
27. L.C. McMillin to E.C. Johnston, March 6, 1943, Fish and Wildlife Service Records, Federal Archives.
28. E.C. Johnston to L.C. McMillin, March 17, 1943. Fish and Wildlife Service Records, Federal Archives.
29. Ward T. Bower to E.C. Johnston, March 30, 1943. Fish and Wildlife Service Records, St. Paul.
30. John R. Stacy, Agent, to E.C. Johnston, March 20, 1943. Fish and Wildlive Service Records, St. Paul.
31. E.C. Johnston to James W. Huston, Resident Engineer, U.S. Engineer's Office, Juneau, April 2, 1943. Fish and Wildlife Service Records, Federal Archives.

32. Frank W. Hynes, Assistant Supervisor, to Ward T. Bower, October 28, 1943. Fish and Wildlife Service Records, Federal Archives.
33. Ward T. Bower to E.C. Johnston, November 3, 1943. Fish and Wildlife Service Records, Federal Archives.
34. Clarence Olson, Agent, to E.C. Johnston, June 8, 1944. Fish and Wildlife Service Records, Federal Archives.
35. Fish and Wildlife Service Records, Federal Archives.
36. "Agent's Annual Report," St. Paul Island, April 1, 1944, Fish and Wildlife Service Records, St. Paul.
37. Ward T. Bower to E.C. Johnston, December 19, 1944, Fish and Wildlife Service Records, Federal Archives.

Chapter 7

TURNING POINT, 1945-1960

The Aleuts' nightmarish memories of the evacuation persisted, but the experience itself laid the groundwork for significant changes in the Pribilof management system. The evacuation not only brought the Pribilof story to the attention of others; it brought the outside world to the attention of the Aleuts, giving them a comparative basis for assessing their circumstances. In the process, they found confirmation for their life-long suspicion that their rights and dignity were being grossly violated. This confirmation catalyzed the Aleuts' political energies; they became determined to change their conditions, to fight for equality and independence.

The political climate was favorable for reform in the Pribilofs. On the heels of the anti-fascist war, many groups in the nation and in the United Nations dedicated themselves to eliminating persisting oppression. The Indian Rights movement proliferated after the war, invigorated by the enhanced political consciousness of some Indian war veterans, the urbanization of Indians, and the development of pan-Indian organizations. National attitudes toward Alaska were also changing as the Alaska independence struggle gained strength and momentum. The defense build-up in Alaska during the war including transportation and communication developments, the emergence of a resident-based construction industry, and major population increases set the stage for the final drive to statehood. Alaska was becoming more urbanized, its institutions more differentiated, and its growing population more demanding of the rights, privileges, and economic opportunities enjoyed by residents in other states.[1]

In this changing political climate, the Aleuts and their supporters found many receptive ears. Among their supporters, Fredericka Martin was the most tireless advocate. A dedicated anti-fascist, Martin had served with the American brigade in Spain and saw the Pribilof struggle as a continuation of the fight against totalitarianism. In the first years after the war, Martin wrote articles describing the Pribilof management as feudalistic paternalism and carried the Pribilof story to one group after another—to the National Congress of American Indians, the President's Advisory Commission on Indian Rights, the Navajo Institute, the United Nations' Ad Hoc Committee on Slavery, the International Labor Organization, and many others.[2] The National Congress of American Indians took a leading role in organizing protest against inequities on the Pribilofs. In one of its first efforts in the Aleuts' behalf, the National Congress in 1947 won the interest of two prominent Washington, D.C. attorneys—James Curry and Felix Cohen. Cohen, formerly a solicitor for the Department of Interior, was considered the foremost authority on Indian law in the nation and had been the major architect of the 1934 Indian Reorganization Act.[3] A third attorney, an Indian from southeastern Alaska, William Paul, joined Curry and Cohen in representing the Pribilovians. Paul had spearheaded the founding of the first native political organization in Alaska in 1912, the Alaska Native Brotherhood and its companion Sisterhood. (This was the sole Alaska native political organization until the early 1960s.) Though organized in southeastern Alaska and interested primarily in Indians of that area, the Brotherhood joined the organizations demanding change in the Pribilofs.

The interaction between these actors—the Aleuts, their attorneys, Fredericka Martin, and Indian Rights organizations—had a snowball effect as each group drew encouragement and inspiration from the support of the others; in the process, they merged themselves into a relatively cohesive force for change, a force that posed a powerful challenge to the Pribilof management bureaucracy.

In the past, the Pribilof management agencies had been largely sheltered from demands and threats from interest groups, within or outside the Pribilofs; they were essentially a closed system. They had minimal interchange with their larger environment except for groups interested in fur seal products and profits and except as such interchanges were forced by the decline of the fur seal and the necessity of designing and adjusting new management regimes. None of this had much to do with the welfare of the Pribilof people except as such "welfare" responses were byproducts of the economic outputs of fur seal harvesting. The system remained closed because of the isolation of the Pribilofs and the absence of groups agitating for reform in the social aspects of the program. There is simply little or no record of any outside agencies or interests calling for such reform. For most of its history, then, the federal administration of the Pribilofs was a closed system within a bureaucratic structure that was largely insulated from its external environment. Even if the administrative system had been exposed earlier to scrutiny from outside, it may not have posed a significant challenge to the social and political aspects of the program because of the tenor of those times, times when fierce exploitation of labor in the interests of industrial development was commonly accepted practice and when national attitudes toward Alaska and especially toward its native inhabitants were colonialist in nature.

Now, with a favorable political climate, an emboldened Aleut community, and a core group of change agents outside the community, the closed, insulated Pribilof administration faced a serious challenge. Let us trace the process of change that ensued: the interplay between change agents and the administrative bureaucracy; the pushes and pulls; the setbacks and triumphs; and how the central actors in this drama, the Pribilof Aleuts, experienced these events.

During the evacuation, a St. Paul Aleut leader joined the Alaska Native Brotherhood, and after repatriation he managed to attend the organization's annual conventions in Juneau. Inspired by these contacts, the Aleut leader, along with his half brother and one or two others, set out to organize a local Brotherhood chapter in St. Paul. One of the organizers gave a colorful description of the first Brotherhood meeting.

> I started running around gathering up young fellows. I met about 46 men for meeting. So we put up meeting and Elary told them all about this ANB—about how it works, and well, we gonna start a little club here, and most of them got up and say we want to be ANB. So allright—$12 a year original donation. We put it up. And the other fellows didn't know nothing so we started talking over this here—about how they handling us here. We started like in ourselves talking.
>
> We put up the petition. The first petition we put up we sent to Juneau. And they have lawyers and secretary. That petition . . . was recopied and bettered and sent to us to have the President sign it, seal it up, send it. And just before St. Paul here know anything about this—from Washington they get wondering what's going on on the Pribilof Islands.[4]

What's going on in the Pribilofs?—indeed, that question was on officials' minds. The pressure for change was felt most keenly at the Washington level; top management was the prime target. And managers had to adapt to the rising crescendo of challenge. They responded in several ways—denial and resistance at first, then small concessions, and later, larger adjustments. Vacillation between resistance, concession, and adjustment characterized management responses to reform demands in the first decade after the war.

In 1947 the attorneys applied to the Commissioner of Indian Affairs for approval to represent the Pribilovians. The Indian Reorganization Act, for the first time, established the right of Indians to have legal council of their own choosing though it was conditional on Interior Department approval. The attorneys encountered repeated delays in their application. One resulted from top management questioning the Pribilovians' eligibility for benefits of the Act, presumably on the basis of the old 'wardship' concept.[5] After eligibility was established, Secretary of Interior Warne refused to recognize this particular group of attorneys, claiming that he had no proof they were lawyers of the Aleuts' choosing. What would constitute proof?—a formal legal contract designating retainer fees.[6] The attorneys' agreement with the Aleuts had been informal until then; they had never raised the question of fees, knowing full well that Aleuts had little money. Obviously, their interest in this case was not generated by the promise of wealth; it was to fight injustice, as Cohen indicated in a letter to the Aleuts: "I was first led to accept your invitation to serve as attorney . . . because of my feeling that your people have suffered great injustices, and my hope that I could help to remedy the worst of these injustices."[7]

To comply with Warne's demand, the attorneys sent a formal contract stipulating fees to the St. Paul people. The Aleuts were distressed; they knew not how to interpret this business of fees. Was this another instance where whites wanted to take advantage of them? Where would they get the money to pay the fees? Was it worth it? One of the leaders raised these questions with Martin who responded with convincing explanations, at least they convinced the Aleuts.

> To revert to the latest attempts to prevent the sealers from bettering their lives, one of the first is Mr. Warne's demand that your attorneys produce a formal, legal contract proving that the attorneys are the lawyers of your choice. This is an important thing to remember when discussing the fee with your associates: that the lawyers asked for no fee or contract when they began working in your behalf and only did so when Mr. Warne demanded it—knowing full well that it would take a long time because of the distance and poor mails for a regular contract to be completed. During this time perhaps Interior or Fish and Wildlife could either discourage the people or frighten them or persuade them to accept some other, less valuable plans . . . When Mr. Warne demanded a contract, the lawyers then had to follow the legal rules for such but you now have their letter ascertaining that they will leave it up to the leaders to decide whether to pay from time to time or some each month, etc. In other words, your lawyers will not push you for money and would not, despite the work they have already done, have asked for money at this time. This is a victory for the Fish and Wildlife Service, a small one if it only causes a delay but a very large one if the sealers let the matter of fees make them distrust the lawyers or stop fighting along the lines we have started.[8]

Reassured, the St. Paul Aleuts consummated their legal contract, although final approval from Interior took nearly two years from the time it was first initiated.

One of the main reasons Aleuts wanted legal counsel was to secure their right to local self-government. This was one of the St. Paul Aleuts' top priorities.

> We are considering our independence and self-governing. The community and Alaska Native Brotherhood council had a meeting and we talked about this matter. We were nine in all and everyone of us agreed that we should have our independence and self-governing community, that we should make our own constitution.[9]

A fearsome undertaking for the Aleuts, given their political inexperience and history of political intimidation. Where would it lead? What unexpected consequences might they encounter? One of the organizers confided these apprehensions to Martin.

> If and after we do get independent I am afraid some people or organization may take advantage of us. Don't think I'm afraid for myself, it's the people of the island I am thinking about. You know there are some people, government or private, that do take advantage of the natives.[10]

Martin succeeded in quelling these fears and the leaders moved on with plans to incorporate for self-government.

Managers were not happy with this development. The proposed constitution for tribal government included provisions that threatened administrative priorities and the old system for controlling Aleuts. The charter called for possessory rights to land and the power to hold, manage, and dispose of all community property; to borrow money from the revolving Indian credit fund; to enter into business, and, most importantly, to sue (and be sued). Managers resisted incorporation, though in a different form than in the past. Too many eyes were now watching, too many ears listening to use direct retaliations; instead they used indirect, covert means to discourage the Aleuts' interest. One of the attorneys gave a revealing account of the use of this tactic.

> We talked about incorporating the village under the Wheeler-Howard Act (Indian Reorganization Act). Mr. Johnston (General Manager) said that the people can do anything they want. . . Most of the rest of the conversation, however, concerned reasons why they should not or did not have to incorporate. First of all, he saw no way to run their own businesses since there is no transportation to or from the islands except by government boat and *government boats will not bring goods to a native-owned store*. Second, he said that since these people live on a reservation they could own no property. . . He said that these people have been dependent for generations—first (upon) the officials of the Russian government and now upon the officials of the federal government.[11]

An Aleut sealer gave a similar report of officials' covert resistance to tribal incorporation.

> We had a meeting by the community club with Mr. Olson (Assistant General Manager), Mr. Benson (Agent), and Father Baranoff. Subjects were about self-government answered by Mr. Benson and were as follows: The island is government property—that we did not have anything if we did have self-government under incorporation. We would not be able to pay for counsel because we wouldn't have enough tax payments; and Mr. Olson asked just what kind of self government (will) we be able to have, to install water line and street or what we had in mind and I told him we had in mind the Act of June 18, 1934. . . Then Mr. Olson asked why? I said so we could negotiate with the federal or territorial government. Olson didn't have anything to say to this.[12]

These tactics seemed to have an effect opposite from that intended, for Aleut leaders' determination became stronger as a result of such resistance.

In the past, the Pribilovians' demands had been limited to small concessions—to increases in supplies or the seal bonus. Now they were asking for some basic changes, not only in the area of self-government, but in economic and educational areas as well. In a petition by the local Brotherhood chapter in 1947 addressed to President Truman, Congress, and the Secretary of Interior, the Aleuts called not only for substantial increases in the seal bonus (from 90 cents on St. Paul and $1.20 on St. George to $1.50 on both islands) and additional supplies, but for a share of the profits from the seal industry, less government control, and transferral of schools from the supervision of the Fish and Wildlife Service to the Bureau of Indian Affairs.[13] They wanted the schools transferred because of the Bureau of Indian Affairs policy to advance Indian opportunities and educate Indians for posts in government.

The Aleuts and their supporters made one demand after another, but no significant action was forthcoming throughout the late 1940s. Thwarted by repeated stalls, petty excuses, silences, and inaction, the Aleuts considered more militant approaches. In early 1949, the sealers announced a strike, the first in many decades. And unlike those strikes in the past that were quietly enacted on the Islands and were readily suppressed by retaliation, this one made the national press.[14] The strike was averted by managers' promise of a new wage system which was in fact introduced.

This degree of assertiveness was certainly novel behavior for the Aleuts. Their political passivity of the past was due not only to intimidation by management but to their long tradition of compliance with the benevolent decisions of chiefs and elders. By their very natures, Aleuts tended to avoid rather than confront conflicts. Harmony within villages was a supreme value and Aleuts had developed sophisticated means for maintaining it—through the use of third-party intermediaries; norms that discouraged complaining, arguing, and confronting; and sanctions that involved ostracizing persons who violated these norms. Like Eskimos, Aleuts are noted for their finely-tuned indirect styles of communication. I remember with poignancy the time an Aleut woman guest responded to an argument between my husband and myself with these words: "If it weren't between husband and wife I would say something." Did she or didn't she say something? However one interprets her remark, it effectively stopped the exchange on the spot with no hard feelings toward her.

This cultural style prevailed among Pribilof Aleuts after World War II. An Aleut leader tenderly described the pattern.

> You asked me what I meant by sensitivity of the people. . . What I mean is . . . they are kind and forgiving no matter how they have been abused. You can abuse them now and next day be kind and do something very satisfying that they will forgive and forget and be friendly again which is a good thing if we don't let it get us down.[15]

Given the Aleuts' long history of conflict avoidance, reinforced by the Pribilof management agencies' authoritarian control, how do we explain this growing assertiveness? Cultural styles persist when they are reinforced by contemporary realities, and the social and political realities of the Aleuts' lives were changing. Though consistently thwarted by management, the Aleuts were also beginning to see chinks in its armor as the forces for change grew and became more clamorous. They were sensing their own potential for cracking that armor. And they believed the realization of that potential would require new leadership styles, more aggressive and militant, styles very different from those of the chiefs of the past whose primary job had been to preserve harmony and avoid rocking the boat.

Yet, with the Aleuts' history of compliance, one might ask how these new leaders acquired traits of assertiveness? In the first place, culture groups that emphasize conflict avoidance do not produce this orientation in every member; there are always deviations from the norm. Cultures produce a range of personalities so that when the need arises for a different type of leader there are usually some, albeit a minority, with the necessary traits. But there are additional reasons for the boldness of the two main leaders in St. Paul, the brothers. Both had spent considerable time living and working away from the islands, during which they gained a new perspective, a new basis for evaluating life at home. And with this perspective came a determination to protect their offspring from living under the same conditions they had known. This determination was buttressed by a reduced fear of management, especially in one of the brothers who had been exiled from the islands; experiencing the worst and surviving undoubtedly emboldened him.

Stalwart and determined they were, nonetheless, an enormous burden fell on the brothers, as one of them movingly described:

> This is why I hesitate sometimes. It is too much of a responsibility for one man. Now that Elary is at the Alaska Native Brotherhood convention, I have the local ANB and the community club to look after and do all the paperwork for both. All I do now is read and review different books and magazines and newspapers for reference . . . they are the only confident advice I have up here. . . Sometimes I feel like you once told me, 'all alone.' Sometimes I feel like giving up everything if it wasn't for my son and wife. As long as I have those two I love so much I'll keep on fighting until we succeed.[16]

The courage and perserverance of these leaders galvanized their supporters to an ever-deepening commitment to their cause. Martin gave eloquent testimony to this effect.

> But what comes out of all those struggles is the phenomenal event that a group of men, thrown back into isolation, harrassed in countless petty ways continually and threatened with worse, had the courage to stand firm and feed ammunition to people many of whom they never saw but to whom they gave their trust. . . It was a bond of friendship, each side gaining strength from the others. When I felt discouraged at the slowness of being held up by petty matters I would think of what St. Paul suffered and how brave Gabe and Elary were, how much harder it was for them—how easy it was for me even when I was stopped a few times . . . It was the bond between Aleut and white friends that the government couldn't break.[17]

Indeed, the Aleuts' supporters conducted an unflagging struggle for reform on the Pribilofs. Managers responded with efforts to frighten and discredit them. Martin says that she was put under surveillance and her telephone was tapped.[18] Aleuts recount instances when agents told them Martin was a communist agitator and should be avoided. In an effort to deny the legitimacy of the reform movement, Clarence Olson the general manager (this position replaced that of superintendent) charged Martin in official communications with suspect motives, using propaganda, arousing the natives to discontent, and the ultimate sin of passing information to them that she had gleaned from conversations with Washington officials.[19] Olson also tried to discredit the Aleuts' demands with similar McCarthy-type invective.

> There we have the formula for apparent discontent similar to what is happening throughout the nation. The pattern is about the same. Our St. Paul workmen are controlled by a small local group under the domination of outsiders who are well schooled in stirring unrest. A continuous flow of advice is pouring in through the mail warning these people that the FWS cannot be trusted. It would be comparatively simple to deal with these people if it were not for the unfair and dishonest influences exerted upon them by outsiders.[20]

Again, these tactics failed to accomplish their intent. Each instance of resistance, each setback by management seemed to increase the reformers' motivation; they were now struggling on many fronts, raising one area of inequity after another. Of all their demands, the most clamorous and insistent was for economic reform. The Aleuts' economic status was still highly ambiguous. The new Fur Seal Act of 1944, similar to its 1910 predecessor, charged the Secretary of Interior with responsibility for paying the Aleuts fair compensation for labor performed as well as for furnishing food, shelter, clothing, fuel, and other necessities of life. The Fish and Wildlife Service had never clarified whether the supplies were wage supplements or gratuities, and if the latter, whether that meant the sealing and foxing bonuses—the Aleuts' only cash income—was compensation for year-round work. Even in response to Secretary Warne's request for clarification of this issue, Director Day of the Fish and Wildlife Service gave contradictory interpretations. In the first part of a memo to Warne, he wrote:

> I do not feel that the free issues of supplies to the resident natives of the Pribilof Islands should be viewed as charitable handouts as Miss Martin has suggested. In effect, such supplies supplement the cash compensation received by these people. . .

Later in the same memo, he contradicted this interpretation:

> Under the provision of this legislation, the free issues of supplies to the natives . . . cannot be considered specifically as payment for services rendered. They are available alike to workmen and unemployed widows. The Bureau of Internal Revenue has ruled that the value of such issues . . . is not subject to federal income tax.[21]

In the same year as the above memorandum was written, the administrative officer of the Fish and Wildlife Service baldly stated that "the sealing and foxing division represents cash compensation not only for the taking of skins but for services of a related nature throughout the year."[22]

If the bonuses were compensation for year-round labor, then by any standards management was in violation of the fair-compensation clause. In 1946, for example, the sealing and foxing divisions produced an average annual income per Pribilof worker of $502, 80 percent below the average annual income of other industrial workers. Even if the value of the supplies, estimated at $68,000 in 1946, had been included, Aleuts' average annual income would have been nearly 60 percent less than that for other industrial workers.[23] And such comparisons do not take into account the recently established fringe benefits and social programs available to other workers but not to the Pribilovians.

In an effort to clear up the confusion about their wage status, Aleuts repeatedly asked for a wage-board hearing, but Warne refused.[24]

In addition to wage-board hearings, the Aleuts' program for economic reform included substantial wage increases, a straight cash wage to replace supplies, elimination of agents' disciplinary authority, and social security benefits.[25] Apparently, by the end of the 1940s, the Aleuts thought better of pressing their earlier demand for a share of the profits from the seal industry, and focused instead on more realizable objectives.

This reform program found support among an ever-expanding group; it now included public as well as private officials. The Alaska Commissioner of Labor, alerted to the situation on the Pribilofs by the Aleuts' attorneys, described labor-management relations there as peonage.

> The terms and conditions of employment, the method of paying wages, provisions for workmen's compensation, disability insurance, old-age assistance and pensions are at such extreme opposites to the generally accepted practices that we must come to the conclusion that the economic status of these workers can only be classed as *peonage*. These conditions contradict the policies of the United States government as demonstrated in our participation in the International Labor Organization and the several activities of the United Nations organizations.[26]

This letter, written to the St. Paul Community Club, came to the attention of the United States Commissioner of Labor, Maurice Tobin. His interest sparked, Tobin asked the Secretary of Interior for an explanation of these charges.[27] International organizations were also having an impact. Investigations by the International Labor Organization and the Committee of Inquiry into Forced Labor culminated later in a United Nations' charge of *slavery* on the Pribilofs.[28]

Secretary Warne responded to these pressures with a proposal for a new wage plan which the Aleuts rejected out of hand. For one reason, while the new plan included a straight cash wage, Warne set the rate of pay so low that it would have entailed an actual reduction in Aleuts' total income. For another reason, the Secretary still retained dominant power to determine wages, though the form was changed. Warne proposed a four-member wage board composed of two Aleuts and two Fish and Wildlife representatives. The hitch was that deadlocks in wage negotiations were to be resolved by the appointment of a third Fish and Wildlife employee, in effect perpetuating the Secretary's power to determine wage rates.[29]

The Aleuts' attorneys were irate about the plan, asserting that it was indefensible by any standards. Citing 1948 Department of Labor estimates of $3,111 a year for an average family at a level of adequate living, they pointed out that Warne's proposed wage rate would mean less than half that amount for the most skilled Pribilof workers and a small fraction of that amount for the least skilled.[30]

Warne defended these proposed low wage rates on the basis of budgetary constraints imposed by Congress. "What can be done," he told Martin, "will depend entirely upon the action taken by Congress."[31] It was true that program funds were determined by annual Congressional appropriation. It was also true that though the times had changed, Congress in the late 1940s applied the same criteria to the Pribilof program as it had in the past—seals and profits, not the welfare of the people. The Congressional Appropriations Hearings for 1949 illustrated the operation of these standards. The chairman asked repeated questions about the net surplus from the seal industry, the size and health of the seal herd, and the expenditures for the program, but not a single question about the economic status or well-being of the Pribilovians. Yet, surplus funds were available for the program. Every year since 1943 the seal industry brought more revenues into the Treasury than the costs of the Pribilof program. The difference between revenues and program costs was striking in 1947; the net surplus from the industry was more than 2.5 million dollars while the appropriation for the program was only $850,000.[32]

Yes, Congress did impose budgetary constraints, but that is only part of the picture. Decisions made in appropriations hearings also reflect the nature and strength of the applicant's appeal. In the 1949 hearings, Director Day of the Fish and Wildlife Service made no mention of wage increases or any other economic demands. He was mute about the movement for economic reform on the Pribilofs. Day asked only for funds to cover physical improvements on the islands, scientific investigations, and additional supplies for Aleuts. Even in discussions of how to use the surplus funds from the seal industry, those over and above the costs of the program, Day made no reference to Aleuts' welfare. Rather, he proposed using these surplus funds to bolster other wildlife refuges.[33]

Thus, while Warne justified the low pay rates proposed for Aleuts in terms of Congressional constraints, he failed to instruct his representative, Day, to alert Congress to the need for wage increases and other economic change. Interior, like Congress, clung to the same market-place criteria for the Pribilof program. It was this orientation that posed the most serious obstacle to meaningful economic change.

Meanwhile, with pressures for Pribilof reform mounting, Interior took a more offensive stance. In an effort to clear its name, the Secretary of Interior in 1949 appointed a special survey group to investigate charges of peonage and slavery. Two of the four members of the group were Department of Interior officials—Director of the Fish and Wildlife Service and Commissioner of Indian Affairs. The other two were the head of the Home Mission Council and the director of a University of Alaska department.[34] The group whitewashed the Fish and Wildlife Service and concluded that Pribilovians were better off economically than most other native groups in the territory.

> The group can find absolutely no basis for the charge that the native Aleuts of the Pribilof Islands are held in "slavery," "bondage," or "peonage". . .
>
> We are forced to the conclusion that much of the criticism of the administration of the Pribilof Islands by the Fish and Wildlife Service is unjust, unwarranted, and without foundation in fact. Some of it may have been valid in the past, but it is not so at present. The bald fact remains that there are not now and never have been any destitute families, any neglected welfare cases, any crime or liquor problem (with the exception of home brew). . . .
>
> On the mainland, the Aleutian Chain, Nunivak Island, Nome and Kotzebue, poverty, disease and want are evident in striking contrast to the conditions on St. Paul and St. George islands.[35]

The Aleuts and their supporters were keenly distressed by the report, believing the investigators overlooked and misrepresented some of the major inequities on the islands. Cohen wrote an impassioned critique of the report to Martin.

> The indignant denial of peonage does not show any particular awareness of the nature of peonage. So far as appears from the report, a government official (the Secretary of the Interior) claims the following rights and powers over each inhabitant: (a) ownership of all land and buildings on the island including the homes of natives; (b) on the basis of such ownership, the right to determine what churches may be built in the native community and who may trade, visit, or meet with the natives; (c) the right to determine what attorneys, if any, the native communities may employ; (d) the right to determine what kind of local government the natives may establish; (e) the right to decide what wages each native shall receive so long as he remains on the island; (f) the right to confiscate his home if he leaves the island. I think that if any white community were thus subject to the decisions of an individual, whether a private person or a public official, who was not himself a member of the group thus controlled, "peonage" would be among the mildest of terms that would be used to describe the facts above listed.[36]

Martin challenged the assumption underlying the economic assessment, asserting that it made no sense to judge the Aleuts' economic well-being by comparing them with native communities that had no steady work or source of income. She believed that Interior sent the group to impoverished native communities to so shock them that anything they saw on the Pribilofs would be acceptable by comparison.[37]

Yes, the Aleuts and their friends were perturbed by the report, but in their distress they may have overlooked positive results stemming from the reports' recommendations for reform, recommendations that denied in part the exoneration of the Fish and Wildlife Service. In its recommendations, the group acknowledged the existence of serious problems and inequities by calling for approval of a corporate charter for St. Paul, higher education for Aleuts, improved race relations, employment of Aleuts in staff positions held by whites, and improved community facilities and services.[38] Furthermore, because two members of the group were Department of Interior officials and one was the Director of the Fish and Wildlife Service, the recommendations, endorsed by all members, had the stamp of a policy declaration. Surely, the Director of the Fish and Wildlife Service was no longer in a position to resist or oppose changes he himself had called for.

And, indeed, he and other Interior Department officials supported these recommendations. In 1950 the corporate charter was approved, albeit with the elimination of possessory rights to land and property; permanent consulting arrangements with the Alaska Departments of Education and Health were established; additional teachers were hired to improve the caliber of education on the islands; plans for a two-year high school for St. Paul were underway; supplies were increased; and most important of all, a new wage plan was put into effect. Top management's strategy was shifting. Resistance and small concessions were giving way to meeting some of the Aleuts' demands, although management still tried to shape these changes to fit the old structure of priorities and control. Yet, as we shall see in the next chapter, these reforms held the seeds for more far-reaching structural change.

One of the first significant acts of the newly established tribal council of St. Paul was a land claims suit against the United States, initiated in 1951. Since first engaging their attorneys, and on the advice of the attorneys, Aleuts had asked for ownership of their land, but the Secretary of Interior made sure that the tribal charter did not open the door for land negotiations: "Since neither Aleut residents nor any other person may acquire land on the Pribilof reservation, references in the charter and Constitution to such transactions have been modified accordingly."[39] With that recourse closed, the Aleuts then filed a legal suit against the United States claiming (1) aboriginal title to lands and adjacent waters, (2) fee title to lands and adjacent waters under Russian law, (3) fishing and hunting rights, and (4) lack of fair and honorable dealings. Three years later the Indian Claims Commission extinguished the claim on grounds that it was lawful for the United States to set aside the Pribilof Islands as a special reservation and lease grounds for commercial purposes.[40] This decision concerned land claims only; it did not address the charge of violation of fair and honorable dealings. The attorneys reopened the case on the basis of the latter charge. In appeals during the next *twenty-four years* the attorneys traversed a web of legal contortions which finally, in 1978, brought forth a favorable ruling, granting the Aleuts 11.2 million dollars in damages for violation of fair and honorable dealings by government.[41] (To avoid an appeal by the government in 1979, the Aleuts settled for $8.5 million).

The new wage plan, initiated in January 1950, was shaped by negotiations that had been in progress since the end of the war, and that received the strongest impetus by a comprehensive wage plan submitted by Martin in 1949 to the Director of the Fish and Wildlife Service and the Secretaries of Labor and Interior. The Martin plan, embodying the major reforms the Aleuts wanted, caused a hubub of deliberations in Washington, within and between agencies,[42] as management came to grips with the reality of the changing structure of interest groups to which it had to adapt. Meaningful economic reform could no longer be forestalled. Martin's proposal was the basis for the 1950 wage plan and subsequent revisions to it.

The new pay plan was a mixture of old and new elements and contained many contradictions and provisions difficult to implement. In relation to the Aleuts' former economic situation, the new plan was a significant breakthrough. In comparison to the economic status of other American workers and federal employees, the Aleuts still lagged very far behind. In essence, the new plan reflected a combination of management strategies—of resistence to basic structural change and of appeasement by partial concessions.

The stated philosophy underlying the plan was to encourage the Pribilovians to exercise their full rights and responsibilities as American citizens, while recognizing the complications this caused, given the Aleuts' status as virtual wards of government. The plan called for a small annual wage with a gradual transition to a full one. Its main features were these: The seal bonus continued, but at a reduced rate. In addition, the Aleuts received a small wage subject to annual wage rate reviews (based on wage rates on the Alaska Peninsula and the consumer price index for a moderate income family in Seattle). The payment of this wage as well as the bonus, however, was contingent on the availability of funds from the sale of seal skins. The supply issues were to be gradually replaced by cash, but at the outset, supplies, except fuel, continued. Indigents were given in kind support as in the past. The Aleuts were recognized as civil servants with federal benefits including retirement. And finally, agents were prohibited from using work demotions and lengthy work suspensions as punishment.[43]

While in the past, the Aleuts' income had often remained stationary or actually decreased, the new plan contained a mechanism that tied their wage levels to those in the larger economy. As a result, the Aleuts' income rose every year after inauguration of the new plan. In St. Paul, for example, estimated average annual income (from all sources) per Aleut worker rose from $1,447 in 1951 to $2,236 in 1955 to $2,979 in 1960. Still it was 32 percent lower than that of the average worker (all industries) in 1960, but the gap was narrowing.[44]

With increasing incomes and civil service status, what was wrong with the plan? What were its inequities? For one thing, the seal bonus, though considered part of Aleuts' wages, was not subject to annual wage rate review. Furthermore, the sealing rate was substantially reduced, from $1.20 and 90 cents on St. George and St. Paul, respectively, to 35 cents in each community. The reduction in seal rates was an apparent effort to offset the costs of the small annual wage. For instance, the 1950 total wage payment in St. Paul was $81,619 while the savings from the decrease in the sealing rate amounted to $52,092, 63 percent of the new wage payment.[45]

A major inequity inhered in making wage payments (bonus and wage) contingent on the availability of funds from the sale of seal skins. No other federal workers were subject to such a condition. Secretary of Labor Tobin was baffled by this contingency.

> I am advised by the Department of Interior that with the adoption of this plan . . . these workers became full-time employees of the United States. It appears rather anomalous, therefore, unless this is required by some interpretation of the Fur Seal Act . . . that the payment of accrued wages should be made dependent upon the availability of funds derived solely from this source.[46]

This letter was written to Martin, but Tobin also asked the Fish and Wildlife Service director for clarification. The director invoked a commonly used rationalization: "Since the government first assumed direct control over sealing and foxing operations on the Pribilofs in 1910, cash compensation to the resident native workmen have been made from this source,"[47] as if the existence of inequity in the past justified its continuance in the present.

Though the Aleuts were accorded civil service status, it was fundamentally unequal to that of other federal workers. It was an unclassified status; that is, Aleuts were not graded in the categories of other federal workers but into classes similar to those used in the past: skilled, semi-skilled, and unskilled. Furthermore, they were classified not by the civil service board, but by agents. Also, unlike other federal employees who consistently received overtime pay, Aleuts received none during sealing season, the time of year when they worked the longest hours. Most important, Aleuts were not eligible for federal retirement benefits for years worked before 1950. Management had made no retirement contributions for those years, but that could have been remedied by a lump-sum payment to the Civil Service Commission, an action that was later taken. The absence of retirement benefits for those years produced serious hardship for older workers, some of whom had been employed in the seal industry for half a century.

Other inequities arose in implementing the plan. Work classifications were to be based strictly on skill and experience, but in actual practice they were based on the needs of management. "There is a limit to the number of skilled carpenters, plumbers, electricians, etc. that can be utilized in our operation . . . and the total number of qualified workmen employed in this category should, in each case, be restricted accordingly"—these were the instructions top management gave to the general manager.[48] As a result of this policy, some skilled workers were classified as unskilled and paid at that rate. Though this system of classification violated pay-plan regulations, a top manager saw nothing wrong with it, justifying it on the basis that it wasn't unique.

> Mr. Anderson mentions dissatisfaction among the workmen arising from the fact that an unskilled workman may . . . be performing the same duties as a skilled workman who receives a substantially higher wage. The existing pay plan for resident Aleut workmen is not unique in this respect . . . I am sure that many parallel situations could be cited for Federal employees in widely separated wage categories.[49]

Discipline of Aleut workers posed one of the thorniest implementation problems. Agents chafed at the loss of former disciplinary authority and asked for it to be restored. Olson concurred even though he recognized it violated pay-plan regulations.

> Pay-plan regulations cannot be followed for fear of allowing drinking and failure to report for work to get entirely out of hand. . . The control and handling of these Aleuts is the number one headache of management and the only reason there has been some measure of success is because management has taken upon itself the responsibility of direct and immediate action.[50]

Olson recommended expanding work suspensions beyond the limits set by the new plan.

One might ask: Why the problem? Why couldn't agents treat Aleuts the same as other federal employees and simply terminate them for incompetence or irresponsibility? Why the attention to special disciplinary measures? Because management was under pressure to keep Aleuts employed. The 1944 Fur Seal Act required Interior to provide for Aleuts' welfare which meant supporting the unemployed. Consequently, management had a vested interest in keeping Aleuts on the job, an objective which they believed required the use of oppressive authority. So we see that even in this regime of reform, when a progressive change, in this case eliminating the use of oppressive authority, conflicted with management's economic objectives, the latter still took precedence.

Despite the persistence of many features of the old priorities and control system, the new pay plan made a significant change in Aleuts' economic welfare. In addition to wage increases and partial civil service status, supplies were being replaced by wages. In 1951 clothing supplies and in 1954 food supplies were eliminated. This is not to say that the old system of gratuities ended. Aleuts still received in kind payments in the form of free housing and transportation, gasoline for outboard engines, and loans of government vehicles, but it was on its way out. Beyond these changes, the new plan introduced concepts that gained a life of their own. By the very establishment of the plan and statement of its philosophy, management committed itself to a regime of reform and to the concept of equal rights for Aleuts, concepts that were a springboard for more basic changes in the future.

The initiation of these economic changes were accompanied by reforms in other areas. Though reluctant at first, management liberalized restrictions on the right to occupancy of the islands for both Pribilof emigrants and other Aleuts who wanted to make their home on the islands. Permission for occupancy, however, was still required and was still denied in many instances.[51] On the education front, management began to encourage high school attendance outside the islands and introduced a ninth grade in St. Paul. The emphasis on higher education may have reflected management's recognition of the imminence of Alaska's statehood and the probable transfer of Pribilof services to state and local management.

These reforms further catalyzed the Aleuts' energies and initiative. They were now starting small businesses—an ice cream parlor, two coffee shops, and a movie theater. With education, business, local self-government and civil service status, the Aleuts' circumstances were certainly changing.

In sum, the Aleuts' awakening political consciousness, the changing political climate after the war, the change in national attitudes toward Alaska and its native inhabitants, and the proliferation of Indian Rights groups—these developments were the springboard for significant changes in the Pribilof management system. Management, trying to maintain its stability, resisted these developments by denying legitimacy to the reform movement, stalling, and using scare tactics. Finally it tried appeasing the Aleuts, at first with small concessions, later more meaningful ones, all within the context of retaining as much of the old system of priorities and control as possible. In so adapting, however, it enunciated principles that kept the wheels of future change ineluctably in motion.

Endnotes

1. For elaboration of the Alaska struggle for statehood, see Ernest Gruening, The State of Alaska (New York: Random House, 1954).
2. See, for example, Fredericka Martin, "Pribilof Sealers—Serfs of the North," Newsletter of the Institute of Ethnic Affairs, Inc. 3 (May-June 1948): pp. 1-4; Fredericka Martin, "Three Years of Pribilof Progress," The American Indians (Spring 1950): pp. 17-26; R.A. Bartlett, Alaska Congressional Delegate, to Fredericka Martin, March 2, 1948; Francis Lopinsky (member of Washington, D.C. legal firm) to Fredericka Martin, November 13, 1952; Maurice J. Tobin, U.S. Secretary of Labor, to Fredericka Martin, March 22, 1949; Fredericka Martin to James Curry and Felix Cohen, November 13, 1949; Fredericka Martin to Editor, Jensen's Weekly, November 22, 1949; Fredericka Martin to Oliver La Farge, December 16, 1949; Fredericka Martin to Ruth Bronson, National Congress of American Indians, November 11, 1947. Fredericka Martin Records.
3. New York Times, October 20, 1953, p. 29; Nation, December 19, 1953, p. 538.
4. Cited in Barbara B. Torrey, Slaves of the Harvest: The Story of the Pribilof Aleuts (St. Paul Island: Tanadgusix Corporation, 1978), p. 136.
5. Francis Lopinsky, attorney in James Curry's firm, to Commissioner of Indian Affairs, February 3, 1949. Fredericka Martin Records.
6. Fredericka Martin to President, St. Paul Community Club, August 6, 1948. Fredericka Martin Records.
7. Felix S. Cohen to President, St. Paul Community Club, May 1, 1951. Fredericka Martin Records.
8. Fredericka Martin to President, St. Paul Community Club, August 6, 1948. Fredericka Martin Records.
9. Excerpts from a letter from a St. Paul sealer, June 22, 1947. Fredericka Martin Records.
10. Ibid.
11. Memorandum to file, January 27, 1948. Sent to Fredericka Martin, signed F.L. (Undoubtedly F.L. is Frances Lopinsky who was in frequent correspondence with Martin at that time.), Fredericka Martin Records.
12. St. Paul Aleut to Fredericka Martin, November 9, 1947. Fredericka Martin Records.
13. Resolution by Camp No. 28, St. Paul Island, Alaska. Alaska Native Brotherhood, August 13, 1947. U.S. Fish and Wildlife Service, Bureau of Commercial Fisheries Records, Federal Archives and Records Center, Seattle.
14. Women's Wear Daily, March 14, 1949, p. 34; March 18, 1949, p. 38.
15. St. Paul Aleut to Fredericka Martin, November 9, 1947. Fredericka Martin Records.
16. Ibid.

17. Fredericka Martin to Dorothy Jones, January 12, 1979.
18. Ibid.
19. Assistant General Manager to General Manager, September 15, 1947. Bureau of Commercial Fisheries Records, Federal Archives.
20. General Manager to Chief, Branch of Alaska Fisheries, May 23, 1950. Bureau of Commercial Fisheries Records, Federal Archives.
21. Director, Fish and Wildlife Service, to Assistant Secretary of Interior, undated. Martin indicated it was written in 1949 or 1950. Fredericka Martin Records.
22. Chief Administrative Officer, Fish and Wildlife Service, to St. George agent, August 8, 1948. Bureau of Commercial Fisheries Records, Federal Archives.
23.

Date	Aleuts	U.S. Production Workers (male nonfarm)
1943	1,294	2,553
1944	835	2,733
1945	1,112	2,674
1946	1,066	2,536
1947	1,144	2,889
1948	1,216	3,049

Sources: Computed from George Rogers, An Economic Analysis of the Pribilof Islands, 1870-1946. Prepared for the Indian Claims Commission, Docket Nos. 352 and 369 (Fairbanks: University of Alaska, Institute of Social, Economic and Government Research, 1976), p. 159; U.S. Department of Interior, Fish and Wildlife Service, Alaska Fishery and Fur-Seal Industries, 1947, p. 60; 1948, p. 50; U.S. Department of Commerce, Bureau of the Census, Historical Statistics of the United States, Colonial Times to 1957, 1960, Series D-659.

24. Martin, "Three Years of Pribilof Progress " 5 (Spring 1950): p. 21.
25. Felix S. Cohen and James E. Curry to President, St. Paul Community Club, November 1, 1948; James Curry to President, St. Paul Alaska Native Brotherhood, September 21, 1949. Fredericka Martin Records.
26. Cited in "News Notes," Newsletter of the Institute of Ethnic Affairs, Inc. 4 (March-April 1949): p. 7.
27. Ibid.
28. New York Times, March 3, 1950, pp. 1 and 16.
29. Felix S. Cohen and James E. Curry to President, St. Paul Community Club, November 1, 1948. Fredericka Martin Records.
30. Ibid.
31. Assistant Secretary of Interior to Fredericka Martin, February 27, 1948. Fredericka Martin Records.

32. Net Surplus from Seal Industry and Annual Appropriations for Pribilof Program:

Date	Annual Appropriations	Net Revenues	Surplus (Revenues over Appropriations)
1943	464,500	523,257	58,757
1944	536,000	701,800	165,800
1945	624,700	673,766	49,066
1946	819,307	1,372,425	553,118
1947	850,000	2,530,773	1,683,773
1948	1,228,000	1,353,000	125,000

Sources: Alaska Fishery and Fur-Seal Industries, 1947, p. 63; 1948, p. 55. Hearings Before the Subcommittee of the Committee on Appropriations, House of Representatives, Part I, 80th Cong., 2nd sess. on the Interior Department Appropriations Bill for 1949, (Washington, D.C.: U.S. Government Printing Office, 1948), p. 871.

33. Hearings Before the Subcommittee of the Committee on Appropriations, Part I., pp. 872-875.

34. Committee members were Dr. Mark Dawber, Home Mission Council; Dr. Loren Oldroyd, University of Alaska; Albert E. Day. Fish and Wildlife Service; and Dr. John R. Nichols, Commissioner, Bureau of Indian Affairs.

35. "Pribilof Islands Survey Reports. Observations and Recommendations." October 28, 1949, pp. 5, 7. Mimeo. Bureau of Commercial Fisheries Records. Federal Archives.

36. Felix S. Cohen to Fredericka Martin, November 2, 1949. Fredericka Martin Records.

37. Fredericka Martin to President, St. Paul Community Club, January 16, 1950. Fredericka Martin Records.

38. "Pribilof Islands Survey Report," pp. 9-11.

39. Secretary of Interior to President, St. Paul Community Club, September 14, 1949. Fredericka Martin Records.

40. Aleut Community of St. Paul v. the United States, Docket No. 350 (1954).

41. The Aleut Community of St. Paul Island v. the United States, Docket Nos. 352 and 369 (1978).

42. Director, Fish and Wildlife Service to Assistant Secretary of Interior, May 22, 1950; U.S. Secretary of Labor to Fredericka Martin, April 26, 1950; Director, Fish and Wildlife Service to General Manager, June 8, 1950; Assistant Secretary of Interior to Assistant to Undersecretary of Labor, February 24, 1950. Fredericka Martin Records.

43. U.S. Fish and Wildlife Service, "Annual Cash Compensation Plan for Res-

ident Aleut Workmen of the Pribilof Islands," 1950, mimeo; Secretary of Interior to Director, Fish and Wildlife Service, May 24, 1951. Bureau of Commercial Fisheries Records, Federal Archives.

44. The average annual income for U.S. workers (all industries) in 1960 was $4,822. U.S. Bureau of the Census. Statistical Abstract of the United States, 85th Annual Edition, 1964, p. 343.

45. Computed by subtracting the total St. Paul sealing bonus paid in 1950 from the amount that would have been paid had the decrease in rate not occurred. Alaska Fishery and Fur-Seal Industries, 1950, p. 58.

46. U.S. Secretary of Labor to Federicka Martin, April 26, 1950. Fredericka Martin Records.

47. Director, Fish and Wildlife Service, to Assistant Secretary of Interior, May 22, 1950. Subject: Letter from Labor Department to Fredericka Martin. Fredericka Martin Records.

48. Chief, Division of Administration, Fish and Wildlife Service, to General Manager, August 8, 1950. Bureau of Commercial Fisheries Records, Federal Archives.

49. Chief, Branch of Alaska Fisheries, to General Manager, October 28, 1953. Bureau of Commercial Fisheries Records, Federal Archives.

50. General Manager to Chief, Branch of Alaska Fisheries, September 20, 1953. Bureau of Commercial Fisheries Records, Federal Archives.

51. General Manager to St. Paul Manager, October 28, 1955; General Manager to Attorney McLean, January 25, 1955. Bureau of Commercial Fisheries Records, Federal Archives.

CHAPTER 8

THE ABANDONMENT POLICY, 1961-1970

The 1960s saw a sweeping reversal in Pribilof policy—to abandon the islands and convert to a seasonal operation. This phase-out policy embodied the long-term goal of resettling the Pribilof Aleuts, except for a small number needed to run the seasonal operation, and the short-term goals of consolidating both villages at St. Paul and emancipating and training Aleuts for their new roles. What motivated management to institute such a dramatic policy switch? The economic imperatives of the past still shaped policy, but the economic conditions under which the program operated threatened portentous change. The Aleuts now represented a potential economic liability, and the seal industry no longer promised a significant source of surplus revenues.

Alaska statehood, achieved in 1958, was one of the developments related to these altered conditions. In statehood negotiation with the federal government, Alaska surrendered its future sovereignty over the Pribilof seals. In exchange, the federal government agreed to pay Alaska 70 percent of the net proceeds from the seal industry. Since the net proceeds before statehood were not impressive, averaging between one and two million dollars in the three preceding years,[1] the payment to Alaska threatened to reduce the net to an inconsequential amount. Furthermore, the government could no longer anticipate increasing revenues from significantly larger harvests. In the 1950s marine mammalogists warned that the seal herd exceeded the level for maximum productivity.[2] Management responded with a population reduction program. The aim was to stabilize the population at a point of maximum yield, estimated between 60,000 and 90,000 animals.[3] While awaiting results of this effort, management set cautious harvesting quotas. Aside from small ups and downs, the quotas declined throughout the 1960s, from a peak of 95,974 in 1961 to only 38,805 by the end of the decade. And federal revenues decreased accordingly.[4] To render the economic outlook yet bleaker, management anticipated constantly rising labor costs, in part from expected wage raises, but mainly because of the expansion of the Pribilof Aleut population. The growth was due not to a migration gain (in fact there was a migration loss) but to natural causes. Between 1950 and 1960 the Pribilof population experienced a 5 percent net migration loss and a 28 percent net natural gain.[5] For the first time, management envisaged a labor force larger than it required. Remember, the Pribilof program carried a legal mandate to support the entire population.

The spectre of "overpopulation," as the labor surplus was called, haunted managers. In 1959, Olson, the general manager, argued for a policy of Aleut population reduction. To buttress the argument, he produced a graph showing the relationship of the Pribilof Aleut population to the seal skin production. For nearly every year between 1906 and 1959, the rate of increase in seal production fell substantially below that for population growth.[6] Rising labor costs in the face of revenue declines comprised the number-one management headache in the 1960s. Olson proposed a solution—resettle the Aleuts.

> The question arises whether the FWS should continue expansion on a scale that will forever accommodate a prolific Aleut population regardless of a supporting economy. Or should the principle of sound economics be followed to limit facilities to a level commensurate with a sealing operation which has already reached its optimum production. . . .
>
> *The big problem we face is to bring about a gradual migration of these Aleuts to places of better employment opportunity.* The time has come when all male residents cannot be absorbed into the Pribilof operation.[7]

Olson's recommendation received support in Washington. Two years later, top management formally embraced the abandonment policy.

> *The question of ultimate disposition of the Pribilof Islands was raised. It was agreed that the long-range goal, to be reached many years in the future, should be the abandonment of the Pribilofs* except for the period necessary each year to prepare for and conduct sealing operations, and for certain year-round maintenance personnel. . . .
>
> Mr. Baker reviewed the future pay plan as it has thus far evolved. He stated that if the Islands as they now stand were abandoned for the portion of the year except that required to prepare for sealing, the actual sealing operation, and the securing of the plant . . . from a preliminary review, it appeared that a saving of approximately 50 percent in labor costs would be realized. The size of this advantage would be reduced to an unknown but certainly significant extent as the necessity arises for recruiting and training seasonal crews.[8]

But what about the legality of the resettlement plan? Section 8 of the 1944 Fur Seal Act required the government to provide for Aleuts' support. Would resettlement constitute a violation of the Act? The Washington Office requested a solicitor's opinion on this matter. The solicitor advised:

> . . . the moral obligation to provide for the welfare of the native inhabitants of the islands, recognized by Section 8 . . . may be fulfilled by a relocation program administered by the Bureau of Indian Affairs and by State assistance to the indigent. *When other provision is made for the support and maintenance of the Island population, no financial obligation remains under Section 8.*[9]

An historical irony, no? For the past fifty years during which the Aleuts were an economic asset, the government insisted on its obligation to support them and, furthermore, defined them as ineligible for benefits provided other federal and nonfederal workers. Now that the Aleuts threatened to become an economic liability, how quickly federal definitions and the Aleuts' status changed. In any case, the solicitor's opinion signalled full speed ahead on the abandonment plan.

This is not to suggest that management was callous about the resettlement plan. On the contrary, top management carefully designed plans to prepare Aleuts for resettlement—to equip them with vocational, political, and attitudinal skills for independence. Aleut emancipation joined abandonment as the twin goals of the 1960s. Though management believed in the compatibility of these goals, they reflected a basic contradiction. The abandonment plan involved consolidation of the villages at St. Paul and resettling of the Aleuts away from the Aleutians, both of which the Aleuts opposed. (And this opposition could have been easily predicted had anyone bothered to assess the Aleuts' views.) Consequently, implementing the policy would entail coercion. And coercion fundamentally contradicts autonomy. The government could not, at one and the same time, promote independence and foist an unwanted program of action on the Aleuts. Management apparently failed to consider this contradiction because it was committed to its notions about the form Aleut independence should take. In managers' thinking, St. George Aleuts could be just as independent after transplantation to St. Paul as before, and, besides, they would gain access to additional services and amenities by making the move. What managers missed or failed to ponder was that imposing their notion of independence on the Aleuts denied the very essence of the concept.

Nevertheless, management reappraised and reformed its ideology and personnel policies to effectuate emancipation. By this time, the management institution had undergone another reorganization. In 1956 the Fish and Wildlife Service established two bureaus, Sports Fisheries and Wildlife, and Commercial Fisheries, each with its own director. The latter retained responsibility for the Pribilof program. Furthermore, the Fish and Wildlife Service abolished its fisheries office in Alaska when Alaska assumed responsibility for its own fisheries management in 1959. The U.S. Fish and Wildlife Service hired the head of the former Alaska office, Donald McKernan, a biologist, as director of the Bureau of Commercial Fisheries.

Immediately, McKernan tried to replace the conservative Olson, who perceived Aleuts as incapable and inferior, with Howard Baltzo. McKernan had worked with Baltzo in the past. A twenty-year veteran of the federal fisheries service, Baltzo had struggled tirelessly against the salmon packers to protect the fishery and had earned a reputation as a principled, courageous, person. However, the substitution of Baltzo for Olson proved difficult to effect. As Olson resisted it, McKernan allowed him to remain titular general manager of the Pribilofs until his retirement a short time later. In the interim, McKernan created a new job title for Baltzo, program director, which carried de facto management responsibilities for the islands.[10]

Baltzo's perception of his function derived from second-hand information.

> I was told that the Department of Interior expected an explosion, that a Communist party group in New York City planned to 'blow the lid' off the Pribilof program; and consequently, the Department wanted to clean up the operation and eliminate injustices as quickly as possible.

Baltzo clearly perceived his role as emancipator of the Aleuts: "Nothing existed in writing until the emancipation was well along, but my job was clear—make the natives independent and bring them into the mainstream."[11] As the new policy direction had not yet filtered down to middle-level administrators, the Washington office granted Baltzo direct and ready access. Frequently Baltzo bypassed the Seattle regional office in making decisions.[12] McKernan and Baltzo acted as a team in the emancipation drive, often against the opposition of the old-guard managers who remained in the Service. A new twist, yes? For the first time in the history of federal government administration of the Pribilofs, the management bureaucracy contained a pro-Aleut faction, or to be more precise, a partially committed pro-Aleut faction, for traces of colonialist mentality persisted.

A first step in the phase-out plan, and of immediate and pressing concern, was to contain rising program costs at this time of severely reduced revenues. The revenue trend was distinctly downward. From 1.5 million dollars in 1960, net revenues fell to only about $442,000 by 1968.[13] Beginning in 1960, to halt the erosion of federal revenues from the seal industry, Congress established a special Pribilof Islands fund made up of the proceeds from the sale of Pribilof products and limited the Pribilof appropriation within the bounds of the fund. Yet, within a few years, program costs surpassed that mandated ceiling. Every year after 1969 the program produced a deficit. Aleuts' wages constituted one of the fastest-rising program costs; for example, in St. Paul the Bureau of Commercial Fisheries wages increased by a staggering 137 percent between 1956 and 1966.[14]

The luxury of simply lowering the Aleuts' wages was no longer even a dim possibility. Top management faced unabated pressure to rectify economic inequities on the islands. Encouraged by the reforms of the 1950s, the Aleuts continued to demand equal treatment. This letter from an Aleut leader to the Secretary of the Interior is illustrative:

> (Competitive) positions are of great advantage to the Aleuts up here but seems like the Department here on the Island don't seem to care to give such positions. An Aleut might happen to get such a position, but he won't be getting the same salary as the employee who is hired from the outside.[15]

Indian rights groups continued their Pribilof reform efforts, and statehood generated new forces for change. From the outset of his political career, Alaska's Senator Bartlett took an avid interest in injustices on the islands, as did the Alaska legislature which in its first session enjoined the federal government to bring the Aleuts' wages up to par with the state minimum wage law requirement.[16]

Yes, meeting these demands conformed to the new policy direction, but how could management respond favorably without increasing labor costs? A reduction in force promised a way out of the dilemma. Management could control expenditures by limiting wage increases and other benefits to a portion of, rather than the entire labor force. Furthermore, a reduction in force promised to facilitate the resettlement goal by creating pressure for emigration, as Baltzo readily recognized: "This (reduction in force) would create the welfare problem but at the same time stimulate interest in relocation and so help to depopulate the village. This latter is . . . an objective of the overall program."[17] A reduction in force now constituted a realistic option. The solicitor's opinion paved the way for negotiations to transfer responsibilities for Pribilof Aleuts to other agencies—responsibilities for education, unemployment benefits, welfare assistance,and public health services. Although the Pribilof program compensated these other agencies, at least the groundwork was laid for ending financial responsibility for Aleuts.

In 1962 management established a new Pribilof compensation plan with three main features—a reduction in force, wage raises, and increased efficiency and skill diversification of the workers:

> The Pribilof Islands Fur Seal Program shall be staffed with the primary objective of improving the quality, efficiency, and economy of operations. . . . The Bureau will not create positions solely for the purpose of providing employment opportunities to the inhabitants of the Pribilof Islands.
>
> Employment . . . shall accordingly be confined to the number of employees required to efficiently carry out essential operations as determined by responsible management officials.[18]

This seems straightforward enough, but unravelling the many strands of inequality often poses more problems than creating them in the first place. Should the sealing bonus be continued? Or with pressure from Bartlett and the Alaska legislature to give Aleuts equal civil service status, had the time now come to eliminate the bonus? The Chief, Branch of Alaska Fisheries, among others said, "no."

> It is our opinion that the sealing bonus as a production incentive for individual native crew members should be continued as an integral feature of Pribilof compensation. Incompatible as this may be with standard Government wage and salary procedures, it is a device widely used in industry and is traditional on the Pribilofs. Of more practical effect, we fear that elimination of this production incentive will result in such greatly lessened accomplishment as to completely outweight administrative benefits.[19]

Another high level official proposed retaining the sealing bonus as a means for funding community facilities: "It is proposed that bonus payments be continued. However, these would be paid into a community fund where they would be used to provide recreational, educational, or other community benefits as determined by the Town Council."[20] How difficult it was for some of the old-guard managers to shed the detritus of colonialist ideology. In their thinking, it was quite acceptable to pay part of Aleuts' wages in a fixed-rate bonus that was not protected by standard wage and cost-of-living increases, and to earmark how the Aleuts were to use this part of their wage. An administrator in the regional office showed more flexibility in converting to new ways of thinking about Aleuts:

> The old method . . . is outmoded because, under the new plan, there will be a number who are on welfare and so are not entitled to the bonus.
>
> The new method fits in better with the idea of teaching the natives the ways of the general economic situation. . . .
>
> Therefore, the arguments of incentive and custom or tradition are outweighed, and the old sealing bonus as such should be done away with.[21]

His opinion reflected the new thinking in Washington, and the sealing bonus was finally laid to rest. In the new plan, the government classified Aleuts by standard civil service criteria and paid them accordingly.

Economic equality meant not only abandoning the sealing bonus but all special benefits, such as noncompetitive prices on food and fuel, free transportation on government vessels, and rent-free houses. Managers were in accord about the need to eliminate these other gratuities, but not about the applicability of certain benefits other federal workers received; for example, the 80 percent isolation rent deduction. Middle-level managers opposed the idea of applying the deduction to Pribilof Aleuts, arguing that it was not intended for persons living in their home communities.[22] McKernan disagreed with his staff: "It must be recognized that the basis for this deduction is the degree of isolation of the individual from a center of population and not how far a person is from his home area."[23] And so another stone was turned in equalizing conditions on the Pribilofs.

Federal employees in Alaska also received a 25 percent cost-of-living allowance. McKernan failed to consider the application of this allowance to Pribilof Aleuts in his draft of the new compensation plan which he sent to the Secretary of the Interior for approval. The Secretary, however, called his attention to this oversight,[24] and forthwith, McKernan granted the cost-of-living allowance to classified employees.

Management, including the Interior Secretary, remained noticeably silent about Aleuts' retirement benefits for the years worked before 1950, probably because correcting this inequity would entail considerable costs. Thus the new compensation plan ignored this issue. But Senator Bartlett plugged away at it, and four years later a new Fur Seal Act required the Pribilof program to cover Aleuts' retirement benefits for the pre-1950 years.[25]

Think of that! With a single stroke of the pen, aside from pre-1950 retirement benefits, the government in 1962 eliminated economic inequality in the Pribilofs. The forces for change within and outside the Fish and Wildlife Service overpowered the traditional-minded, reflecting not only the power of public opinion but also top management's determination to phase out the Pribilof program, which required emancipating the Aleuts.

Economic equality, however, proved to be a mixed blessing, for it was accompanied by growing rates of poverty and unemployment. Before 1963 the Bureau of Commercial Fisheries employed virtually every able-bodied Pribilof man on a full-time basis. After that it hired an ever-shrinking proportion to work full time. In 1961 in St. Paul, the Bureau employed ninety-four permanent workers and thirty-seven temporary ones. Five years later the ratio was reversed; the Bureau employed only forty-four permanent workers and seventy-four temporary ones.[26] The full-time St. Paul workers in 1966 received an average wage of $8,500 and the long-term seasonal workers, an average wage of $2,600. An additional twenty-five persons, mostly students, found short-term seasonal jobs with the Bureau at an average annual wage of $630.[27] Furthermore, income from other sources failed to compensate for these low wages. Though there was now some off-island employment, a few small businesses, and transfer payments—retirement, unemployment, and welfare—income from these other sources represented less than 20 percent of the St. Paul Aleuts' total income in 1966.[28] In other words, the Bureau still paid more than 80 percent of the Aleuts' total wages. A detailed economic analysis of St. Paul, reveals the distribution of gross household income averaged for 1966 and 1967:* 20 percent of all households earned less than $4,000 a year; 22 percent, between $4,000 and $8,000; 35 percent from $8,000 to $12,000; and 23 percent, more than $12,000.[29] Consider that! Nearly half the households earned less than $8,000 a year and an average household contained 6.3 persons.[30] Yes, economic reform on the Pribilofs engendered a new set of economic problems. From that time forth, underemployment and inadequate income plagued the Pribilovians.

The training component of the economic reform package encountered many obstacles.** Placing high priority on this goal, McKernan emphasized

*In interpreting the distribution, keep in mind that St. Paul households contained an average of two members in the labor force.

**The Fish and Wildlife Service had established the training priority in 1956.

training both for relocation and for management positions on the islands. The rub was that, eager to unload responsibilities for Pribilof programs onto other agencies, management relied on the Bureau of Indian Affairs to fulfill the training function. And the Bureau of Indian Affairs program failed to excite the interest of the Aleuts or to provide training for staff positions on the islands. In 1961 McKernan acknowledged the Bureau of Indian Affairs' failure in this regard:

> Management officials . . . felt that the BIA relocation and training program fulfilled this need but such a program, while certainly worthwhile from a relocation standpoint, has not produced the training requested by the Director. The Director reiterated his request for a positive training program to qualify Pribilof Aleuts for positions presently held by staff employees.[31]

Believing that staff disinterest subverted the training goal, McKernan exhorted his managers:

> The fact that nothing has been accomplished cannot be justified or excused. It can only be attributed to indifference or disagreement with my views. If there is some reason why this program is not going forward, please advise me in full. If not, I expect immediate action.[32]

Undoubtedly, McKernan sought to inspire middle-level managers to more conscientious efforts in convincing Aleuts to pursue training. One wonders if middle-level managers, threatened by the injunction to train Aleuts for their own positions, subverted the training goal. In a recent interview Baltzo suggested an alternative explanation, that the slow progress reflected administrators' reluctance to coerce the Aleuts in any way: "We encouraged them, we tried to persuade them as honestly as we could . . . but we bent over backwards to make them sure we wouldn't feel offended if they didn't adopt our views."[33] But whatever efforts staff might have made, the success of the training program was inherently limited by the lack of funds for implementation. The St. Paul agent called attention to this reality: "You write now as if there was funds available for this sort of thing . . . but we have not heard about it. Why can't we get help for those already trying to get an education on their own?"[34] By this time a significant number of Aleuts were pursuing education and training with no help from the Bureau. Yet, McKernan continued to upbraid staff for failing to inspire Aleut interest in the admittedly inadequate Bureau of Indian Affairs training program. And, indeed, few Aleuts responded; for example, in 1961, the program director indicated that only four Aleuts were enrolled in formal vocational training.[35]

The failure of the training program can be attributed to management's pursuit of conflicting goals—to train Aleuts for staff positions on the islands and at the same time to transfer responsibilities for the training to another agency over which it had no control and whose program was inadequate. Evidently the interest in transferring responsibilities held dominance and the training program faltered.

Nevertheless, McKernan's insistence on training Aleuts for staff positions within the villages produced some results through on-the-job training. Although reluctantly at first, administrators equipped Aleuts to manage and operate the Pribilof facility. A highly significant development, this, representing as it did, along with full civil service status and wage equality, a major breakthrough in removing inequality on the islands.

Baltzo actively sought to eliminate other practices symbolizing inequality. Unlike Olson who had spent only about six weeks of each year on the islands, Baltzo, convinced that his mission required knowledge and understanding of Aleuts, lived at St. Paul for six months of each year. Furthermore, unlike past managers, Baltzo declined living in the manager's house atop a hill overlooking the flatlands where the Aleuts resided. He divided the hill-top house into apartments, and with his family moved to a modest dwelling in the town. Reversing the deeply entrenched pattern of social segregation, Baltzo and his wife invited Aleuts to visit and socialize.

Legalizing alcohol on the islands was one of Baltzo's first priorities. The ban on drinking applied to all residents, white and Aleut, but, Baltzo said, it was enforced only against the Aleuts. Baltzo considered this to be gross discrimination, and perhaps too he perceived the repeal of prohibition as a step in acculturating Aleuts to prepare them for relocation. Reflecting persisting colonialist mentality, Baltzo's staff, however, adamantly opposed him on this issue, arguing that repeal was against the best interests of the Aleuts. "That is beside the point," Baltzo recalls telling them, "the Aleuts are free citizens."[36] Evidently McKernan supported Baltzo, and in May 1962, although thirty years later than the rest of the country, the government repealed prohibition in the Pribilofs.[37]

The Aleuts responded enthusiastically, not only because package liquor was now available, but because of the symbolic meaning of the repeal, as a sign of equality with the white overlords. And although Aleuts had been denied self-government for many decades, they displayed a remarkable readiness to assume responsibility for liquor control. Immediately, both communities enacted regulations that limited sales to beer, one case a week per person; limited the place of sales to the canteens; prohibited sales on Sundays and during working hours; and denied purchase rights to persons who disturbed the peace or neglected their families. Furthermore, the Aleuts organized a local constabulary and judiciary to enforce regulations.[38] At first the community councils assumed this responsibility, but they met with limited success. For one reason, Aleuts are reluctant to inform or testify against their fellows. For another, Aleut police hesitate to engage in actions such as arresting drunkards that might alienate their fellows. The records of the St. George Community Council reveal repeated instances of the ineptness of local law enforcement. Here are several examples.

June 29, 1963, St. George Community Council

> . . . that council should do something about police force and judge. The reason they wanna quit from the force . . . said it was personal reason so council subjected that they'll straighten that out on next council meeting.[39]

* * *

August 5, 1964, St. George Community Council

> Meeting was about . . . absence of village judicial and enforcement authority. Successors need to be appointed and they must be supported in carrying out their official duties.[40]

St. Paul experienced a similarly disappointing outcome with a local police force, and in 1965, in cooperation with the Bureau of Commercial Fisheries and the Alaska Department of Public Safety, the community hired a state trooper, each of the three parties paying an approximately equal share of the trooper's salary.[41] The trooper provided job training to several local residents, and when he left St. Paul in 1971, the community resumed responsibility for police functions. Judicial functions by then were handled in a conventional manner; offenders were sent to Anchorage for hearing or trial. And the long and atrocious history of agent juridical control died.

Baltzo also successfully promoted an end to federal restrictions on visitors to the islands. This effort arose not at his instigation but in response to pressure from a new and potentially powerful interest group—the Alaska natives. Until 1960, the Alaska Native Brotherhood in southeastern Alaska remained the sole native organization with a pan-Indian orientation. Then came the Statehood Act which authorized Alaska to select 104 million acres of land and required it to disclaim any right or title to native lands. However, Congress had never clarified native land rights. To protect and advance their land interests, natives from every part of the state organized local and regional associations. Accompanying these developments was the first statewide native newspaper, Tundra Times, which published scathing editorials about injustice on the Pribilofs. In 1964, when management denied an Aleut candidate for the State Legislature access to the Pribilofs, the Tundra Times publicly decried the act.[42] Soon after that, Alaska's Governor Egan dispatched the State Human Rights Commission to the Pribilofs to investigate civil rights violations. These pressures brought immediate results. Baltzo recommended lifting the ban on visitors and the Washington office followed suit.

Yes indeed, these actions connoted new management ideology and behavior. In place of contempt and oppression, management responded positively to the demands of the Aleuts and their supporters and reversed a number of discriminatory practices. But this responsiveness had limits. Management harbored its own conception of what form Aleut independence should take, and when its notions conflicted with those of the Aleuts, management was not only unresponsive but devious. The consolidation plan exemplified this response.

Management's eagerness to consolidate the two villages at St. Paul reflected not only economic considerations—it was far less costly to provide one set of services and amenities than two, especially in villages with such small populations—but also interest in facilitating resettlement. St. Paul was a more acculturated community than St. George, and, apparently, managers believed that consolidation at St. Paul would speed up the St. George Aleuts' acculturation and thereby prepare them for resettlement. In the course of implementing the resettlement policy, consolidation appears to have taken on a symbolic value, as a test of the feasibility of the resettlement policy; if management couldn't convince St. George Aleuts to emigrate to nearby St. Paul, then how could it hope to persuade them to move away from the Pribilofs? Consequently, management placed high priority on consolidation.

According to Baltzo, the consolidation policy originated locally rather than in Washington. After several St. George families requested to move to St. Paul, Baltzo and other field administrators conceived the plan. At first, Baltzo said, members of both communities agreed to the idea, and Baltzo proceeded to carry it out.[43] Washington officials rather quickly embraced the consolidation goal. As early as 1962 high-level managers advanced the policy at a meeting with the Alaska Congregational Delegation.

> Keep in mind that the long-range objective is the placement of the island operation on a seasonal basis. . . . *In this connection we would suggest that we take positive steps toward consolidating the two island communities by setting a target date of perhaps 1975 or 1980 as the date by which we would propose complete transfer of St. George residents to St. Paul.* In the meantime new houses and other construction not essential to the sealing operation would be built only at St. Paul.[44]

That same year, managers promoted the consolidation issue at St. George. The Community Council expressed concern: "There was still talk about moving over to St. Paul whoever wants to but this they did not say, if we really don't want to nobody been force."[45] Thereafter, minutes of community council meetings reveal consistent opposition to the idea.

> March 12, 1963
>
> Community council meeting with Mr. Bob Carrol (community development officer hired by the Bureau of Commercial Fisheries). Discussions were about relocating of St. George people to St. Paul. Something we are all going to take action against.[46]

* * *

January 28, 1964

Subject—To discuss about trying to move us families to St. Paul. And three families are moving to St. Paul on this coming boat as volenters. All members doesn't want to go to St. Paul. . . . President said that every member of community club has got to be at the meeting. To fight all together, to have more power. Bob Carrol was trying to force to say, yes, when he goes around the houses and questions us. . . .

They promise us that anybody going to St. Paul will hold their job they had over here. And they said B.C.F. is trying to drop this island. All members are plan to send out letter to authorized persons.[47]

The old guard, the new guard, Baltzo, McKernan, up and down the line, managers seemed united in effecting the consolidation. They induced St. George Aleuts to move to St. Paul with promises of jobs and houses, promises that engendered resentment and concern in St. Paul, for the Aleuts there were still reeling from the reduction in force. Moreover, they faced a constant housing shortage; when people married, often there was no place for them to live other than with relatives. Managers used many subtle pressures to persuade St. George Aleuts to move: "Our request for a furnace was met with a suggestion that we move to St. Paul," recalled a St. George woman.[48] Covert threats were common:

They have been asking individually certain people, "Are you going over to St. Paul?" When the answer is "No," then they answer back to them, "You just think so." It seems like it is forcing them to move over this way.[49]

Once St. George Aleuts did move to St. Paul, island managers (the new title for agents) immediately burned their houses so there was no returning. A special investigating committee appointed by the governor in 1965 confirmed this practice: "Bureau of Commercial Fisheries officials informed the Commission that it has been the policy to demolish a dwelling at St. George every time there is a net reduction in the number of families requiring housing space there. The objective is a gradual shift of almost all the inhabitants of St. George to St. Paul."[50] United States Senate hearings held on the Pribilofs in 1965 regarding Senator Bartlett's proposed new fur seal act lent furthur corroboration. Bartlett himself seemed unaware of the demolition practice.[51]

Senator Bartlett. You mean the houses over there have been demolished.

Mrs. Susie Merculief. Yes.

Senator Bartlett. Were they in good condition?

Mrs. Susie Merculief. Yes. Most of them were. Only two of them were pretty old . . . . I could have moved to one of those houses that were destroyed, from the one I am living in now because it is very old. . . .

Excuse me, that is another reason, too, they don't like to move over there. If they want to return to St. George, they don't have a house to return to, to live in. It is destroyed as soon as the person leaves. . . .

Mr. Foster. Is that the policy . . . to destroy every house of anyone who moves from St. George?

Mrs. Susie Merculief. I understand they were supposed to destroy two houses every year and two built over here every year. . . .

Senator Bartlett. Let me interrupt you right there. Let's ask the Bureau of Commercial Fisheries if that is the fact.

Mr. Baker. . . . The thought was, however, to hold constant the total number of housing units on the Pribilof Islands, feeling that from the standpoint of the fur seal industry this was adequate or more than adequate to provide housing for the industry people.

That has been the policy, Mr. Chairman.

Senator Bartlett. The Committee doesn't quite understand yet why it is necessary to tear down a house, old as it may be, but still serviceable and usable. Why was that done? Your answer hasn't explained this to me at all. Was it a move to force the people over there and to make them stay here?

Mr. Baker. No sir, it was not intended that way at all.

Senator Bartlett. Who ordered the houses destroyed and why were they destroyed?

Mr. Baker. Any home that is left on St. George at the time the family moves to St. Paul obviously must be maintained. It cannot just sit idle without deterioration.

If it is maintained . . . there is an added expense to the government.

Senator Bartlett. What form would this maintenance take? Why would it be so expensive?

Mr. Baker. My understanding is that the buildings have to be kept heated in order to prevent deterioration through dampness and cold. If this is to be done, it must be done by the Bureau. . . .

Senator Bartlett. As a matter of public policy, since this is Government property, let's say dampness got into the house and it deteriorated a bit, it could still be there standing and it could be utilized with a little refurbishing if a need arose. If it is destroyed, that can't be done.[52]

Exposure at the Bartlett hearings put a stop to the demolition of houses, but not to managers' pressure to move St. George Aleuts to St. Paul. And these endeavors met with some success. Between 1964 and 1970, thirteen St. George families involving sixty-eight individuals moved to St. Paul.[53] Still the majority stubbornly remained despite the persistence of the consolidation goal.

St. Paul Aleuts also feared losing their houses if they emigrated, not because of demolition but because management might assign the houses to other persons. Consequently, they hesitated leaving the village even for temporary employment. At the same time, the reduction in force produced pressure to take outside jobs. Aleuts again urged management to give them title to their homes.

> Inquiry was made about the possibility of buying a house from the government and making monthly payments. The Council members were advised that the possibility of transferring title to the houses was considered and dropped because of government ownership of the land and the lack of authority for doing so. . . .
>
> The Council was concerned about arrangements that could be made for an individual leaving the island temporarily to work to retain his home on the Island. . . . No encouragement was given on this score.[54]

Despite management's intransigence on this issue, Pribilof Aleuts increasingly left the villages for temporary work; survival required it, but few left permanently. Ironically, between 1960 and 1966 (the Bureau kept migration data only until 1966) only thirty St. Paul Aleuts permanently left the village, while, after the restriction on immigration had been lifted, 107 (more than one-third from places other than St. George) moved permanently to St. Paul.[55] The resettlement plan was not only losing ground, but the reverse was taking place—permanent immigrants outnumbered emigrants.

Managers imposed their notion of Aleut independence in yet another way, by promoting religious diversification. In 1965 the Assemblies of God applied for a permit to build and administer a church at St. Paul. After checking the legality of the application, McKernan offered full support: "You are authorized and encouraged," he wrote his second in command, "to assist and cooperate with the Alaska Assemblies of God and any other religious denomination which may desire to establish a church on St. Paul Island."[56]

Baltzo claimed that the Fish and Wildlife Service never actively encouraged this application but that managers were caught in a bind because of the emphasis on equality. Baltzo remarked: "How could we advocate equality for the Aleuts and deny it to the Assemblies of God? The minister claimed that the whites on the island had a right to a church of their own."[57] Further, Baltzo pointed out, the Assemblies of God attorneys threatened a court suit if their application were denied.[58]

However, the advent of the Assemblies of God mission represented more than happenstance. As early as 1949, the director of the Fish and Wildlife Service as well as other Department of Interior officials in the special survey group advocated religious diversification on the Pribilofs. Apparently convinced that Aleuts' acculturation required religious diversification, the group recommended: "The way must be administratively clear for them (managers) to furnish additional religious and social leadership among the natives."[59] Thus, McKernan acted on a policy that had been set down over a decade earlier.

Dorothy Rose Jones

A CENTURY OF SERVITUDE

By: Debor

Professor: Dorot

Date: April

The Aleuts first learned of the Assemblies of God application, not from the Bureau, but from friends in Fairbanks. They were irate. Aleuts were ardently devoted to the Russian Orthodox Church. As one feature after another of their traditional way of life disappeared, they clung ever more tenaciously to the church as a cultural bulwark. The church represented not just a valued religious institution but also a cultural one of great significance. They immediately protested the application to the Secretary of the Interior. The Russian Orthodox bishop followed suit:

> As Bishop of Sitka and Alaska and the spiritual shepard of all of the permanent inhabitants of St. Paul I ask you, Mr. Udall, to be kindly toward the members of my religion and to give your orders for the protection of my spiritual flock from the troubles and temptations to which they are now being subjected. Will you please explain to me how the United States of America can be a party to, or condone and sanction, these troubles and temptations.[60]

Flatly dismissing the Aleuts' and the Bishop's appeals, management granted the permit to the Assemblies of God. In 1966 the new church was built, but no Aleuts joined. Apparently thwarted and hostile at the Aleuts' disinterest, the pastor of the new church harrassed the Russian Orthodox Aleuts. In April 1967, during the Russian Orthodox Good Friday and Easter services, the pastor blew a bullhorn over a loudspeaker near the Russian church. An Aleuts' letter to the pastor about this intrusion merits citing for its brilliant irony.

> While the Congregation of our Orthodox Believers were in church, in reverence of our Lord's Passion and long suffering, we heard a loud noise coming from a loud speaker attached to the side of your house.
>
> It was a great help, reminding us of the Bible: "Then was Jesus led up of the spirit into the wilderness to be tempted by the devil." Matt. 4:1. . . . We are aware of the consequences of unbelief. "And many false prophets shall rise and shall deceive many. And because iniquity shall abound, the love of many shall wax cold." Matt. 24:11,12.
>
> If you should think of playing more, during our services, think of those and also remember the Unity of Believers. "Now I beseech you brethren, by the name of Our Lord Jesus Christ, that ye all speak the same thing, and that there be no divisions among you, but that ye be perfectly joined together in the same mind and in the same judgement." I: Cor. 1:10.
>
> . . . It is understood by everyone involved, that permission was granted to you on "revocable land use permit, and primarily for persons on the Island who are not affiliated with the local Russian Orthodox church."
>
> You know as well as I do that the local community council did not adhere your request for them to endorse your idea to establish a church here.
>
> You may remember the time when you and Mrs. . . . visited my house inviting my family to attend your "opening day service," it was then I chatted with you both letting you know that I was not interested in going and I further stated that there

must be places where there is no church and the people could use of conversion faith, and if I remember correctly, there was such a place where you stated that "the people worship their cows and will not butcher them for food, etc." It was then I stated that if I was a pastor interested in helping people to find God that I would go to such a place and at the same time I questioned why you did not plan establishing your church there, instead of here where we've had our faith from time immemorial.[61]

Clearly, religious diversification produced a different consequence than management had anticipated; it had, in fact, created an enormous aggravation for management. Baltzo responded to the bullhorn incident with a memo entitled, "Competitive Christianity."

> Since returning from St. Paul Island . . . I have been filled in on the distressing details of Reverend . . . 's bullhorn operation on Russian Orthodox Good Friday and Easter. . . . Had I been aware of this incident when in Seattle . . . I would not have reassured you as I did that local friction would probably die out as contesting parties got to know each other better. Mr. . . . 's interference with the Russian services was obviously deliberate, his disturbance of the peace extremely blatant, and his explanation patently untruthful and defiant.
>
> It seems clear that we have a difficult personality to deal with.
>
> I have been defensive of the AOG church here in the past only because I believed that freedom of religion is guaranteed at St. Paul just as surely as anywhere else under the U.S. Constitution. I cannot share (the Bishop's) opinion that his organization has sole and exclusive right at this location. As things now stand, however, I think (the pastor) has proven to be his church's own worst enemy because his initial modest congregation has now dwindled to almost none. . . .
>
> I would greatly appreciate your advice on effective remedial action. . . . In the meantime, local leadership is trying to exercise objective judgement and ameliorate personal feelings of outrage.[62]

In reply to this letter, Baltzo's superior asked if there were any terms or conditions of the permit which would allow the Bureau to cancel it.[63] Apparently there weren't, for the mission remained, albeit with no Aleut members. And clearly the "religious and social leadership" of the pastor and the presence of a Protestant sect contributed nothing to Aleuts' acculturation and desire for relocation.

Management policies in the 1960s reflected the same economic imperatives as in the past though the direction changed under significantly altered circumstances; both the Aleuts and the seal industry threatened to become economic liabilities. In response to this reality, the Bureau adopted a new policy direction calling for abandonment of the islands and conversion to a seasonal operation. The latter was within its power to effectuate, but not the former. Given the growing influence of outside interest groups, including new forces of change generated by Alaska statehood and the establishment of the relatively pro-Aleut faction within the institution, management had to respect the Aleuts' determination to remain permanently in their communities.

Integral to the abandonment policy was the goal to emancipate the Aleuts, to develop and train them either for resettlement or for managing the seasonal operation. Emancipation ran into trouble when management's notions conflicted with those of the Aleuts—regarding consolidation of the two villages and religious diversification. Otherwise, management's efforts to promote Aleut independence brought a virtual end to the colonial relationship on the Pribilofs. What the Bureau of Commercial Fisheries failed to redress, the new Fur Seal Act of 1966 accomplished. While the new act retained the section 8 provision, it resolved most persisting traces of inequality. One of its main purposes was to facilitate the Aleuts' self-sufficiency and self-government. The act provided for *the transfer of government land and houses to Aleuts*; legal steps for *township incorporation* under Alaska law, which meant taxing privileges; and *retirement credits* for the years worked before 1950. Finally, the act further reduced the Aleuts' dependence on the Bureau by transferring responsibility for their health to the United States Public Health Service and for their education to the State of Alaska.

Thus, the Bartlett Act, as the new act was called, officially ended *de jure* inequality in the Pribilofs. Putting it into effect, however, was still ahead and involved grappling with new forces of change in the 1970s.

Endnotes

1. "Calculation of Payment to Alaska in Terms of Number of Sealskins, 1945 to 1964." Bureau of Commercial Fisheries Records, Federal Archives and Records Center, Seattle.
2. "Review of Fur Seal Operations and Administration of the Pribilof Islands." Report to the Congress of the United States by the Comptroller General of the United States. June 1961, p. 25; "Annual Report of Sealing Operations, Pribilof Islands, Alaska, 1968," p. 2. Bureau of Commercial Fisheries Records, Federal Archives.
3. The new plan included, for the first time, the killing of female seals. The specific objective of the plan was to reduce the population to a level that would produce about 400,000 pups annually. The expected result was an increase in the total harvest and then stabilization with an estimated sustained yield of 55,000 to 60,000 males and 10,000 to 30,000 females. Federal Register, Vol. 38, No. 147, August 1, 1973, p. 20599.
4. "Employment-Administration of Pribilof Islands—July 1970." Compiled by Bert Johnson, September 17, 1970, p. A-25 (annual seal harvest quotas),

p. A-3 (net revenues and payments to Alaska). National Marine Fisheries Service Records, Seattle.

5. Computed from data in Don C. Foote, Victor Fischer, and George Rogers, St. Paul Community Study: An Economic and Social Analysis of St. Paul, Pribilof Islands, Alaska (Fairbanks: University of Alaska, Institute of Social, Economic and Government Research, 1968), p. 31; Census data, Bureau of Commercial Fisheries Records, St. George Island.

6. General Manager to Chief, Division of Resource Management, August 6, 1959. Supplement to July 15, 1959 Memorandum, Bureau of Commercial Fisheries Records, Federal Archives.

7. General Manager to Chief, Division of Resource Management, July 15, 1959, Bureau of Commercial Fisheries Records, Federal Archives.

8. "Minutes," Meeting in Director's Office, March 15, 1961. Bureau of Commercial Fisheries Records, Federal Archives.

9. Regional Solicitor to Associate Solicitor, Territories, Wildlife and Parks, May 3, 1961; Associate Solicitor to Director, Bureau of Commercial Fisheries, May 25, 1961. Bureau of Commercial Fisheries Records, St. Paul Island.

10. Personal Communication, Howard Baltzo, November 10, 1978.

11. Ibid.

12. Ibid.

13. "Employment-Administration of Pribilof Islands—July 1970," p. A-3, National Marine Fisheries Service Records, Seattle.

14. Foote, et. al., St. Paul Community Study, p. 55.

15. St. Paul Aleut to Secretary of Interior, June 24, 1960, Fredericka Martin Records.

16. Senate Joint Resolution No. 9, March 30, 1961.

17. Program Director to Island Managers, June 9, 1961, Bureau of Commercial Fisheries Records, Federal Archives. In reviewing a draft of this chapter, Baltzo clarified his thinking of that time: "You gave the impression that to save a few dollars, we sacrificed the natives. From the point of view of middle-level staff, the budget was a sacred thing. It was determined from Washington. As far as the administrators in the field were concerned, it never occurred to us we were weighing dollars against lives."

18. "Compensation Plan for Employees of the Pribilof Islands Fur Seal Program," Section 3. Approved by Interior Secretary, June 14, 1962. Bureau of Commercial Fisheries Records, Federal Archives.

19. Chief, Branch of Alaska Fisheries, to Regional Director, March 14, 1961, Bureau of Commercial Fisheries Records, Federal Archives.

20. "Revised Pribilof Compensation Plan," January 19, 1961. Bureau of Commercial Fisheries Records, Federal Archives.

21. Regional Office Staff Member to Program Director, May 9, 1961. Bureau of Commercial Fisheries Records, Federal Archives.

22. Acting Regional Director to Director, October 30, 1961; "Memo," from Program Director, October 27, 1961; Program Director to Regional Director, June 14, 1961; Bureau of Commercial Fisheries Records, Federal Archives.

23. Director to Regional Director, December 7, 1961. Bureau of Commercial Fisheries Records, Federal Archives.
24. Secretary of the Interior to Director, Bureau of Commercial Fisheries, December 4, 1961. Bureau of Commercial Fisheries Records, Federal Archives.
25. Fur Seal Act of 1966, P.L. 89-102, 80 Stat. 1091 (November 2, 1966).
26. Foote, et. al., St. Paul Community Study, p. 57.
27. Ibid., p. 59.
28. Ibid., p. 63.
29. Ibid., p. 66.
30. Ibid., p. 70.
31. "Minutes, Meeting in Director's Office," March 15, 1961. Bureau of Commercial Fisheries Records, Federal Archives.
32. Director, Bureau of Commercial Fisheries, to Regional Director, March 15, 1961. Bureau of Commercial Fisheries Records, Federal Archives.
33. Personal communication, Howard Baltzo, October 13, 1979.
34. St. Paul Agent to Regional Office Staff Member, April 7, 1961. Bureau of Commercial Fisheries Records, Federal Archives.
35. Program Director to Regional Director, April 5, 1961. Bureau of Commercial Fisheries Records, Federal Archives.
36. Personal communication, Howard Baltzo, November 10, 1978.
37. Program Director to President, St. George Community Council, April 5, 1963. Bureau of Commercial Fisheries Records, St. George.
38. President, Aleut Community of St. Paul, "Proposed Liquor Control Law for Pribilof Islands," N.D. In 1962 file, Community Council Records, St. Paul; Minutes, St. George Community Council, May 15, 1962; May 19, 1962; September 17, 1963. Community Council Records, St. George.
39. Community Council Records, St. George.
40. Ibid.
41. Program Director to Assistant Director for Resource Development, October 17, 1965. Bureau of Commercial Fisheries Records, Federal Archives.
42. Tundra Times, November 23, 1964, p. 1.
43. Personal communication, Howard Baltzo, October 13, 1979.
44. "Minutes of Meeting," Bureau of Commercial Fisheries with Alaska Congressional Delegation, June 12, 1962. Bureau of Commercial Fisheries Records, Federal Archives.
45. "Minutes," St. George Community Council, May 5, 1962. Community Council Records, St. George.
46. Community Council Records, St. George.
47. Ibid.
48. Field notes, St. George, 1978.
49. U.S. Congress, Senate, Hearing before the Committee of Commerce on S.2102, 89th Cong., 1st and 2nd Sess., 1966, p. 79.
50. Economic and Social Conditions on the Pribilof Islands, Report by Special Commission Appointed by the Governor of Alaska (Juneau, 1965), p. 9.

51. According to Baltzo, Bartlett did not oppose the consolidation policy, only the house demolition practice. Personal communication, Howard Baltzo, October 13, 1979.
52. Hearings, S.2102, pp. 76-77.
53. "Employment-Administration of Pribilof Islands—July 1970," p. A-8, National Marine Fisheries Service Records, Seattle.
54. "Presentation of Pribilof Islands Compensation Plan," April 4, 1962, Bureau of Commercial Fisheries Records, Federal Archives.
55. Foote, et. al., St. Paul Community Study, pp. 31 and 33.
56. Director to Regional Director, April 1, 1966. Bureau of Commercial Fisheries Records, Federal Archives.
57. Personal communication, Howard Baltzo, October 13, 1979.
58. Ibid.
59. "Pribilof Islands Survey Report. Observations and Recommendations," October 8, 1949, p. 7. Bureau of Commercial Fisheries Records, Federal Archives.
60. Bishop, Russian Orthodox Church, to Secretary of the Interior, February 6, 1967. National Marine Fisheries Service Records, Seattle.
61. Iliador Merculieff to Reverend . . . , Assembly of God Mission, St. Paul Island. April 28, 1967. National Marine Fisheries Service Records, Seattle.
62. Program Director to Assistant Director for Resource Development, May 19, 1967, National Marine Fisheries Service Records, Seattle.
63. Regional Director to Program Director, June 8, 1967, National Marine Fisheries Service Records, Seattle.

CHAPTER 9

CENTENNIAL, 1971-Present

In 1870 potential profits from commercial sealing sparked traders' fantasies; one hundred years later the spectre of financial doom in the seal industry haunted their successors. In 1870 the federal government established Pribilof policy without seriously considering the Aleuts' interests; one hundred years later it had to negotiate policy directly with the Aleuts. Yes, Pribilof history had taken a 180-degree turn.

Cost consciousness, always a dominant factor in the Pribilof program, had in the past been cloaked by broader goals. Even as late as the 1960s, when cost containment was the motivation underlying the abandonment policy, cost issues did not achieve policy rank in their own right. But by the 1970s, on the brink of financial disaster, management adopted an explicit cost-reduction policy.[1] Abandoning the islands no longer comprised a management goal because most of the Aleuts simply refused to be resettled. Similarly, the consolidation goal, while persisting rhetorically, now represented a management hope rather than reality for the same reason. Two other elements of the abandonment policy—converting to a seasonal operation and transferring responsibility for island administration to the Aleuts—persisted as subgoals of the cost-reduction policy.

This policy reorientation reflected a growing hopelessness about the seal industry. Something was seriously wrong with the seals. The seal population reduction program instituted in the late 1950s had gone awry. The program had been shaped by predictions derived from seal survival rates of the past. But for unexplained reasons, the survival rate fell below the desired level, and nothing seemed to reverse the trend. Planned population reduction was clearly out of control. In response to this uncertainty, management consistently decreased the size of the harvests. From a peak of over 95,000 seals in 1961, the harvest shrank to only about 25,000 by 1978—and remained relatively low throughout the 1970s.[2]

Speculating about the declining survival rates, marine mammalogists considered these causes:

- The disorganized state of fur seal research.
- The reduced availability of seal food due to commercial utilization of species upon which the seals feed.
- Disruption of the nursing cycle by research activities.
- Long-term changes in the ocean environment.
- Changes in the seals' gene pool resulting from harvesting, which is an unnatural cause of mortality.[3]

But no one knew for sure, and the survival rate failed to recover its former level.

With relatively fixed program costs, the reduced harvests inevitably eroded federal revenues. Every year since 1969, the Pribilof program has operated in the red. The deficit grew from almost one-half million dollars in 1970 to nearly four million in 1976.[4] As a result, Congress significantly reduced the Pribilof budget, by $100,000 in 1973 and a staggering $420,000 in 1977 (representing about 14 percent of the total program budget for that year).[5]

Why not pull out of the seal business entirely? Why not close down the operation? In addition to financial pressures to do so, portions of the conservation lobby called for just such an action. The Sierra Club proposed protective legislation that would prohibit all hunting of Pacific sea mammals without special permission of a Marine Mammal Commission except by aborigines who hunted for subsistence. Taking an even harder line, the Friends of Animals and The Society for the Prevention of Cruelty to Animals agitated for an end to all killing of marine mammals, without exception. The Friends of Animals filed a suit against the Secretary of Commerce asking for an injunction to stop the seal harvests.[6] The Commerce Secretary was implicated because in 1970 the Bureau of Commercial Fisheries, renamed the National Marine Fisheries Service, was transferred to the National Oceanic and Atmospheric Administration in the Commerce Department. These environmental groups, clamoring for an end to Pribilof sealing throughout the 1970s, were joined later in the decade by the Greenpeace movement whose members threatened to sail their ship to the islands in dramatic protest against the seal slaughter.[7] These groups are now pressing for a new fur seal act that would permanently end commercial sealing on the Pribilofs and terminate the United States' participation in the international fur seal treaty. The controversy they have stirred is attracting national interest. Indeed, St. Paul Island appeared to be under seige during the 1979 harvest. Listen to this account in the Tundra Times.

> The annual Pribilof fur seal harvest began shortly after 5:00 a.m. Tuesday morning . . . . Except for the presence of what appeared to be more cameras than seals on the harvesting grounds, the harvest was conducted without incident. Even a local Aleut film crew was on hand to film the large number of outside photographers, newsmen, and environmentalists there to witness the harvest . . .
>
> Leading the onslaught is a contingent from the environmentalist group, Friends of Animals. Also on hand are representatives from the Committee for Humane Legislation and the Greenpeace organization.
>
> In addition, biologists and enforcement officers from state and federal agencies . . . are on hand, as well as representatives from the national press, including a CBS camera crew, and reporters from The Associated Press, National Geographic, and

Life magazine. To top if off, three large plane loads of tourists . . . have descended on the island.[8]

Compelling pressures, these, but the seal business was not yet finished! The United States' involvement in the International Fur Seal Treaty requires fulfilling international obligations. Furthermore, management was not at all convinced that cessation of harvests would protect the seal resource and restore former survival rates. In fact, this issue was under investigation at St. George. In 1972, the North Pacific Fur Seal convention established St. George as a seal research station and prohibited all seal killing. By this means scientists could compare the effects of harvests on one island and no harvests on the other.[9] There was an additional consideration for continuing harvests. Until the Aleuts achieved economic self-sufficiency, the government was legally responsible for their welfare. Since resettlement was no longer a realistic option and since the Aleuts remained economically dependent on the seal industry, the government hesitated to cut off this dominant source of livelihood. Nonetheless, recognizing the bleak prospect for the industry, management forged full speed ahead in promoting Aleuts' self-sufficiency.

The 1966 Fur Seal Act paved the way for this transition. It called for transferring land and property to the Aleuts as soon as they become a viable community. Viability was defined in terms of municipal incorporation under Alaska law. Actually, three types of municipal organization were available to the Aleuts. One was the traditional village council, the community club, which still operated in St. George. The second was tribal incorporation under the Indian Reorganization Act. Tribal governments lacked taxing powers but they were eligible for federal credit and loans, could operate profit-making businesses, and could sue (and be sued). St. Paul organized a tribal government in 1950 and gained considerable experience in managing local enterprises—the canteen, store, hotel, tavern, gas station, and repair shop. In addition, the tribal government assumed partial responsibility for several municipal services, including police and fire protection. It was the St. Paul tribal government that filed a suit against the federal government in 1950 charging seventy-six years of servitude. To participate in the suit, St. George joined St. Paul's tribal government in 1970. The third type of municipal organization, that intended by the Fur Seal Act, was incorporation under Alaska statutes. This form provided taxing privileges and eligibility for state revenue-sharing funds, but prohibited profit-making ventures. Encouraged by their tribal government experience and frustrated by the limitations that inhere in that form of organization, St. Paul in 1971 applied for a municipal charter and a year later became a second-class Alaska city.[10]

The seven-member city council, headed by a mayor, assumed responsibility for the municipal services formerly provided by the tribal government, plus several others—garbage collection and maintenance of roads, street lights, water system, recreation hall, and a mini-television station. The city and tribal governments co-existed, each with separate funding sources and functions, the one to provide services and the other to operate local businesses. The St. George people hesitated to incorporate under Alaska law; the advantage would be taxing powers, but there was nothing to tax there save store purchases, and the people opposed that idea.

While St. Paul was in the process of forming a municipality, the National Marine Fisheries Service and the Aleuts deliberated the transfer of land and properties under the Fur Seal Act. But nothing concrete had been accomplished by 1971 when the passage of the Alaska Native Claims Settlement Act cast a different light on land rights and conveyance.

The Native Claims Settlement Act was landmark legislation in the United States, reflecting the federal government's unique relationship to the native people and aboriginal lands in Alaska. Unlike its relationship to Indians in the continental United States, the federal government never made treaties with the Alaska natives. It simply declared most of the land in Alaska federal property. The natives' only recourse to gaining recognition of their land rights lay in filing land claims suits with the Indian Claims Commission. The Tlingit and Haida Indians of southeastern Alaska successfully pursued this course. But the Commission could compensate Indians only in money, not land; and the Alaska natives wanted land, which would require an Act of Congress.;

Interest in settling the Alaska land question intensified after statehood and especially after the discovery of vast oil reserves on Alaska's north slope in 1968; for no oil could be transferred across disputed lands. With this impetus, Congress enacted the Alaska Native Claims Settlement Act.

A very convoluted piece of legislation it was, but these are the central features: The Act gave the natives 40 million acres of land and nearly one billion dollars—$462.5 million from the Treasury to be distributed over an eleven-year period and $500 million from a 2 percent royalty on mineral development in the state. The act required the twelve native regional organizations in the state, each representing a geographic area roughly corresponding to cultural areas, to form profit corporations, and the villages to do likewise. The act also allowed for the organization of regional and village nonprofit associations. The regional corporations were to select 16 million acres of land; and the village corporations, the rest. The cash was to be distributed first to the regional corporations which, in turn, were to allot at least half to the village corporations and a small proportion to individual shareholders. Regional corporation income from investments was to be distributed by the same rules as the cash compensation.[11]

The new legislation assured the Pribilovians far more land than would have been available under the Fur Seal Act; consequently, Aleuts abandoned negotiations on that score and focused on land selections under the new law. At first, management and the Aleuts deliberated informally on land and property conveyance. Then in 1977 they formed a Joint Management Board comprised of three members each from the two village corporations—Tanaq in St. George and Tanadgusix in St. Paul—and one from the National Marine Fisheries Service.[12] Essentially, the federal government claimed only those lands and properties necessary to conduct the seal business and meet international obligations. In these retentions, management worked out joint-use agreements with the Aleuts.[13] The village corporations selected nearly all the remaining land, 95 percent of the land in St. Paul and 97 percent in St. George,[14] all of which selections were approved in 1976. At the same time, the National Marine Fisheries Service and the Aleuts negotiated conveyance of title to the Aleuts' houses and other properties and facilities on the islands. Management agreed to bring the houses and facilities up to certain structural standards and the St. Paul airport up to Federal Aviation Agency standards before the transfer; however, budget reductions prevented fulfillment of some of these promises. The conveyance of property is not yet complete, bogged down primarily by repeated administrative delays, but settlement is expected any day. Think of that—for the first time since the purchase of Alaska, the Pribilof Aleuts are to own their land, houses, and other island properties and facilities!

The major hitch in the transition to Pribilof self-sufficiency is economic. The Aleuts' acquisition of land and property, although a milestone, failed to generate a viable economy. Aleuts presently consider unemployment and underemployment their most clamant problem. The National Marine Fisheries Service still remains the major employment source, but in 1978 it provided only thirty-six full-time permanent jobs on the two islands; nearly four times that number worked at part-time and temporary jobs,[15] and this doesn't include those who would have been in the labor force had jobs been available. Furthermore, with its eye on pulling out of the seal business, management now plans to accelerate the reduction in force. Other employment sources on the islands—the schools, village corporations, city and tribal councils hire an insignificant number of permanent workers—a total of thirty-two in 1978,[16] and these sources cannot be expected to significantly increase their work force.

Now that Pribilof employees occupy civil service status and hold some responsible positions, permanent workers earn a relatively adequate wage, an average of $17,403 in 1975. But the wages of temporary and part-time workers are grossly insufficient, averaging only $4,620 in that year.[17] Some of the underemployed pick up additional temporary work from other local sources and a few engage in off-island employment, but most derive the major portion of their income from National Marine Fisheries Service employment.

Clearly, the seal industry can no longer provide a stable economy in the Pribilofs, and future prospects, especially with pressure from the conservation lobby to halt all sealing, look grim. All parties concerned with the maritime Pribilofs, including the Aleuts, are keenly aware that the fishing industry offers the only viable economic alternative. But the Pribilofs lack a boat harbor, which the Aleuts consider necessary for the scale of operations and the shore-based fish-processing facility that they envisage. In the absence of a harbor, the only alternative for a local fishing industry would entail use of extremely large vessels, large enough to withstand the rough Bering Sea waters and anchor near St. Paul. The Pribilovians not only lack funds for such a purchase but strongly oppose the idea. Fish-processing facilities on a vessel that large would require a labor force far in excess of that locally available; it would entail use of a considerable number of imported workers.

Pribilovians agonize over the possibility of such a development. Over the past decade, they have watched the far-reaching disruption caused by such a development in Dutch Harbor-Unalaska, now a major fishing port, where imported workers outnumber the Aleut community by ten or twenty to one during the height of fishing season. "We don't want the Dutch Harbor syndrome here," proclaimed an Aleut leader.[18] Consequently, the Pribilovians devote their energies to promoting the construction of a boat harbor which would allow smaller-scale fishery operations that the community could manage and control. Indeed, gradual, controlled fisheries development is the village corporations' development goal.

As a first step, at the Aleuts' urging, Senator Bartlett introduced a bill in 1967 to fund a feasibility study for a St. Paul boat harbor. The bill passed; the Corps of Engineers undertook the study, but funds were insufficient for its completion. And that is where matters stood for over a decade until in 1978 Congress appropriated additional funds to complete the study. This decade of delay only to accomplish a feasibility study disheartened the Aleuts. More discouraging was the Corps' cost estimate for constructing the harbor, between 15 million and 20 million dollars.[19] Where would the Aleuts find such a sum?

The state is one possibility, but preliminary discussions indicate that at best the state would fund only a small part of the costs. The Aleuts' resources are far too limited to underwrite the costs. The city and corporation income is in the thousands, not the millions, and furthermore, investing in the harbor would deplete their funds, leaving nothing for fisheries and fisheries-related development. The tribal government is the most affluent local organization due to its receipt of over 8 million dollars in damages from its suit against the government. Filed in 1950, the suit wasn't settled until 1978. Finding in favor of the Aleuts, the Indian Claims Commission awarded 11.2

million dollars damages. However, at the threat of a Justice Department appeal, the Aleuts settled for 8.5 million dollars. But only about 20 percent of the settlement money is available for community development; the remainder will be distributed to individuals, primarily because a substantial portion of persons who lived on the islands during the years for which damages were paid have moved elsewhere. If most of the funds were used for local projects, these persons would be denied compensation.[20] In any event, even diverting a portion of these funds to the boat harbor would leave the major costs still uncovered, which means federal government involvement is necessary.

Aleut leaders express concern that even if funding is procured, the completion of the project is still years away. They estimate that the necessary impact studies and federal legislative and appropriation process will take at least five years, and the engineer's estimate eight years for the actual construction.[21] In the meantime, corporation leaders search for interim development plans geared to their philosophy of gradual, controlled fisheries development.

Investment planning by the village corporations must take into account not only contemporary economic needs on the islands but also the profit potential. Without profits, the corporations face the danger of losing their lands when they become taxable in 1991. This apprehension creates tension in investment planning, for investments on the islands are very risky. Tanadgusix focuses on projects both within and outside St. Paul. Locally, it operates the seal byproducts plant and an apartment complex, both of which produce profit on a small scale. But its main local investment, the tourist trade, which involves operating a hotel and restaurant, has yet to show a profit, even though the size of the tourist trade continues to grow. At the same time, the corporation is exploring the possibility of investing in a marine service base at Chernofsky on Unalaska Island, but this venture, if it proves successful, will not significantly affect the economy in St. Paul. Tanaq Corporation has even fewer options for local investment. Without a seal harvest, there is no byproducts plant. And without a tourist trade to speak of, the hotel and restaurant are not promising sources of profit. Tanaq did purchase an airplane which provides both a much-needed service and profit, as the corporation leases the plane to a commercial airlines for part of the year. Tanaq also undertook an ill-fated purchase of a 50-foot salmon fishing vessel, but it proved inadquate for the Bering Sea and is now for sale.

The regional corporation's investments affect the Pribilof economy only peripherally. The region purchased the National Marine Fisheries Service freight vessel and now handles all freight to the islands, as well as a large fishing vessel with processing capacity. Currently, it is involved in negotiations with the Economic Development Administration for loans for fisheries development. But none of these efforts produce solutions to the basic economic problem of the islands—the seal industry no longer provides an adequate economic base, and there is no other industry there.

The economic future of the Pribilofs, indeed, is up in the air, figuratively speaking; literally, it is in the sea. And fisheries development itself may create more problems than it solves should the "Dutch Harbor syndrome" occur. Controlled fisheries development at the least will involve a boat harbor that can accommodate small-scale fishing enterprises, and funds for the harbor are uncertain.

Meanwhile, a different kind of economic frustration plagues St. George. The moratorium on sealing deprived the Aleuts access to seal meat, important not only from economic necessity in these slack times, but as a valuable cultural symbol. The issue of St. George Aleuts' subsistence rights was not clearcut. Eager to protect the purity of its research experiment, the National Marine Fisheries Service sought to avert the Aleuts' demand to engage in subsistence sealing on St. George. At the same time, the Marine Mammal Protection Act of 1972[22] assured aborigines subsistence rights, providing they used aboriginal hunting methods. However, unlike the hunting of other marine mammals, seal hunting was a land-based operation; consequently, it wasn't clear that it was protected in this legislation. To further complicate the picture, the federal government was still legally responsible for the Aleuts' welfare; most of those on St. George were poor and seal meat was their main staple. Management initially resolved these disparate considerations by delivering seal meat captured at St. Paul to St. George.

The St. George Aleuts found this scheme wholly unacceptable.

> I was on the ship . . . when the seal meat was loaded on board. The meat wasn't even covered and therefore exposed to air, sun, and houseflies. The rotting meat was then loaded onto the ship by the same kind of filthy nets used on shore . . . placed on the deck of the ship. Dog food is given more consideration. . . .
>
> The food was exposed for over eight hours before reaching its destination . . . rotten, dried up, dirty, and fly ridden.[23]

The St. George people insisted on their subsistence rights. Management reluctantly submitted, providing they limit their catch to 200 animals and follow the letter of the law regarding the use of aboriginal methods, which meant canoes propelled by oars or sails and the use of handthrown spears.[24] Aleuts probably never used these methods in seal hunting; if they had, their memory of it is long dead. Under these conditions the subsistence seal hunt was doomed not only to fail but to humiliate the Aleuts. Even a high-level manager seemed embarrassed by this idle exercise.

> One male seal was killed and retrieved.

> Reportedly other seals were struck by spears and wounded but were not retrieved. From the description, some of these seals may have died from their wounds.
>
> If the purpose was to demonstrate the inefficiency of such a method of food-getting, then the point was well made. On the other hand, if this hunt was considered in any sense to have been an enactment of an ancestral technique, then it was a farce. It is improbable that aboriginal Aleuts would have used unwieldy *bidars* for hunting craft, or would have access to the high concentration of fearless seals as afforded by the rookery. Also it seems unlikely that they would have used spears such as those employed.[25]

Red-faced, management quickly abandoned this plan and again proposed delivering seals captured at St. Paul to St. George. The St. George Aleuts counterproposed sending their own men to St. Paul to kill food seals, but this proposal created another obstacle, for it involved additional expenditures. Cost conscious as never before due to severe budget reductions, the St. George manager responded to this proposal with an indirect threat that the Aleuts would have to underwrite the costs:

> We do have an agreement with you and if you prefer to send your own crews over we have to support it. There's only one thing, of course, there is a little expense involved with it which means those kind of expenses gotta come from somewhere . . . and that means a little less work for some of the part-time people here and on St. Paul.[26]

Little enough work was available as it was; the Aleuts rejected any further cutbacks and reasserted their subsistence rights under the Marine Mammal Protection Act. Again management acquiesced, although first it sought and won permission from the North Pacific Fur Seal Convention for land-based seal hunting at St. George. Currently, St. George Aleuts collect their seals at home, to a limit of 200 animals, and use harvesting methods to which they are accustomed. How astonished would have been the great grandparents of these contemporary Aleuts to witness their power in the negotiations with management and management's responsiveness to their demands.

We have in this period of transition to Aleut independence focused on modernization in the Pribilofs, involving such matters as city government and investment capital. What was happening to the Aleuts' culture in the process? Curiously, modernization was accompanied by a cultural revitalization movement. Perhaps it's not curious at all, for with independence came the power to shape their lives. Aleuts had never lost interest in protecting and promoting their culture; they were simply helpless in the face of cultural suppressions imposed by the federal government. The St. George Aleuts' insistence on subsistence sealing is one manifestation of their determination to perpetuate their culture. Sealing represents more than a means of securing food; it is a way of life and a source of raw materials for the production of clothes and artifacts. And there were other manifestations. One was the Aleuts' interest in reconstructing their history. Tanadgusix published a history entitled, Slaves of the Harvest.[27] Several Aleuts are themselves collecting historical data. For example, a St. Paul man recently visited Funter Bay to gather data on the evacuation; another is preparing classroom materials from historical records on the island. After years of suppression of their language, they now seek to reinvigorate it through bilingual programs in the schools and parents' efforts in the home. And they remain devotedly committed to the Russian Orthodox Church, which they view as a powerful cultural symbol. These, then, are the visible ingredients of contemporary Pribilof culture—history, hunting, food, religion, language, and artifacts.

Indeed, this is the way St. Paul school children perceive their culture, revealed in themes the teacher assigned to seventh and eighth graders in 1972 entitled, "What is an Aleut?" Here are two examples.

> He (an Aleut) is like a person and is a Native of the Alaska chain. We have traditions—the ladies go to the recreation hall and have arts and crafts. They make fur hats, parkas, shoes, and mittens, and the same costumes. We go to church, church school, and learn about the church. . . . We have our own community, and our family life is pretty good too. And we're hunters. We go out and hunt sea lions, birds, when the hunting season opens up and in the summer (we) go out sealing and get food for our family and get the skins baked and throw them in big tanks to be salted and then we blubber and pack them and send them out. In the summer we go on vacations. We go to St. George and visit for about a week or . . . until the boat comes back.

* * *

> I am Aleut. We are out in the middle of the Bering Sea and we love it. We love the cool winds and the warm sun. Sometimes we go reindeer, seal lion, fox trapping, and duck hunting. Sometimes we go swimming when the water gets warm. One time it was so hot that you could take off your jacket. Even in the winter it gets warm but we never take off our jackets because it would be kind of chilly.

Yes, these Aleut students appear to value their environment and way of life. We found the same attitude among the adults. And this explains why they have maintained many elements of their culture despite decades of suppression by the federal government and why they have refused to move from the islands despite a bleak economic outlook and powerful pressures to do so by the government.

I found the Pribilof Aleuts quite prideful and self-respecting. Standing erect, shoulders square, they speak with dignity and respect about their lives and struggles and those of their fellows. This degree of dignity, pride, and self-respect probably stems from the Pribilof Aleuts' tendency not to blame themselves for their misery. Rather, they direct the finger of blame at an external source, the United States Government. In other native communities in Alaska and elsewhere, the process of deculturation and oppression has been far more insidious, the forces responsible for deprivation more difficult to identify. And as a result, many of these other native groups tend to assail themselves for their condition, becoming demoralized in the process. This is not to suggest that the direct, readily identifiable form of oppression in the Pribilofs is good for people; it always takes a heavy toll. But it is to underscore the importance that oppressed people anywhere resist the tendency to join their oppressors in blaming themselves.

Endnotes

1. "Employment-Administration of Pribilof Islands—July 1970." Prepared by Bert Johnson, September 17, 1970, Pribilof Islands Program, National Marine Fisheries Service Records, Seattle.
2. Don C. Foote, Victor Fischer, and George Rogers, St. Paul Community Study: An Economic and Social Analysis of St. Paul, Pribilof Islands, Alaska (Fairbanks: University of Alaska, Institute of Social, Economic and Government Research, 1968), p. 22; "Pribilof Islands Report: Meeting with the State of Alaska," June 4, 1975, p. 10, National Marine Fisheries Service Records, Seattle; Annual Report of the Pribilof Islands Management Program, Pribilof Islands, Alaska, 1975, p. 1, 1976, p. 1, National Marine Fisheries Service Records, Seattle; Walter Kirkness, Program Director, Pribilof Islands Program, to Dorothy Jones, July 31, 1979.
3. Federal Register, 38, no. 47, August 1, 1973, p. 20599.
4. "Pribilof Islands Report: Meeting with the State of Alaska," June 4, 1975, p. 10, National Marine Fisheries Service Records, Seattle; Walter Kirkness to Dorothy Jones, July 31, 1979.
5. Director, National Marine Fisheries Service, to Assistant Administrator for Marine Resources, March 1, 1973; "NMFS Task Development Plan: Pribilof Islands Operations—Administration of St. Paul," October 19, 1977, p. 4, National Marine Fisheries Service Records, Seattle.
6. U.S. Congress, Senate, Hearings Before the Subcommittee on Oceans and Atmosphere of the Committee on Commerce; Ocean Mammal Protection, 2 parts, 92nd Congress, 2nd sess., 1973, Part I, p. 750.
7. The Seattle Times, Sunday, June 17, 1979, p. D-4.
8. Tundra Times, June 27, 1979, p. 1.
9. "Press Release," Office of Secretary of Commerce, March 28, 1973, National Marine Fisheries Service Records, Seattle.
10. St.Paul incorporated as a fourth-class city in 1971. A year later the State Legislature eliminated that class, and all fourth-class cities automatically became second-class.
11. For an excellent discussion of the features of the act, see Gerald A. McBeath and Thomas A. Morehouse, Alaska Native Self-Government (Anchorage: University of Alaska, Institute of Social and Economic Research, 1978), pp. 86-109. Also to be published as The Dynamics of Alaska Native Self-Government (Lanham, Maryland: University Press of America, 1980).
12. The joint Management Board's first formalized agreements were the following:

a. Joint use by the Parties of roads, docks, scoria pits, sanitary land fills and other areas on the islands appropriate to joint management.

b. Recreational, subsistence, official, and other uses, by the Parties of land on the Islands not owned by the Party desiring the use thereof.

c. Provision for tourists, research personnel, official guests, and other visitors to the Islands.

d. Protection of the fur seal herds and the fur seal research program from undue interference.

e. Such other items of mutual concern to the Parties as may properly come before the board.

"Cooperative Agreement between the Native People of St. Paul Island and St. George Island, Alaska and United States Department of Commerce, National Oceanic and Atmospheric Administration, National Marine Fisheries Service, to Establish the Pribilof Islands Joint Management Board," December 22, 1976, National Marine Fisheries Service Records, Seattle.

13. "Meeting with Tanadgusix Corporation, Tanaq Corporation, the Aleut Corporation and Aleutian Planning Commission regarding the Alaska Native Claims Settlement Act," February 21, 22, 1974, National Marine Fisheries Service Records, Seattle.

14. The village corporations also selected lands on the Aleutian Islands of Umnak and Unalaska.

15. "Permanent Employees, St. Paul Island, Alaska, 1978"; "Temporary Employees, St. Paul Island, Alaska, 1978"; "Permanent Employees, St. George Island, Alaska, 1978"; "Temporary Employees, St. George Island, Alaska, 1978." Tanadgusix Corporation Files, St. Paul; Tanaq Corporation Files, St. George.

16. Ibid.: Field Notes.

17. "Pribilof Islands Report: Meeting with the State of Alaska," June 4, 1975, p. 16, National Marine Fisheries Service Records, Seattle.

18. Larry Merculieff, Tanadgusix Corporation, personal communication, July 27, 1979.

19. Ibid.

20. Ibid., Agafon Krukoff, Aleut Corporation, Personal Communication, July 26, 1979; Mike Lekanoff, Aleutian-Pribilof Islands Association, Personal Communication, July 15, 1979, August 6, 1980.

21. Larry Merculieff, Personal Communication, July 27, 1979.

22. 86 Stat. 1027. Public Law 92-522 (October 21, 1972).

23. Tundra Times, August 8, 1973, p. 1.

24. "For the Record," Resource Management Specialist, October 2, 1975, National Marine Fisheries Service Records, Seattle.

25. Ibid.
26. "Meeting of NMFS Program Director and St. George Community about Subsistence Sealing" (transcript of tape recording of meeting), June 8, 1978.
27. Barbara Boyle Torrey, Slaves of the Harvest: The Story of the Pribilof Aleuts (St. Paul Island: Tanadgusix Corporation, 1978).

CHAPTER 10

IN SUM, WHAT HAPPENED ON THE PRIBILOFS?

Understanding why and how a situation of hidden, internal colonialism developed in the democratic United States rests on identifying the forces associated with its emergence, its persistence despite sweeping reforms in the rest of the country, and its disintegration.

Pribilof colonialism reflected, in part, national colonialist attitudes towards Alaska. All the ingredients for colonial rule existed in the territory—the presence of actual and potentially valuable commercial resources; the absence of local capital, certain necessary technology, and access to markets; and a small, unorganized labor force. Control of the territory became centralized in government agency-Congressional committee-private corporate alliances built on their mutual self-interests. The Pribilof program not only mirrored this colonialist stance but assumed a much harsher form because of the remoteness of the islands and because the Pribilof people are a racial and cultural minority. In that era the general public considered Indians wholly uncivilized, as wards of the government not eligible for political, civil, and human rights.

In this atmosphere, designers of the Pribilof program focused on economic gain, not only for private industry but for the government as well. Why the emphasis on profits to government? Because officials were uncertain about the wisdom of the Alaska purchase and apprehensive that it would, as opponents of the purchase had predicted, drain the Treasury. Remember, at that time seal skins were the only viable commercial product in the territory; if the federal government failed to realize revenues from them, indeed, the costs of administering the new territory might well have taxed the treasury. Accompanying this motivation was the real opportunity to achieve a profit. Given the easy availability of the entire seal herd, profits from the industry, whether realized by private companies or the government, hinged on protection of the resource. Such protection was clearly the business of the federal government. And government involvement in the program provided Congress with justification to enact legislation not only to protect the herd, but, since seal management cost money, to also extract a certain share of the profits. Legislators perceived this opportunity as a means to underwrite both the costs of the seal management program and other administrative costs in the territory. The government's major mission in the Pribilofs, then, was profits and conservation of the resource that produced them.

The Pribilof program encountered periodic and often uneasy tensions between these two main goals. When the herd was in good condition, management concentrated on maximum revenues from the industry. When it wasn't, then, as a public interest institution, management focused on conservation, even if it meant a sizable revenue loss. In favorable years in the industry, Congress expected the program not only to pay for itself but to create a surplus. In lean years, Congress expected the program to cut costs to the bone. These Congressional pressures generated a marketplace standard of profitability that became deeply ingrained in the structure of the program and gave rise to attitudes and norms markedly different from those in most other federal programs, especially in the social welfare field.

The presence of a skilled labor force, of course, facilitated the government's economic goals. However, just as tension at times arose between seal conservation and profits, so it did in the government's dual role as protector of the Aleut people and as entrepreneur in a labor-management relationship. As public protector, in recognition of the Pribilof Aleuts' dependent status and in line with federal policy towards other American Indian groups, the government assumed responsibility for the Aleuts' welfare. In terms of bread and butter issues, this protector role was congruent with the entrepreneurial one in the first lease period when the industry produced a handsome profit for both the government and the private company. Thereafter, the two roles increasingly clashed as management perceived economic advantage from keeping Aleuts in a subjugated status. These tensions, between protecting seals, making profits, and looking after the Aleuts' welfare were the fount that gave heart and structure to the Pribilof program.

Wearing its entrepreneurial hat, the government sought unlimited control over the Aleuts' economic behavior. To discourage defiance and resistance and to enforce compliance, managers dominated the Aleuts' political and juridical institutions; they controlled the Aleuts' use of money and manipulated their work classifications. These actions were not strikingly out of line with certain national norms. It was a time of intense exploitation of labor in the interests of capitalist development, exploitation that was commonly accepted. Workers' rights, let alone Indians' economic rights, had gained scant public recognition. However, management advanced its domination to unconventional limits by coercing the Aleuts to work part of the year for no pay. In the post-Civil War period, such slave labor practices hardly would have won public support. Thus, national norms influenced management practices only in part. The isolation of the islands and management's insulation from interest groups that might expose and protest such actions also shaped management practices. Managers wanted unlimited control, the opportunity existed, and they took it.

The periods of tension between economic imperatives and the Aleuts' welfare gave birth to other forms of oppression. During the second private lease when the seal population precipitously declined and the government suffered a revenue loss, management introduced wage payments in kind rather than cash. A response to an economic depression, yes?, apparently conceived as an emergency measure. Yet, this practice became stubbornly entrenched into the fabric of the program, undoubtedly because managers discovered unanticipated benefits. Initially, they introduced in kind payments to reduce labor costs. When paid in cash, Aleuts could and did use some of it for purchases by mail or at Unalaska. Payments in kind eliminated this practice. Furthermore, in kind payments enabled managers to effectively decrease wages by reducing the quantity and quality of supplies. The practice also provided a flexible device for manipulating wages in response to economic ups and downs without an outright reduction in the Aleuts' wage rate. Managers found this practice increasingly appealing after the 1910 Fur Seal Act which stipulated fair compensation for Aleuts' labor and after the 1911 International Fur Seal Treaty under which the program was expected to provide a sufficient surplus to meet international obligations.

Another more implicit motivation appears to have increased the attraction of in kind wages. Top managers were certainly aware of the consequences of in kind payments to Aleuts' pride and morale. Lembkey, among other agents, repeatedly pointed to its demoralizing effects. That top managers instituted this practice during an economically depressed period is one thing. That they perpetrated it after the seal herd was restored and the treasury was again receiving substantial revenues is another matter, strongly suggesting that this practice produced other benefits for management. Since they knew of its demoralizing effects and since the original economic motivation for instituting in kind payments no longer applied, it seems logical to conclude that managers wanted this outcome, that at some level of awareness they considered it useful to render Aleuts sufficiently abject to submit to the oppressive conditions imposed.

The establishment of in kind wages presaged a profound change in the Aleuts' economic status—first from wage earners to wards, then to colonial subjects as the system became entrenched. The labor-management system on the islands assumed all the earmarks of a typical colonial relationship. The federal government controlled the natural resources, paid the Aleuts increasingly low wages in relation to other comparable United States workers, undermined them psychologically, and dominated their political life to assure control of their labor.

By the time of the reforms in the 1920s and 1930s, this colonial system had developed a life of its own, one which made it self-generating, resistant to changes in national mood and attitudes, even in national laws. Wages and hours legislation, collective bargaining rights, the Social Security Act, welfare reform, and an enlightened Indian policy failed to dent the system. While the situation of other workers dramatically improved, that of the Pribilof Aleuts deteriorated.

Most social organizations begin as entities designed to fulfill certain functions and goals. To survive they must take into account and adapt to the demands of the interest groups that surround them. But the Pribilof system was uniquely isolated and insulated from such demands. Its functions were highly specialized and did not attract general interest. Its operation took place in a remote part of the country, unseen by others. Management maintained a policy of secrecy about the program and required special permits for all visits. Through staff selection policies, centralized control, and attractive rewards in status and prestige, top management succeeded in neutralizing middle and lower-level managers. And the Russian Orthodox Church, the only outside organization with knowledge about conditions on the islands, remained silent in its avoidance of secular involvements. All of these factors protected management from having to respond to interest-group pressures and from having to update its practices to conform to changes in national laws and attitudes.

That was the situation at the time of the World War II evacuation of the Pribilof Aleuts, a time when management, in its most execrable acts to date, exposed the Aleuts to subhuman conditions in camps. In an incredible denial of the evidence of their senses, managers believed that they were as immune from public scrutiny and criticism in a populated area immersed in the war effort as they had been on the isolated Pribilof Islands, and tried to keep the Aleuts virtually imprisoned in the camps. Believing that other institutions would support their peculiar relationship with the Aleuts, managers asked the draft board to exempt Aleuts from military service; when that failed, they tried to prevent the Aleuts from taking jobs outside the camps; when that failed, they importuned the United States Employment Service to place the Aleuts in groups isolated from other workers and to pay their wages in a lump sum to the federal agents; when that failed, managers kept tabs on the Aleuts who left the camps and threatened them with permanent loss of Pribilof residency rights if they hesitated to return to the islands when management commanded.

With these pressures, the Aleut sealers returned to the islands for the 1943 sealing season despite the presence of the Japanese in the Aleutians, and nearly all the Aleuts returned for good in 1944. Once back on the islands, still with its head in the sand, management assumed that it could restore the former colonial relationship.

But the tide had ineluctibly turned. Visitors to the evacuation camps threatened to expose the anachronistic Pribilof management system. Fredericka Martin, who during her stay on the islands in 1941 made a pervasive commitment to reform the Pribilof system, wrote articles decrying conditions on the islands and sought and won support from an ever-growing number of sympathizers. The Indian Rights movement took up the banner of the

Aleuts' cause and attracted the interest of prominent attorneys, including Felix Cohen, the foremost authority on Indian law in the nation. And the Aleuts themselves, emboldened by their experiences and contacts in Juneau during the evacuation, resolved to emancipate themselves from federal government control. These forces combined to shake Pribilof management from its lethargy, to awaken it to the reality of a new interest group environment. At first, managers resisted change, attempting to discredit the Aleut activists and their supporters. But reform pressure mounted until they were forced to adapt to some of the demands. They introduced a wage reform in 1950 and a more meaningful one in 1962 that gave Aleuts nearly equal status to that of other federal workers.

At the same time, other developments influenced the federal government to fundamentally alter its Pribilof mission. Although the same economic imperatives operated as in the past, they now dictated a change in course, from tenaciously holding on to the Pribilof enterprise to getting out of the business as quickly as possible. The Pribilof program now threatened to burden rather than relieve the federal treasury. The Statehood Act of 1958 accorded Alaska 70 percent of the net proceeds from the seal industry, which meant a powerful reduction in treasury revenues. Furthermore, the federal government could no longer anticipate the same level of productivity in seals due to an unexplained and persisting decline in the seal survival rate. And labor costs threatened to continually rise not only because of economic reforms but because the Aleut population continued to grow. From the 1950s on, the labor supply exceeded the demand, and management believed itself responsible for supporting the entire population.

Management proposed converting to a seasonal sealing operation and abandoning the islands for the rest of the year. This plan involved relocating Aleuts to other places, but when most of the Aleuts refused to be relocated, the abandonment idea was discarded. It was replaced by a plan to transfer responsibilities for island management, excluding the seals, to the Aleut people. Beginning in 1960, management policy emphasized emancipating the Aleuts in order to equip them for management responsibilities. Aleut independence, Aleut training, Aleut political autonomy—these became the policy motifs of the 1960s and 1970s. What the reformers left undone, management completed in response to the unfavorable economic outlook in the seal industry.

But Aleut emancipation and federal government withdrawal from island management introduced a new set of problems. Before the 1962 pay plan reform, the government provided full-time permanent jobs for virtually every able-bodied Pribilof man. After that it provided such employment only for those workers actually needed, an ever-shrinking number over the years, now representing a small proportion of the labor force. Unemployment and underemployment now assail the Aleuts; it constitutes their major contemporary problem.

As the Pribilof economy is based on a single industry, and that industry absorbs only a small part of the labor force on a fulll-time basis, most people concerned with the plight of the Aleuts call for the establishment of an alternative fishing industry. But that offers no easy resolution. The costs of developing other fisheries on the Pribilofs would far exceed anything that the Aleuts could underwrite or that the government currently supports. True, the Alaska Native Claims Settlement Act of 1971 provides some funds, and the Pribilof Aleuts' receipt of 8.5 million dollars in damages from their suit against the federal government provides additional resources. But all their funds combined are insufficient to build even a boat harbor at St. Paul, let alone purchase boats and processing facilities.

To compound their economic problem, even the Aleuts' meager income from the seal industry is now threatened by humane societies demanding an end to all seal killing on the Pribilofs and the United States' withdrawal from the International Fur Seal Treaty. If the latter transpires, pelagic sealing will undoubtedly resume and the entire fur seal herd may well face extinction.

This 110-year history of the Pribilof Islands has depicted the evolution of a colonialist system sponsored and promoted by the federal government, the persistence of that system when it frightfully violated national norms and laws, and the destruction of the system when individuals and groups exerted pressure for change and when the unfavorable condition of the seal industry convinced management that it was in its economic interest to emancipate the Aleuts. I wish the story could end there, with all problems solved and the Aleuts living happily thereafter. Instead, we conclude with a note of deep concern for the Aleuts' economic future and a plea to the government who profited from the Aleuts' labor for a century to help them establish a viable economic alternative.

BIBLIOGRAPHY

All federal government records cited from St. Paul Island were hand-copied.

Baran, Paul A. The Political Economy of Growth. New York: Monthly Review Press, 1957.

Barth, Tom F.W. Geology and Petrology of the Pribilof Islands, Alaska. Geological Survey Bulletin 1028-F. Washington, D.C.: Government Printing Office, 1956.

Blum, Jerome. Lord and Peasant in Russia from the Ninth to the Nineteenth Century. Princeton: Princeton University Press, 1961.

Bryan, Alan L. "An Archeological Reconnaisance of the Pribilof Islands." Anchorage: Alaska Department of National Resources, Division of Parks, n.d.

Bryant, Charles. "On the Fur Seal Islands." The Century Illustrated Monthly Magazine (November 1889 to April 1890, Inclusive): 902-905.

Cohen, Felix S.; Ickes, Harold L.; Margold, Nathan R.; Handbook of Federal Indian Law. Washington, D.C.: Government Printing Office, 1942. Third printing.

Colyer, Vincent. Report of the Honorable Vincent Colyer, United States Special Indian Commissioner, on Indian Tribes and Their Surroundings in Alaska Territory, from Personal Observation and Inspection, 1869. H. Exec. Doc. No. 1414, 41st Cong., 2nd sess., 1869.

Daniels, Roger. The Decision to Relocate the Japanese Americans. Philadelphia: J.B. Lippincott, 1975.

Economic and Social Conditions on the Pribilof Islands. Report by Special Commission appointed by the Governor of Alaska. Juneau, 1965.

Elliott, Henry W. The Seal Islands of Alaska. Section IX, Monograph A. Tenth Census of the United States. Washington, D.C.: Government Printing Office, 1881.

Fedorova, Svetlana G. The Russian Population in Alaska and California, Late Eighteenth Century-1867. Kingston, Ontario: Limestone Press, 1973.

Foote, Don C.; Fischer, Victor; and Rogers, George W. St. Paul Community Study: An Economic and Social Analysis of St. Paul, Pribilof Islands, Alaska. Fairbanks: University of Alaska, Institute of Social, Economic and Government Research, 1968.

Gruening, Ernest. The State of Alaska. New York: Random House, 1954.

Gsovski, Vladimir. Russian Administration of Alaska and the Status of Alaska Natives. Washington, D.C.: Government Printing Office, 1950. Also issued as S. Doc. No. 152, 81st Cong., 2nd sess., 1950.

Haas, Theodore. "The Legal Aspects of Indian Affairs from 1887-1957." The Annals of the American Academy of Political and Social Science: American Indians and Indian Life (May 1957): 12-22.

Hrdlička, Aleš. The Aleutian and Commander Islands and Their Inhabitants. Philadelphia: Wistar Institute of Anatomy and Botany, 1945.

Jones, Dorothy. A History of United States Administration in the Pribilof Islands, 1867-1946. Prepared for the Indian Claims Commission. Docket Nos. 352 and 369. Fairbanks: University of Alaska, Institute of Social, Economic and Government Research, 1976.

Jones, Dorothy. Aleuts in Transition: A Comparison of Two Villages. Seattle: University of Washington Press, 1976.

Jones, Lester E. Report of Alaska Investigations in 1914. Washington, D.C.: Government Printing Office, 1915.

Jordan, David Starr; Stejneger, Leonard; Lucas, Frederick A.; Moser, Jefferson F.; Townsend, Charles H.; Clark, George A.; Murray, Joseph. The Fur Seals and Fur Seal Islands of the North Pacific Ocean. 4 parts. Washington, D.C.: Government Printing Office, 1898. Also issued as Treasury Department Doc. No. 2017, part 1. The History, Condition, and Needs of the Herd of Fur Seal Resorting on the Pribilof Islands, by David Starr Jordan and George Archibald.

Katz, Michael B. The Irony of Early School Reform: Educational Innovation in Mid-Nineteenth Century Massachusetts. Cambridge: Harvard University Press, 1968.

Kikuchi, Charles. The Kikuchi Diary. Urbana, Illinois: University of Illinois Press, 1973.

Lantis, Margaret. "The Aleut Social System from 1750 to 1810, from Early Historical Sources." In Ethnohistory in Southwestern Alaska and the Southern Yukon, pp. 139-272. Ed. Margaret Lantis. Lexington: University of Kentucky Press, 1970.

Lurie, Nancy O. "The World's Longest On-Going Protest Demonstration."

In Beliefs, Behaviors, and Alcohol Beverages: A Cross-Cultural Survey, pp. 127-144. Ed. Mac Marshall. Ann Arbor: The University of Michigan Press, 1979.

Martin, Fredericka. Martin's Records can be found in two places. One is the Fredericka Martin Collection, Rasmuson Library, University of Alaska, Fairbanks. The other is c/o Fredericka Martin, Casa 13 de las 14 Casas Cuauhtemoc 715, Cuernavaca, Morelos, Mexico.

Martin, Fredericka. "Recapitulation of Errors of Administration and Abuse and Exploitation of Pribilof American Aleuts by the United States Government, 1867 to 1946." Unpublished manuscript.

Martin, Fredericka. "Pribilof Sealers—Serfs of the North." Newsletter of the Institute of Ethnic Affairs, Inc. (May-June, 1948): 1-4.

Martin, Fredericka. "Three Years of Pribilof Progress." The American Indian (Spring 1950): 17-25.

Martin, Fredericka. "The Wind is No River." Unpublished manuscript.

McBeath, Gerald A.; and Morehouse, Thomas A. Alaska Native Self-Government. Anchorage: University of Alaska, Institute of Social and Economic Research, 1978. To be published as Dynamics of Alaska Native Self-Government. Lanham, Maryland: University Press of America, 1980.

Memmi, Albert, The Colonizer and The Colonized. Boston: Beacon Press, 1965.

"Mixed Fur Seal Records, Annual Reports, Pribilof Islands, 1786-1960." Record Group 22, item 420. Alaska Division. Federal Archives, Washington, D.C.

National Resource Committee, Regional Planning Part VII. Alaska, Its Resources and Development. No. 1. Report of the Alaska Resources Committee. Washington: D.C.: Government Printing Office, 1937.

"News Notes." Newsletter of the Institute of Ethnic Affairs, Inc. (March-April, 1949): 7.

Okun, Semen B. The Russian-American Company. Trans. by Carl Ginsburg. Boston: Harvard University Press, 1951.

Osgood, Wilfred H.; Preble, Edward A.; and Parker, George. The Fur Seal and Other Life of the Pribilof Islands, 1914. Bulletin of the Bureau of Fisheries, vol. xxxiv, 1914. Washington, D.C.: Government Printing Office, 1915. Also issued as Bureau of Fisheries Doc. No. 820, and S. Doc. No. 980, 63rd Cong., 3rd sess., 1915.

Pribilof Islands Daily Log. On microfilm, Rasmuson Library, University of Alaska, Fairbanks.

Rogers, George W. The Future of Alaska: Economic Consequences of Statehood. Baltimore: The Johns Hopkins Press, 1962.

Rogers, George. An Economic Analysis of the Pribilof Islands, 1870-1946. Prepared for the Indian Claims Commission. Docket Nos. 352 and 369. Fairbanks: University of Alaska, Institute of Social, Economic and Government Research, 1976.

Rosengren, William R. "The Careers of Clients and Organizations." In Organizations and Clients: Essays in the Sociology of Service, pp. 117-135. Ed. Mark Lifton. Columbus, Ohio: Charles E. Merrill, 1970.

Sarafian, William. Russian-American Company Employee Policies and Practices, 1799-1867. Ann Arbor: University Microfilms, 1970.

Shenitz, Helen A. "Pribilovians, the Forgotten People of Alaska." Paper presented at the Alaska Science Conference, Fairbanks, Alaska, August 3, 1965.

Shenitz, Helen. "Alaska's Good Father." In Alaska and its History, pp. 121-130. Ed. Morgan Sherwood. Seattle: University of Washington Press, 1967.

Sims, Edwin W. Report on Alaska Fur Seal Fisheries. H. Rpt. 251, 59th Cong., 2nd sess., 1906.

Spicer, Edward H.; Hansen, Asaek T.; Luomala, Katherine; Opler, Martin K. Impounded People, Japanese Americans in the Relocation Centers. Tucson: University of Arizona Press, 1969.

Tikhmenev, Petr A. Historical Review of the Formation of the Russian-American Company and Its Activities up to the Present Time. 2 parts. St. Petersburg: St. Petersburg Printing Office of Edward Weimar, 1861. Part I. Trans. Michael Dobrynin. Bancroft Library, University of California, Berkeley. Part II. Trans. Dmitri Krenov. Seattle: Public Works Administration, 1939-1940. Both parts recently issued as A History of the Russian-American Company. Trans. and ed. by Richard A. Pierce and Alton S. Donnelly. Seattle: University of Washington Press, 1978.

Tompkins, S.R. Alaska Promyshlennik and Sourdough. Norman: University of Oklahoma Press, 1945.

Torrey, Barbara. Slaves of the Harvest: The Story of the Pribilof Aleuts. St. Paul Island: Tanadgusix Corporation, 1978.

U.S. Department of Commerce and Labor, Bureau of Fisheries. The Fisheries of Alaska. For the years 1906-1910.

U.S. Department of Commerce and Labor. Appendix A to Hearings on House Resolution No. 73. 62nd Cong., 1st sess., 1911.

U.S. Department of Commerce and Labor. Hearing Before the Subcommittee on Appropriations. 67th Cong., 2nd sess., 1922.

U.S. Department of Commerce, Bureau of Fisheries. Alaska Fisheries and Fur Industries. For the years 1911-1919.

U.S. Department of Commerce, Bureau of Fisheries. Alaska Fishery and Fur-Seal Industries. For the years 1920-1939.

U.S. Department of Commerce. Hearing Before the Subcommittee of House Committee on Appropriations. 73rd Cong., 2nd sess., 1934.

U.S. Department of Commerce, Bureau of the Census. Statistical History of the United States from Colonial Times to the Present, 1965.

U.S. Department of Interior Fish and Wildlife Service. Alaska Fishery and Fur-Seal Industries. For the years 1940-1970.

U.S. Treasury Department, Special Agents Division. Seal and Salmon Fisheries and General Resources of Alaska. 4 vol. Washington, D.C.: Government Printing Office, 1898. Also issued as: U.S. Congress, H. Doc. No. 92, 55th Cong., 2nd sess., 1898. Also issued as U.S. Census Office, 10th Census, 1880, Vol. 8. Washington: D.C.: Government Printing Office, 1884.

U.S. Congress, House. The Alaska Commercial Company. H. Rpt. No. 623, 44th Cong., 1st sess., 1876.

U.S. Congress, House, Committee on Foreign Relations. Minority Report No. 37, 50th Cong., 2nd sess., 1869.

U.S. Congress, House. Fur Seal Fisheries of Alaska. H. Exec. Doc. No. 136, 41st. Cong., 2nd sess., 1869.

U.S. Congress, House. Fur Seal Fisheries of Alaska. H. Rpt. No. 3883, 50th Cong., 2nd sess., 1889.

U.S. Congress, House. Hearing Before the Committee on Expenditures in the Department of Commerce and Labor, House of Representatives, on House Resolution No. 73 to Investigate the Fur Seal Industry of Alaska. 62nd Cong., 2nd sess., 1911-1912.

U.S. Congress, Senate. Hearings Before the Committee on Conservation of Natural Resources on Bill S. 7242 entitled "An Act to Protect the Seal Fisheries of Alaska and For Other Purposes." S. Doc. No. 605, 61st Cong., 2nd sess., 1910.

U.S. Congress, House. House Miscellaneous Doc. No. 11. 41st Cong., 2nd sess., 1869.

U.S. Congress, House. The Fur Seal Industry of Alaska. H. Rpt. No. 1425. 62nd Cong., 3rd sess., 1913.

U.S. Congress, Senate. Fur-Seal Skin Sales. S. Doc. No. 213, 67th Cong., 2nd sess., April 10, 1922.

U.S. Congress, Senate. Hearings Before the Subcommittee on Oceans and Atmosphere of the Committee on Commerce: Ocean Mammal Protection, 2 parts. 92nd Cong., 2nd sess., 1973.

U.S. Congress, Senate. Message from the President of the United States. S. Exec. Doc. No. 67, 53rd Cong., 3rd sess., 1895.

U.S. Congress, House. Russian America. H. Exec. Doc. No. 177, 40th Cong., 2nd sess., 1868.

U.S. Congress, House. Seal Fisheries of Alaska. H. Exec. Doc. No. 83, 44th Cong., 1st sess., 1875.

U.S. General Services Administration, Office of Finances, Accounting Division. Accounting Report on Pribilof Islands: Aleut Community of St. Paul Island and Aleut Tribe v. United States, Docket Nos. 352 and 360, 1977.

Veniaminov, Ivan. Notes on the Islands of the Unalaska District. 3 vol. St. Petersburg, 1840. vol. 2. Trans. Richard Geogehan. Rasmuson Library, University of Alaska, Fairbanks. Also trans. B. Keen and Assye Kardinelowska. Human Relations Area File, Yale University, New Haven.

INDEX

Abandonment, policy of, 139, 140, 141, 148, 154, 155, 159, 177
Acculturation, 147, 149, 152, 154
Act to Prevent the Extermination of Fur Seals (1870), 15
Admirality Island, Alaska, 107
Agents: background of, 19, 57; as commissioners, 79, 87n56; salaries of, 19, 55, 57
Alaska, 36, 119, 120; laws of, 82, 155; national attitudes towards, 84, 119, 120, 134, 173; purchase of, 1, 3, 114, 163, 173; resources of, 1, 3, 65, 162, 173; statehood of, 119, 134, 135n1, 139, 142, 148, 154, 162, 177; state of, 140, 141, 148, 150, 164; legislation by state of, 75, 143, 148, 169n10
Alaska Commercial Company, 10, 15, 16, 20-29 *passim*, 35, 37, 49n14
Alaska Commissioner of Labor, 127
Alaska Congregational Delegation, 149
Alaska Department of Education, 130
Alaska Department of Health, 130
Alaska Department of Public Safety, 148
Alaska Human Rights Commission, 148
Alaska Native Brotherhood, 120, 121, 122, 123, 125
Alaska Native Claims Settlement Act (1971), 162-163, 169n11, 178
Alaska Native Sisterhood, 120
Alaska Natives, 3, 17, 19, 61, 111, 129, 130, 148, 162, 168-69; land of, 162; national attitudes toward, 120, 134; under Russian rule, 4, 5, 19
Alaska Peninsula, 5, 12n11, 131
Alaska Territorial Department of Health, 108
Alaska Trader's Protective Association, 35
Alcohol, 25, 26, 55-56, 111, 129, 147. *See also Quass*
Aleutian Islands, 1, 5, 11n1, 25, 82, 107, 110, 113, 114, 129, 141, 170n14, 176
Aleut language, 27, 58, 59, 80, 168
Anchorage, Alaska, 148
Anti-Monopoly Association of Pacific Coast, 35
Artels (temporary hunting settlements), 5, 6
Arts, 33n70, 168
Assemblies of God, 152-154
Atka, Alaska, 8
Attu, Alaska, 107

Baidarka (skin boat), 6, 11n2
Baltzo, Howard, 141-154 *passim*; 156n17, 158n51
Barabara (traditional Aleut house), 20, 27, 30n28
Baranoff, Father Makary, 123
Barshchina (work obligation), 6
Bartlett, E.L., 143, 145, 150, 151, 155, 158n51, 164
Benefits: entitled Aleuts, 127, 131, 132, 133, 140, 143, 144, 145
Benson, Dan, 111, 115, 123
Berenberg, Dr. Sam, 74
Berenberg, Mrs. Sam, *See Martin, Fredericka*
Bering Sea, 1, 37, 38, 48n11, 55, 165, 168
Bering, Vitus, 4
Boutwell, George, 9, 17
Bryant, Charles, 19, 20, 24, 28, 41
Bureau of Commercial Fisheries, 46-83 *passim*; 107, 109, 115, 142-155 *passim*; 160
Bureau of Fisheries, 67-83 *passim*; 107, 109, 115
Bureau of Indian Affairs, 124, 129, 140, 146
Bureau of Internal Revenue, 126
Bureau of Sports Fisheries, 141
Bureau of Wildlife and Commercial Fisheries, 141
Buterin, Karp, 23
Buynitsky, S.N., 35

Campfire Club of America, 51
Canteens, 78-79, 147, 161
Cape Newenham, 11n1
Carrol, Bob, 149, 150
Censorship of press, 114
Chemawa Indian School, 59-61
Chernofsky, Alaska, 165
Chief(s) in Aleut political organization, 5, 7, 16, 19-24 *passim*; 40, 46, 59, 124, 125
Chief of Alaska Fisheries, 109-115 *passim*; 143
Christianity, 5, 18, 27, 32n70, 59, 152, 154. *See also* Assemblies of God; Russian Orthodox Church
Christoffers, H. J., 76, 77

Citizenship: Russian, 19; U.S., 19, 78. 114, 131, 147
Civil Service Commission, 133
Civil Service Status, 131, 132, 134, 143, 144, 147, 163
Clothing, 43, 50n31, 53, 69, 70, 108, 126, 134, 167, 168
Cohen, Felix, 119, 121, 129, 177
Collective bargaining, 76, 175
Colonialism, 65-84; 115, 120, 144, 147, 155, 173-178
Colyer, Vincent, 19
Commander Islands, 52
Committee for Humane Legislation, 160
Committee of Inquiry into Forced Labor, 127
Community club, 78-79, 123, 125, 127, 161
Conservation of fur seals, 3, 4, 8-9, 16, 17, 19, 29, 48n11, 51, 66, 67, 160, 164, 173, 174. *See also* Fur seals, management of
Consolidation, plan of, 139, 141, 149-152, 155, 158n51, 159
Council(s) in Aleut political organization, 5, 130, 144-149 *passim*; 153, 161, 163
Crompton, C.E., 60, 61
Curry, James, 119

Dawber, Mark, 137n34
Dawes Act. *See* Indian Allotment Act
Day, Albert E., 126, 128, 137n34
Deculturation, 168-169
Desty, Robert, 35-36
Drunkenness, 25, 26, 55, 79, 80, 147
Dutch Harbor, Alaska, 107, 164, 166

Economic Development Administration, 165
Education: of Alaska Natives, 61; of Aleuts, 15, 27-29, 45, 57-61, 80-82, 123, 124, 130, 134, 143, 144, 146, 155; under Russian administration, 18, 33n70. *See also* Russian school; Schools
Egan, William A., 148
Elliott, Henry, 20, 21, 37, 57
Enemy aliens, 107, 110
English language, 58, 59
Environmental groups, 160
Evacuation of Pribilof Islands, 107-115, 116n4, 119, 121, 168, 176, 177

Fassett, H.C., 53, 54
Federal Aviation Agency, 163
Fishing industry, 164-166, 178
Food: of Aleuts, 43, 50n31, 60, 65, 69-73, 76, 79, 82, 108, 109, 126, 134, 144; of government employees, 72, 73; seal meat as, 3, 21, 37, 48n11, 52, 70, 166-67
Fort Ross, California, 4
Fouke Fur Company, 52, 74
Fratis, John, 83
Freedom of movement, 6, 65, 76-77, 78, 80, 110-112, 134
Freedom of religion, 152-154
Friends of Animals, 160
Fuel, 53, 55, 69, 126, 131, 134, 144
Funsten and Brothers, 52
Funter Bay, Alaska, 107-115 *passim*; 167
Fur Seal Act: of 1910, 51, 67, 175; of 1944, 126, 132, 133, 140; of 1966, 145, 155, 161, 162, 163
Fur Seal Advisory Board, 51
Fur seal harvest: 9, 21, 57, 85n10, 114, 120; seasonal operations plan of, 139, 140, 149, 154, 155, 159, 177
Fur seal industry, 1, 3, 4, 7-10, 21, 110-113, 120, 123, 124, 139, 154, 159-67, 173, 178
Fur seals: population of, 1, 35, 36, 51, 62, 66, 128, 139, 155, 159, 160, 174, 175, 177; management of, 15, 16, 37, 38, 46, 48n11, 112, 139, 170n12; research on 159, 161, 170n12. *See also* Conservation of fur seals

Gabrielson, IRA, 115
Galakkionoff, Alex, 27
Gavitt, William, 25
Glidden, H.A., 23
Grant, Ulysses S., 10
Great Britain, 4, 37, 38, 48n11, 51
Greenpeace, 160

Hanna, G. Dallas, 56
Harbor, 164, 178
Hatton, P.R., 56
Health: of Alaska Natives, 129; of Aleuts, 4, 39, 70, 72, 108, 114, 143, 155
Hitchcock, Frank H., 62n3
Home Mission Council, 129
Honcharenko, Agapius, 35, 36
Housing: 16, 20, 27, 30n28, 36, 53, 60, 73, 74, 76, 108-109, 114, 126, 134, 144, 147, 149, 150, 163; demolition of, 150-151, 158n51; ownership of,

Housing (cont.)
20, 129, 152, 155; used by U.S. Navy, 107; vandalized, 114
Hynes, Frank W., 113, 114

Ickes, Harold L., 109, 114
Ikatan, Alaska, 82
Income, average annual, 21, 39, 40, 41, 67, 127, 132, 136n23, 138n44
Independence, 119-134, 139, 141, 142, 149, 152, 155, 167, 177
Indian Allotment Act, 44
Indian Claims Commission, 131, 162, 164
Indian Citizenship Act (1924), 78
Indian law, 120, 177
Indian Removal Act, 44
Indian Reorganization Act (1934), 65, 78, 120, 121, 123, 161
Indians, 12n11, 18, 19, 26, 40, 52, 62n5, 78, 119, 124, 173, 174; as wards of U.S. government, 44-46, 47, 173; organizations of, 119-120, 134, 142; rights of 45, 57, 119, 121, 142, 174, 176, 177; U.S. citizenship of, 45, 78
Interest groups, 113, 120, 130, 131, 148, 154, 174, 177
International Fur Seal Treaty, 160, 161, 175, 178
International Labor Organization, 119, 127
International obligations of U.S., 51, 54, 68, 161, 163

Japan, 51, 52
Japanese, 107, 110, 113, 114, 176
Japanese-Americans, 107, 115
Job training, 57, 61, 68, 139, 146, 177
Johnston, Edward, 123
Joint Management Board, 163, 169-170 n12
Jones, Lester, 56
Jordan, David Starr, 62n3
Juneau, Alaska, 107, 110, 111, 112, 121, 177
Justice, administration of, 24-26, 79, 80, 147, 148, 161

Katz, Michael, 28, 58, 59
Kiska, Alaska, 107
Kodiak Island, Alaska, 12n11
Kochergin, Gavril Stepetin, 77
Kotchootin, Mary, 39
Kotzebue, Alaska, 129
Krukof, Nellie, 82
Krukoff, Nicholas, 26
Krukoff, Peter, 25
Kushing, Aga, 26

Land, ownership of, 123, 129, 130-131, 155, 161, 162-163, 170n14
Lembkey, Walter, 41, 42, 43, 53-58 *passim*; 175
Lucas, Frederick A., 62n3
Lurie, Nancy, 26

McGovern, C.J., 55, 56
McIntyre, H.H., 18
McIntyre, William, 28
McKernan, Donald, 141-152 *passim*
McLenny, P.L., 56
McMillin, Lee C., 111, 113
Mandregan, Francis, 77
Mandregan, Neon, 39
Marine Mammal Commission, 160
Marine Mammal Protection Act of 1972, 166, 167
Marriage, 27, 39, 43, 65, 76, 83
Martin, Fredericka, 71, 74, 77, 78, 119-132 *passim*; 176
Medical care, 16, 36, 53
Merriam, C. Hart, 62n3
Melividov, Alex, 39
Melovidov, Anton, 24
Melovidov, Solomonia, 81
Merculief, Paul, 76
Merculief, Mrs. Susie, 150, 151
Miller, John, 10

National Congress of American Indians, 119
National Marine Fisheries Service, 160, 162, 163, 165, 166
National Oceanic and Atmospheric Administration, 160
Navajo Institute, 119
Nederazoff, Martin, 23
Negotiations: between Alaska and U.S. government, 139, 159; between Aleuts and U.S. government, 123, 128, 130, 131, 162-169
Negotiations, international, by U.S. government, 38, 47, 48n11
New Deal, 65
New York City, 142
Nichols, John R., 137n34
Nome, Alaska, 129
North American Commercial Company, 36, 37, 40, 47, 50n31, 51

North Pacific Fur Seal Convention, 51, 52, 161, 167
Nunivak Island, Alaska, 129

Obrok (cash payment), 6
Office of Indian Affairs, 61, 82
Okhotsk, Siberia, 8
Okun, Semen, 5
Oldroyd, Loren, 137n34
Olson, Clarence, 123, 126, 133, 139, 140, 147

Paul, William, 120
Payments: in bonuses, 123, 126, 127, 131, 132, 143, 144; in kind, 44, 46, 52-55, 61, 63n10, 67-70, 126, 127, 131, 134, 175; in wages, 7, 13n28, 16, 21, 22, 31n42, 39, 41-43, 47, 55-70 *passim*; 83, 111, 126-132 *passim*; 143-145, 163-164, 175
Pelagic hunting, 8, 35, 36-37, 47, 51, 52, 62n5, 178
Peonage, 127, 129
Philemenof, Leonty, 83
Political organization, 46, 47, 66, 84, 174. *See also* Chiefs in Aleut political organization
Popoff, Matfay, 26
Popoff, (widow), 25
Population of Aleuts: decline of, 4, 27, 31n42, 32n64, 39, 40, 49n24, 109; increase of, 72, 139, 177; planned reduction of, 139-140
President's Advisory Commission on Indian Rights, 119
Press coverage, 35, 55-56, 148, 160-61. *See also* Censorship of press
Pribilof, Gerasim, 8
Pribilof Islands: archeological records of, 11n2; location of 1, 11n1
Priest, Russian Orthodox, 22, 27, 28, 40, 58, 74
Proctor, A.H., 55, 56, 81
Puerto Rico, 116n4
Punishment, 22-23, 25, 26, 28, 47, 68, 76, 79, 80, 115; exile as, 22, 26, 27, 39, 46, 47, 77, 79, 80, 112, 115, 125; fines as, 26, 28; work as, 26; work demotions as, 77, 80, 132

Quass (home-brewed beer and wine), 17, 25, 26, 129. *See also* Alcohol

Redfield, William C., 56
Redpath, James C., 25
Reform, movements of, 120-134, 142, 175, 176, 177
Relief, 116n4, 46, 49-50n31, 52, 65, 143
Repatriation, 112-116, 121
Reservation, Pribilof Islands as, 3, 130, 131
Resettlement, plan of, 139-155 *passim*, 159, 161, 168, 177
Revenues, to U.S. government, 3, 9, 10, 15, 16, 20, 36-38, 47, 52, 54, 62, 67, 68, 128, 137n32, 160, 173-77 *passim*; losses of, 38, 51, 54, 85n16, 109, 139, 140, 142
Rights: of Aleuts, 18, 22-29, 39, 41, 47, 65, 75-84, 110-116, 119, 131, 134, 148, 176; of Indians, 45, 121, 142, 174, 176, 177
Rookeries of fur seals, 1, 3, 8, 9, 22, 38, 167
Roosevelt, Franklin D., 107
Roosevelt, Theodore, 51
Russia: administration of Pribilof Islands by, 1, 4-9, 12n11; discovery of Pribilof Islands by, 1; participation in fur seal treaty by, 51
Russian America, 4, 5, 6
Russian-American Company, 4-9
Russian fur trade, 4, 6, 9
Russian language, 19, 27, 80
Russian Orthodox Church, 27, 32-33n70, 50n31, 58, 66, 74, 153-154, 168, 176. *See also* Priest, Russian Orthodox
Russian School, 28, 58, 59, 80

St. Matthew Island, 11n1
San Francisco, California, 1, 16, 35, 40, 50n31, 54
Schools, 16, 18, 28, 33n70, 57-61, 80, 81, 124, 130, 134, 163, 168. *See also* Education of Aleuts; Russian School
Segregation: racial, 73, 75, 81, 84; social, 73-75, 147
Selective Service, 110, 176
Selective Service Act, 110
Self-government, 78-79, 122-134, 144, 147, 155, 161-165, 169n10, 177
Serfdom in Russia, 5, 6-7
Sexual abuse, 25, 55-56
Seward's Folly, 3
Shabolin, Neon, 39
Shaisnikoff, Paul, 24
Shane, Fecla, 39
Shelikhov, Grigor, 8

Shenitz, Helen, 74
Siberia, 1, 4
Sierra Club, 160
Sims, Edwin W., 62n3
Sitka, Alaska, 153
Skills, 8, 21, 33n70, 113, 133, 141, 143, 166-167, 174
Slaves, Aleuts as, 35, 54, 80, 127, 129, 174
Slaves of Aleuts, 6, 12n12
Smithsonian Institution, 4
Social Security Act, 75, 175
Social Security benefits, 127
Society for the Prevention of Cruelty to Animals, 160
Solicitor of the United States, 75
Stejneger, Leonard, 62n3
Stephan, Terentia, 23, 24
Stimson, Henry M., 109, 110
Subsistence, 6, 8, 21, 40, 48n11, 72, 160, 166-167, 170n12
Supplemental Appropriation Act (1941), 116n4
Swineford, Alfred P., 23, 36

Taft, William H., 51
Tanadgusix Corporation, 163, 165, 167
Tanaq Corporation, 163, 165
Terakanoff, Kerrick, 23, 26
Tetoff, Neon, 23
Tlingit and Haida Indians, 162
Tobin, Maurice J., 127, 132
Tongue, L.N., 56
Tourism, 165, 170n12
Townsend, Charles H., 62n3
Treaty of Cession, 19, 48n11, 78
Truman, Harry S., 123

Udall, Stewart L, 153
Umnak, Alaska, 170n14
Unalaska, Alaska, 8, 25, 26, 31n42, 33n70, 39, 43, 77, 82, 83, 107, 164, 170n14
Unalaska Island, Alaska, 11n1, 165
Unimak, Alaska, 11n2
United Nations, 119, 127
United Nations' Ad Hoc Committee on Slavery, 119
U.S. Army, 110; Corps of Engineers, 113, 164
U.S. Congress, 3, 4, 44, 51, 52, 54, 57, 61, 123, 128, 129, 148; appropriations by, 40, 52, 53, 68, 128, 137n32, 142, 160, 165; hearings of, 1, 15, 16, 17, 29, 35, 36, 37, 38, 69, 128, 150; legislation by 3, 10, 15, 29, 162-63, 165, 173, 174
U.S. Department of Commerce, 75, 109, 160
U.S. Department of Commerce and Labor, 42, 46, 51, 82
U.S. Department of Labor, 56, 127, 128, 131
U.S. Department of Interior, 59, 61, 109, 114, 121-133 *passim*; 142, 144, 152
U.S. Department of Justice, 45, 46, 56, 165
U.S. Department of Treasury, 3, 4, 9, 10, 15-39 *passim*; 44, 45, 49n14, 50n31
U.S. Department of War, 107, 109
U.S. Employment Service, 110, 111, 176
U.S. Fish and Wildlife Service, 78, 109-145 *passim*; 152
U.S. Navy, 107, 109
U.S. Public Health Service, 155
U.S. Surgeon General, 114
University of Alaska, 129

Veniaminov, Ivan E., 11n2, 25, 27, 33n70
Village corporations, 163, 170n14
Villages, 8, 114, 115, 124
Virgin Islands, 116n4
Visitors, 82, 129, 148, 170n12, 126
Volkoff, Markel, 24
Volyer, Vincent, 9

Wage system, reform of, 124, 126-134, 139, 142, 143, 147, 177
Wards of U.S. Government: Aleuts as, 44-46, 47, 50n40, 78, 110, 121, 131, 175; Indians as, 47, 173
Warne, William E., 121, 122, 126, 127, 128, 129
Washington, D.C., 59, 119, 121, 126, 140, 142, 144, 148, 149
Whitney, Alvin D., 56
Whitney, Alvin D., Mrs., 56
Wicker, Frank, 9
World War II, 23, 47, 51, 73, 84, 107-11, 112, 115, 119, 124, 131, 176

Yurts (multi-family housing units), 30n28

ABOUT THE AUTHOR

Dorothy Knee Jones, a professor of sociology at the Institute of Social and Economic Research, University of Alaska, has for many years conducted studies of the Aleuts on both the Aleutian and Pribilof islands. Her close contacts with the Aleuts during her 10-year residency in the Aleutians and her various field studies have given her a compassionate understanding of the Aleut peoples.

Professor Jones has published numerous books and articles on the Aleuts, Alaska Natives, and women. Two recent publications of note are Aleuts in Transition (University of Washington Press, 1976) and The Status of Women in Alaska (principal author, for the Alaska State Commission on Human Rights, 1977).

Active in the women's movement, Professor Jones is also a feminist psychotherapist. She is a member of the Governor's Commission on the Status of Women and was a delegate to the 1977 International Women's Year in Houston.

A mother of three (Scott Cole, Lori Larsen, and Chuck Jones) and grandmother of one (Chanti Ford), Professor Jones now resides in Eagle River, Alaska with her husband Bob (Sea Otter) Jones, a U.S. Fish and Wildlife biologist of three decades.